THE STONES BEAR WITNESS

(BLAND COUNTY, VIRGINIA)

VOLUME 1

Parke C. Bogle

and

Jo Ann Tickle Scott

Heritage Books
2024

HERITAGE BOOKS

AN IMPRINT OF HERITAGE BOOKS, INC.

Books, CDs, and more—Worldwide

For our listing of thousands of titles see our website
at
www.HeritageBooks.com

A Facsimile Reprint
Published 2024 by
HERITAGE BOOKS, INC.
Publishing Division
5810 Ruatan Street
Berwyn Heights, MD 20740

Originally published 1987

International Standard Book Number
Paperbound: 978-0-7884-7773-7

FOREWORD

In 1987, with the help of Melissa Lester, I started out to copy as many of the Bland County Cemeteries as possible. We succeeded in copying most of the larger ones when an unexpected illness halted my endeavors. My undying gratitude goes to Melissa Lester for her help in this task and for her continuing aid to me. Thanks goes also to my young nephew, Philip Bogle who climbed high hills to copy dates for me. My thanks to Alma Newberry Waddell for filling me in on some of the old Newberry cemeteries and for names of those who had no stones.

In 1998, Mrs. Jo Ann Tickle Scott took on the task of finding and copying about 100 burial spots in the county. We now have a total of 106. The Bland County Historical has expressed a desire to have these records. My thanks goes to Zereda Earnest for information she has supplied.

I realize that to catalogue every burial spot in the county is impossible but there are those who remembered these dear old people and gave us the pertinent information. We must remember that during the Reconstruction period after the Civil War, times were hard and money was scarce. Many could not afford to purchase the ready-made stones for the graves of their loved ones. The names and dates that were often chiseled on plain field stones were marks of love and devotion. How difficult and time consuming it must have been to do these etchings. By these stones, they are remembered! No doubt we have made mistakes in copying these old stones. We ask your indulgence when you find an error. Remember that the stones are very old and some are eroded so badly that the dates are almost illegible. We will appreciate it if you let us know when you find a mistake and make any corrections or additions that you may know about. Our addresses are found below.

I would like to dedicate this work to my patient and loyal husband, George Bogle, who has gone without his meals while I spent hours at the computer entering the cemetery data and while I was off for days at a time visiting courthouses and obtaining documentation. Also to my children who seem to be tired of hearing no conversation except about dead people, I dedicate this endeavor.

Parke C. Bogle
1117 High Street
Pulaski, VA 24301
Telephone- 540-980-6974
Email- <parkebog@swva.net>

I, also would like to thank my husband, Emery Scott, for his patience in allowing me the freedom to pursue this endeavor. His understanding has made my work a little easier. I dedicate this work to him. Also to my children whose ancestors lie deep in the Bland County soil, I dedicate this compilation. My thanks to the many people who have helped me and especially to Donna and Bob Distel, Donald Helvey, Buzz and Milly Richardson and Bob Munsey.

Jo Ann Tickle Scott
Route 2, Box 28
Bland, VA 24315
Email- <jotickle@naxs.com>

CRABTREE GAP

TAZEWELL

COUNTY

COUNTY

625

625

647

625 Cedars

3

42

622

2

42

625

622

622

1

628

622

625

623

623

610

622

622

622

JEFFERSON

4

742

625

624

COUNTY

610

626

WYTHE

COUNTY

816

i

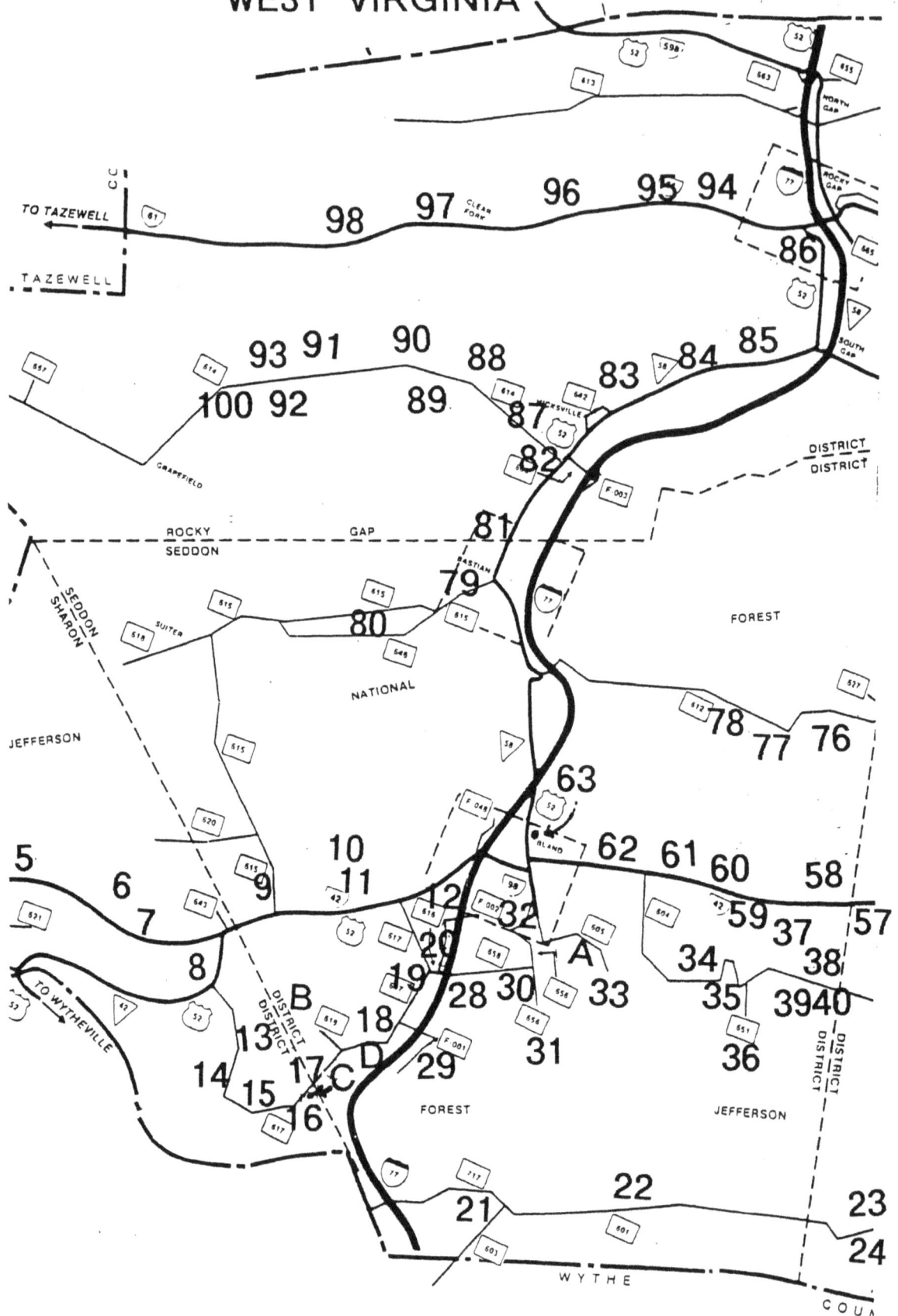

WEST VIRGINIA

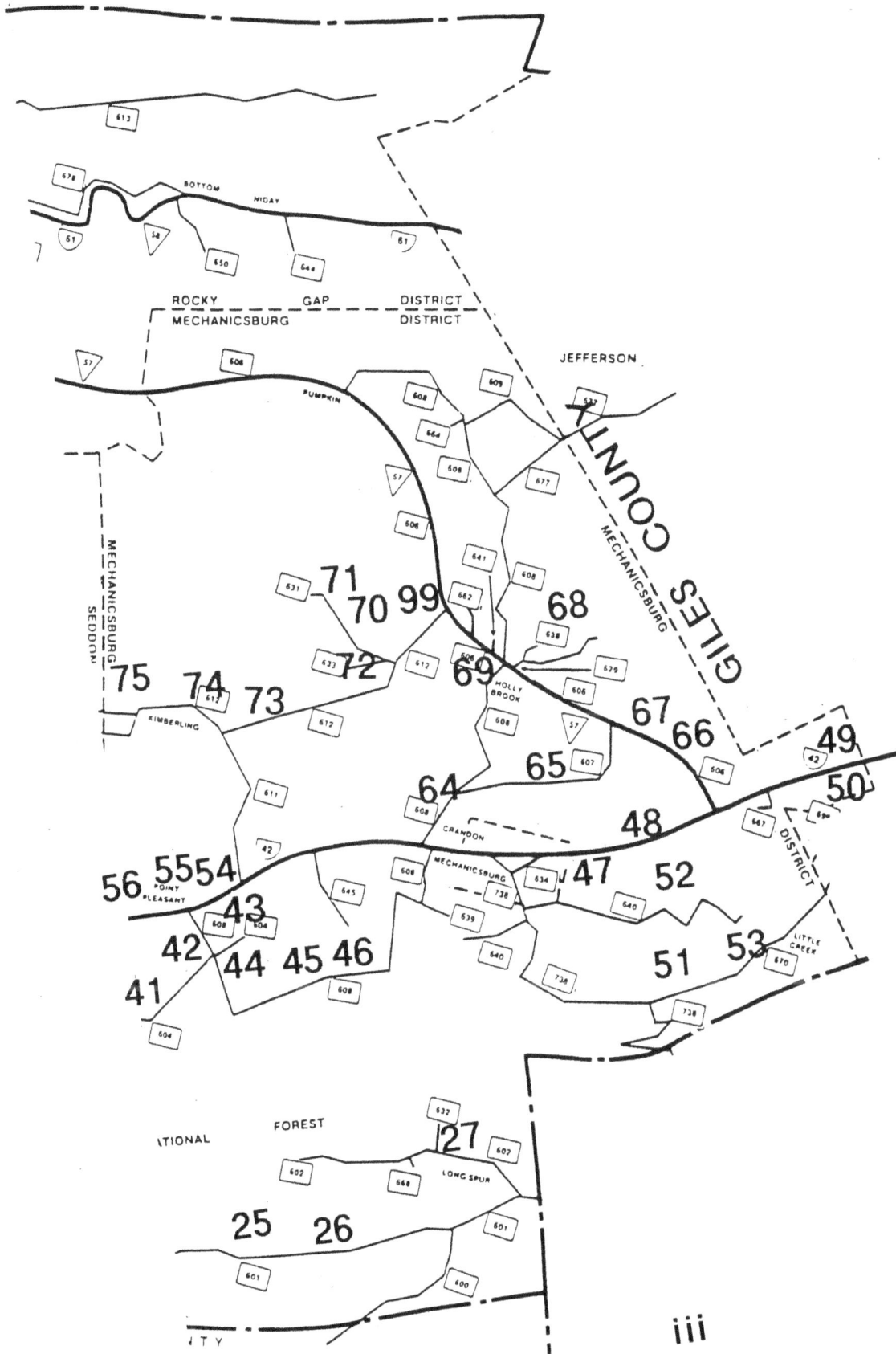

ROCKY GAP DISTRICT
MECHANICSBURG DISTRICT

JEFFERSON

GILES COUNTY

MECHANICSBURG SEDDON

MECHANICSBURG

BOTTOM   MIDAY

PUMPKIN

71
70 99
72
69
HOLLY BROOK
68
67 66
65
64
CRANDON
48
47 52
49
50
DISTRICT
75 74 73
KIMBERLING

56 55 54
POINT PLEASANT
43
42
44 45 46
41

51 53
LITTLE CREEK

27
LONG SPUR

FOREST
NATIONAL

25 26

iii

Cemetery Map Index

1. Bethany
2. Sharon
3. Crabtree
4. Red Oak
5. Bethel
6. Repass 1
7. Repass 2
8. Stowers (Trinity)
9. Robinett (Rt.615)
10. Grayson
11. Stowers
12. Kegley
13. Waddle 3
14. Waddle 2
15. Hayton Waddle
16. Waddle 1
17. Davis
18. Newberry (Capt. Henry)
19. Newberry (A.T.)
20. Steel (Crockett)
21. Burton (Rt. 603)
22. Blankenship
23. Strader's Chapel
24. Hancock
25. Hidden Valley 1
26. Hidden Valley 2
27. Goshen
28. Newberry's Chapel
   (Rudder & Dillow-Woods)
29. Kegley (abandoned)
30. Dillow-Bogle
31. Grayson
32. Kitts
33. Oaklawn
34. Burton (Giles)
35. Wyrick
36. Pauley
37. Kitts - Tickle
38. Tickle - Bogle
39. Thompson
   (Community Cem.)
40. Munsey (E.M.)

41. Hutsell
42. Hoge - Harman
43. Robinett (Rt 608)
44. Central Ch. Cem.
45. Harman Cem.
   (High Rock)
46. Penley (Way)
47. Mechanicsburg
48. Mustard (Community)
49. Allen
50. Strock
51. Miller (Walker's Mtn.)
52. Mustard (Walker's Creek)
53. Bogle (Walker's Creek)
54. Neal
55. Hoge's Chapel
56. Updyke
57. Bruce - Petree
58. Slave (Ben Birds)
59. Bird (D.W.)
60. Havens (G.C.)
61. Muncy
62. Penley #2
63. Bland - Temple Hill -
   Morning Star
64. Hobbs
65. Morehead #1
66. Mitchell Farm Cem.
67. Shiloh
68. Mountain Field
69. Harman Burrying Ground
70. Clark
71. Ramsey
72. Finley
73. Morehead (L.K.)
74. Miller (Dr.L.J.)
75. Helvey (Henry)
76. Meek Miller Farm Cem.
   (L.D. Helvey)
77. Salem Church
78. Helvey (L. J.)
79. Hornbarger

80. Kidd
81. Rose Hill
82. Hicks
83. Gross
84. Compton
85. Shufflebarger
86. Honaker - Tuggle
87. Justice
88. Looney (H.J.)
89. Bogle (Wolf Creek)
90. Childress
91. Kidd (A.T.)
92. Green Valley Ch.
93. Levitt
94. Clear Fork Bapt. Ch. Cem.
95. Sunny Point
96. Stimson
97. I.F. Stowers
98. Steele
99. Nunn
100. Burress (Beckner's Store)

Grave Sites
A. Nancy Rhinehart
B. Isabella Waddle & Child
C. Infant Overbaugh
D. Evelyn Thompson

iv

BETHANY CHURCH CEMETERY
[One mile down Route 626, off State Routy 42, west of Ceres, Va.
{Copied in 1991 by Parke C Bogle and checked by Jo Ann Tickle Scott}

ATKINS, Maggie J.- (3-16-1933 -   )
ATKINS, Rose Francis- (11-3-1900 - 12-7-1969)
ATKINS, Robert Carson- (4-2-1857 - 5-8-1936)
ATKINS, Lydia- (3-31-1821 - 12-6-1891) W/o J.M. Atkins, age 70 yrs.
      8 mos. and 5 das.
ATKINS, James M.- (5-12-1817 - 1-18-1882) Age 64 yrs. 8 mos & 6 das

ATWELL, Carrie U.- 6-28-1877 - 6-3-1960)
ATWELL, John Henry- (11-3-1876 - 11-9-1949)
ATWELL, Leland S.- (7-13-1897 - 12-26-1965)
ATWELL, Alphi E.- (8-31-1892 - 9-16-1898) D/o J.E & L.J. Atwell.
ATWELL, Jessee James- (1889 - 1973)
ATWELL, Garnet D.- (9-5-1914 - 9-30-1939)
ATWELL, Essie A.- (2-28-1874 - 8-20-1944)
ATWELL, G. Stewart- (11-11-1874 - 1-11-1965)
ATWELL, Hilda Mae- (12-29-1902 - 12-13-1904) Daughter
ATWELL, Gurvis J.- (1-20-1907 - 11-29-1970)
ATWELL, Elizabeth Jackson- (1-14-1906 - 3-30-1980)
ATWELL, Alvis A.- (4-19-1907 -m   )
ATWELL, Mary C.- (8-29-1909 - 8-10-1988)
ATWELL,, John E.- (1868 - 1961)
ATWELL, Laura J.- (1869 - 1940)
ATWELL, Denzil L.- (2-4-1896 - 10-20-1934)
ATWELL, Donald Keith- (born & died 7-3-1927)
ATWELL, Dana Lynn- (4-26-1935 - 4-30-1935)

BALES, Laura P.- (1893 - 1955)
BALES, Paris Dailey- (1897 - 1988)
BALES, Ruth G.- (1-17-1922 - 3-28-1988)
BALES, Vance C.- (8-9-1918 - 1-21-1970)
BALES, Wiley Legard- (10-14-1925 - 3-8-1990)

BARGER, Infant son of Donald & Louisa Barger (died 9-15-1959)

BARNETT, Elizabeth- (5-23-1853 - 3-15-1932)
BARNETT, Belena C.- (7-29-1888 - 5-29-1943)

BAUMGARDNER, H.M.?- (4-10-1844 - 7-30-1928)
BAUMGARDNER, Mary E.- (5-24-1847 - 8-19-1914) W/o M.L. Baumgardner.

BEEN, John S.C.- (no dates- CSA Co F. Va. Infantry)

BEVIL, William S.- (12-25-1887 - 10-7-1936)
BEVIL, Mary P. Tibbs- (2-14-1890 - 7-31-1986)
BEVIL, Brown- (3-5-1918 - 9-26-1992)

BLESSING, L. Belle- (2-3-1869 - 2-8-1900) Wife of E.F. Blessing.
BLESSING, 9 small unmarked stones on Blessing plot.

BOGLE, Nannie U.- (1874 - 1957)
BOGLE, Joseph G.- (1870 - 1952)

BRIDGES, James W.- (1876 - 1940) Father
BRIDGES, Laura H.- (1891 - 1967) Mother

BROOKS, William F.- (1866 - 1956)

BRUCE, William Watson- (12-2-1921 - 10-6-1987)
BRUCE, Geneva C.- (11-11-1932 - 5-25-1959)
BRUCE, Tyra V.- (4-18-1869 - 2-13-1896) { Notation on stone says,
     " Killed in Billings, Montana while coupling cars. "
BRUCE, Sarah A.- (9-13-1837 - 3-28-1891) Wife of H.F. Bruce. { Dau.
     of G.W. Suiter and Esther Newberry Suiter. }
BRUCE, Herald F.- (9-8-1836 - 8-22-1925) Hus. of Sarah.
BRUCE, Emmer Grey- (dates illegible) { Dau of Sarah & Herald }
BRUCE, Callie Adeline, (dates illegible) Died 11-9-1882. { Date
     taken from the Archives, Virginia State Library }
BRUCE, James H.- (10-23-1830 - 7-5-1910) Age 79 yrs 8 mos 12 das.
BRUCE, Mary M.- (2-6-1831 - 6-2-1897)
BRUCE, Wriley W.- (7-2-1869 - 3-18-1912)
BRUCE, Dora Umbarger- (12-7-1875 - 5-7-1965)
BRUCE, Family of Claude Bruce- One huge stone, no markings on it.
BRUCE, Myrtle S.- (3-16-1895 - 3-23-1964)
BRUCE, Joubert O.- (10-3-1899 - 6-25-1974) Father
BRUCE, Beulah H.- (12-29-1898 -   ) Mother
BRUCE, Shirley G. (1912 - 1997) FHM
BRUCE, James Wayne- (7-1-1925 - 9-22-1992)
BRUCE, Irene- (7-30-1929 -   ) {W/O James Wayne Bruce}

BURTON, Erica Lynn- (11-19-1993 - 2-17-1994)

CASSELL, Infant son of D.A. & S.A. Cassell (12-21-1949)
CASSELL, H. Bailey- (1890 - 1975)
CASSELL, Anna B.- (1897 - 1973)
CASSELL, Douglas A.- (11-6-1921 - 7-28-1976)
CASSELL, Louisa Jane Umbarger- (9-4-1862 - 12-11-1881)
CASSELL, Infant son of Mr. & Mrs F.H. Cassell- (1-19-1946)
CASSELL, Davis H.- (1889 - 1945)
CASSELL, Pearl L.- (1896 -   )

CATRON, Ettie M. Umbarger- (9-7-1867 - 1-21-1931) Wife of R.M.
CATRON, R.M.- (9-7-1867 - 4-12-1939)
CATRON, Margaret I. Eperson- (7-8-1865 - 3-23-1950) Wife of R.M.

CLEMONS, Levine Robins- (1926 - 1963)
CLEMONS, Joseph Henry- (1882 - 1962)
CLEMONS, Josephine Neel- (1885 - 1970)
CLEMONS, Joanie S.- (born & died 12-15-1975)
CLEMONS, FHM illegible. No stone.

BETHANY CHURCH CEMETERY
[One mile down Route 626, off State Route 42, west of Ceres.]

CLEMMONS, Ella Louise- (1931 -   )
CLEMMONS, Amber Leigh- (10-10-1977 - 10-17-1977)

COOLEY, Malinda N.- (1809 - 1884)
COOLEY, Wm. Henry- (2-1-1850 - 9-10-1885)
COOLEY, Merilda- (5-30-1882 - 3-22-1927)

COX, Winton B.- (9-22-1909 - 2-7-1985)
COX, Maude B.- (1-7-1913 - 2-13-1994)
COX, Donald R.- (12-29-1958 - 6-28-1975) Beloved son.
COX, Walter W.- (7-29-1884 - 12-15-1954)
COX, Mary J.- (9-25-1890 - 6-12-1972)
COX, Herman M.- (6-23-1909 - 4-28-1969)
COX, Enoch Asberry- (8-29-1869 - 9-24-1955)
COX, James A.- (1908 - 1986) FHM
COX, Ruby L.- (1923 - 1983) FHM
COX, Robert M.- (1876 - 1962)
COX, E. Grace- (1883 - 1960)
COX, A.W.- (CSA marker, no birth or death dates)
COX, Catherine- (10-16-1842 - 11-8-1885) Age 43 yrs 22 days
COX, Ella Marie- (4-15-1915 -   )
COX, Forest Lincoln- (4-1-1906 - 12-17-1981)
COX, George C.- (CSA, no dates)
COX, Lee M.- (1871 - 1927)
COX, Susan M.- (1872 - 1948)
COX, Estill Huey- (6-13-1907 - 6-10-1968)
COX, Infant son of Mr. & Mrs. S.S. Cox. (7-1-1946)
COX, Bennie D.- (1-9-1941 -   )
COX, Barbara W.- (3-6-1946 - 4-21-1992) {W/O Bennie D. Cox}
COX, Sherman S.- (4-20-1916 - 10-18-1992)
COX, Ella Harding- (8-16-1918 - 2-6-1995)
COX, William Harvey- (2-1-1856 - 9-10-1885)

CREAL, Jettie Myrtle- (12-10-1895 - 3-23-1964)

DURHAM, James O.- (1896 - 1980) { US Army WW I }

EPPERSON, William P.- (8-16-1871 - 9-3-1947)
EPPERSON, Ellen N.- (1-7-1861 - 12-27-1942)
EPPERSON, Robert S.- (8-26-1897 - 11-4-1888)
EPPERSON, Helen M.- (12-8-1913 - 2-13-1989)
EPPERSON, Charles Edward- (9-9-1971 - 9-9-1971)

FIELDS, David Clint- (10-7-1909 - 2-28-1977)
FIELDS, Alverta Cox- (9-1-1912 - 9-17-1986)

FORTNER, Levator S.- (2-5-1909 - 11-25-1984)
FORTNER, Mary E.- (7-30-1913 -   )
FORTNER, Dianna L.- (1-14-1952 -   )

BETHANY CHURCH CEMETERY
[One mile down Route 626, off State Route 42, west of Ceres, Va.

GILLESPIE, Nancy Adeline- (2-6-1868 - 3-11-1925)
GILLESPIE, Reese Samuel- (1-13-1870 - 6-8-1930)
GILLESPIE, John M.- (1-15-1842 - 6-1-1893)
GILLESPIE, Julia Ann- (5-24-1858 - 8-14-1943)

GOOD, Cleo Atwell- (1-6-1903 - 2-18-1948)

GORDEN, Merilda- (5-30-1882 - 3-22-1927) { Name may be CORDEN. }

GROSECLOSE, B. Dodd- (1878 - 1963)
GROSECLOSE, Kate F.- (1888 - 1960)
GROSECLOSE, Evelyn Cassell- (5-5-1923 -   )
GROSECLOSE, Luther Wayne- (1-22-1918 - 2-13-1986)
GROSECLOSE, Edna W.- (1887 - 1943)
GROSECLOSE, Robert L.- (1880 - 1931)
GROSECLOSE, Mary L.- (6-24-1850 - 12-5-1919)
GROSECLOSE, Henry- (?-11-1828 - 6-13-1901) Age 72yrs 9 mo & 2 das.
GROSECLOSE, A.S.- (2-8-1884? - 10-29-1897) S/o H.A. & M.A. Groseclose
GROSECLOSE, Grace W.- (1889 - 1933)
GROSECLOSE, Charles S.- (1882 - 1961)
GROSECLOSE, Curtis Eugene- (1915 - 1933)
GROSECLOSE, Infant- (2-10-1909 - 2-10-1909)
GROSECLOSE, Wilmer- (11-9-1911 - 10-22-1914)
GROSECLOSE, Rosmary- (10-28-1944) {Infant of Herbert & Ruth}
GROSECLOSE, Herbert Blair- (5-31-1913 - 7-24-1995)
GROSECLOSE, Ruth King- (1-10-1915 -   ) {W/O Herbert B. Groseclose}

HANCOCK, James F.- (1889 - 1973)
HANCOCK, Madie M.- (1895 - 1959) {Nee Hanshew, w/o James F. }
HANCOCK, William Byron- (1918 - 4-9-1998 {S/O James F & Madie}
HANCOCK, Lois McFarland- (2-10-1916 -   )

HANSHEW, Aileen Morris- (4-26-1930 - 8-6-1955)
HANSHEW, R.E.- (2-14-1890 - 11-20-1974)
HANSHEW, Georgia W.- (5-2-1896 - 7-13-1971)
HANSHEW, Charles W.- (6-10-1870 - 4-5-1950)
HANSHEW, Lettie M. Umberger- (1-4-1873 - 2-1-1935){W/o Chas. W. -}
HANSHEW, Polly M. Wilson- (3-12-1830 - 3-24-1907) {Age 77 yrs 12 das
                    Wife of Daniel Hanshew.}
HANSHEW, Daniel- (2-22-1828 - 5-24-1895) Age 67yrs 3 mos 2 days.
HANSHEW, Infant son of C.M. & V.R. Hanshew- (died 8-19-1931)
HANSHEW, Infant son of C.M. & V.R. Hanshew- (died 7-14-1933)
HANSHEW, Infant son of C.M. & V.R. Hanshew- (died 8-7-1934)
HANSHEW, Infant son of C.M. & V.R. Hanshew- (died 10-18-1940)
HANSHEW, Marlin- (1-21-1901 - 11-16-1975)
HANSHEW, Oralena Vare- (2-26-1899 - 11-26-1974)
HANSHEW, Olon P.- (1-22-1906 - 2-18-1981)
HANSHEW, Clara U.- (7-15-1910 - 3-19-1975)
HANSHEW, G.(C?) T.- (7-4-1888 - 9-12-1899)
HANSHEW, J.D.- (8-31-1888 - 8-2-1910) Killed by an engine.

HANSHEW, Amassa B.- (9-25-1873 - 5-3-1918)
HANSHEW, John T.- (4-20-1841 - 4-7-1925)
HANSHEW, Margaret L.- (6-5-1849 - 2-9-1941)
HANSHEW, Hezakiah F.- (1867 - 1926)
HANSHEW, Nannie R.- (1870 - 1967)
HANSHEW, Eunice V.- (12-31-1878 - 5-7-1927)
HANSHEW, Lorin Benton- (8-22-1914 - 9-20-1993)
HANSHEW, Ella Mae- (1921-   )   {Md. 2-23-1937, w/o Lorin B.}

HARMON, Albert R.- (2-22-1892 - 5-26-1961)
HARMON, Callie V.- (11-5-1873 - 5-30-1895) Wife of George Harman,
        age 23 yrs, 6 mos & 25 days.
HARMON, Infant child of George & Callie Harman. (Dates illegible)
HARMON, Robert Paxton- (3-2-1935 - 1-28-1983) U.S. Army.

HARNER, William Ray- (10-20-1898 - 7-26-1986) WW I & II
HARNER, Floy B.- (4-25-1903 -   ) Wife of William Ray H--

HARRIS, Charles L.- (7-22-1927 - 12-5-1970)

HAYTON, Cecil Leon- (3-31-1920 - 5-30-1990)
HAYTON, Felicia A.- (9-9-1930 -   )
HAYTON, Andrew Brown "Brownie"- (4-19-1911 - 9-12-1990) Age 79, FHM
HAYTON, Ollie Kate Williams- (10-29-1900 -1-27-1952) W/o Grat Hayton
HAYTON, Andrew Jackson- (12-27-1867 - 9-14-1944)
HAYTON, Mary Dell Kitts- (6-6-1875 - 1-20-1952) W/o Andrew J. Hayton

HOUDASHELL, Fred M.- (10-17-1900 - 2-5-1956)
HOUDASHELL, Tess- (7-2-1900 - 11-29-1968)

HUBBLE, Mamie R.- (8-17-1893 - 9-14-1914) W/o H.B. Hubble.
HUBBLE, W.A.- (1901 - 1978)
HUBBLE, Mary U.- (1907 - 1955)
HUBBLE, William A. Jr.- (9-24-1925 - 1-24-1992) { US Navy}
HUBBLE, Edith L.- (6-21-1926 -   ) {W/O Wm. A. Jr.}

HULL, Dorcas Harman- (4-4-1935 - 10-28-1963)

KIMBERLIN, Claude W.- (4-24-1902 - 5-14-1974)
KIMBERLIN, Berma A.- (10-24-1902 -   )

KING, Thomas- (2-17-1891 - 2-18-1980)
KING, Lillian V.- (8-31-1892 - 1-16-1976)
KING, John Greever- (9-11-1854 - 5-24-1927)
KING, J. Ellen- (1857 - 1940)
KING, William P.- (1852 - 1936)
KING, Charles David Owen- (1-13-1931 - 7-12-1994)

KITTS, Samuel L.- (4-2-1847 - 5-15-1906)
KITTS, Augusta DeAvor- (9-1854 - 9-8-1883)

BETHANY CHURCH CEMETERY
[One mile down Route 626, off State Route 42, west of Ceres, Va.]

KITTS, James Glen- (7-24-1877 - 7-30-1899?)
KITTS, Martha- (1850 - 1906) {Mother}
KITTS, George- (1850 - 1897) {Father}
KITTS, Amanda Wilson- (3-12-1862 - 11-2-1947)

LAMBERT, Clifford Basil- (3-27-1932 - 11-27-1988)
LAMBERT, Linda D.- (1965 - 1969)
LAMBERT, Delightful Victoria- (7-8-1906 - 4-30-1996)

LEONARD, G.W.- (1910 - 1967)

MCFARLAND, Eliza M.- (4-13-1833 - 2-5-1901)
MCFARLAND, B.P.- (2-14-1854 - 4-13-1930)
MCFARLAND, Mattie K.- (1893 - 1976)
MCFARLAND, L. Dunn- (1877 - 1958)
MCFARLAND, Rosa May King- (2-21-1887 - 3-11-1920) Age 33 yrs, 18 das.
MCFARLAND, Laura- (9-15-1876 - 9-12-1930)
MCFARLAND, Loranza D.- (1829 - 1904) {51st VA Inf. CSA}

NEEL, Anna Ruth- (6-17-1932 - 11 14-1990) Age 58.

NOONKESTER, Nancy Ann- (1888 -   )
NOONKESTER, Belle Tibbs- (5-5-1878 - 8-29-1908) {Mother}

PALMER, Charles- (3-4-1916 - 11-25-1964)

PATTERSON, Elizabeth F. Umbarger- (5-1-1828 - 8-1907) W/o William P

PERRY, Nancy McFarland- (1870 - 1945)

REPASS, Zeyn- (7-1-1894 - 2-8-1966) WW I
REPASS, Okie Kitts- (4-12-1896 - 6-4-1985) Wife of Zeyn Repass.
REPASS, Roy F.- (12-14-1901 - 10-15-1933)
REPASS, Roger A.- (1-15-1891 - 4-10-1961)
REPASS, Eula E.- (1-8-1897 - 5-15-1932) Wife of R.A. Repass.
REPASS, Arthur Glen- (4-7-1870 - 12-1-1948)
REPASS, Margaret May- (5-11-1880 - 5-20-1954)
REPASS, Infant dau. of A.E. & Sue Repass. (died 4-14-1953)
REPASS, Layfayette Digby- (12-3-1882 - 7-22-1937) Father
REPASS, Ardelia B.Baumgardner- (8-24-1887 - 9-5-1953) W/o L.D. Repass
REPASS, Malinda C- (3-13-1836 - 2-17-1897) {W/O Fredrick F. Repass
    and d/o Micajah Saunders.}
REPASS, Ella M.- (2-6-1861 - 3-4-1880) {D/O F.F & M.C. Repass.}
REPASS, Morris D.- (1878 - 1961)
REPASS, Gray U.- (1886 - 1967)
REPASS, Robert O.- (1-27-1921 - 1-25-1945) WW II
REPASS, Orville Dupree- (12-21-1917 - 2-28-1945){Army Air Corps WW II
REPASS, Hectorine I.- (7-15-1867 - 8-31-1924)
REPASS, Elias- (11-28-1825 - 7-3-1906)
REPASS, Adeline E.- (9-19-1839 - 4-9-1900)

BETHANY CHURCH CEMETERY
[Down Route 626, off State Route 42, west of Ceres, Va.]

REPASS, Elva T.- (1899 - 1980)
REPASS, Esther- (died 6-9-1880, age 84 yrs, 11 mos, & 11 days.)
        { Nee Gullian, w/o Reuben Repass, divorced.}
REPASS, Ira Guy- (1875 - 1943)
REPASS, Infant son, parent's names illegible. (died 11-4-1902)
REPASS, Ibby T.- (9-9-1845 - 11-29-1902) Wife of Dr. I.M. Repass.
REPASS, I.M.- (6-7-1836 - 6-26-1890) He was a doctor.

SHUFFLEBARGER, J. Glen- (9-11-1903 - 9-5-1972)
SHUFFLEBARGER, Mable A.- (5-3-1900 - 12-21-1986)

SHUPE, Inez T.- (10-9-1912 -   ){W/O John A., md 10-4-1930}
SHUPE, John A.- (10-6-1906 - 6-23-1987)

SMITH, Almetta C.- (6-28-1928 - 9-15-1976){ Wife & Mother}
SMITH, Frank A.- (9-26-1912 - 4-7-1995) {Father} US Army WW II

STOWERS, Roy Brown- (1905 - 1906)
STOWERS, Nellie Glee- (1897 - 1897)
STOWERS, Mattie Washington- (1894 - 1905)
STOWERS, Elbert- (died 2-1-1902)
STOWERS, Adam A.J.- (12-1869 - 3-1899)
STOWERS, James Lawrence- (1895 - 1897)
STOWERS, Hattie Matilda- (11-28-1898 - 7-23-1971)
STOWERS, Trula Mae- (2-8-1901 - 6-30-1960)
STOWERS, Amanda McFarland- (11-27-1865 - 1-29-1929)
STOWERS, James Madison- (1-12-1840 - 11-20-1911)

TIBBS, Samuel F.- (9-12-1876 - 8-10-1965)
TIBBS, Odessa I.- (7-17-1876 - 9-29-1961)
TIBBS, Curtis W.- (12-18-1912 - 6-10-1988) Dad.
TIBBS, Cleta C.- (10-22-1918 -   ) Mom.
TIBBS, Herman- (3-20-1899 - 6-10-1949)
TIBBS, Loma A.- (2-8-1901 -   )
TIBBS, Henry- (no dates, CSA stone)
TIBBS, Adrian Morris- (10-20-1940 - 11-18-1993) {US Navy}

TURLEY, Reese T.- (1-29-1857 - 3-4-1946)
TURLEY, Louisa Barnett- (1-30-1854 - 3-29-1911) Wife of Reese T.
TURLEY, William R.BV.- (9-29-1899 - 2-3-1920)

UMBARGER, Katherine Walker- (3-18-1886 - 10-1-1960)
UMBARGER, Eli Franklin- (10-1-1881 - 6-10-1960)
UMBARGER, "Granny" Cleo- (7-15-1910 - 1-19-1987)
UMBARGER, Hubert Hall- (9-16-1909 - 1-25-1966)
UMBARGER, Carl Sherman- (11-14-1912 - 3-9-1983)
UMBARGER, Russell Layman- (5-12-1938 - 5-15-1938) S/o C.P. & R.E. U
UMBARGER, Asby P.- (9-11-1865 - 4-20-1949)
UMBARGER, Ruby P.- (8-27-1883 - 4-24-1956)
UMBARGER, James J.- (7-25-1859 - 8-7-1932)

UMBARGER, Jonathan R.- (1991 - 1991) FHM
UMBARGER, Jesse H.- (6-21-1888 - 10-2-1975)
UMBARGER, Hattie B.- (5-22-1889 - 12-12-1960)
UMBARGER, Brittany- (died 7- 1986)
UMBARGER, John F.- (3-22-1833 - 9-5-1915)
UMBARGER, Rachel D.- (8-12-1857 - 3-27-1926)
UMBARGER, Elmer Golden- (9-23-1909 - 8-9-1996) {US Navy}
UMBARGER, Nellie- (9-22-1918-   )
UMBERGER, Herman Frazier Fred- (4-8-1916 - 12-2-1982)
UMBERGER, Thomas P.- (1825 - 1921)
UMBERGER, Elizabeth A. Brooks- (1841 - 1920) W/o Thomas P. U-
UMBERGER, Charles Augustus- (4-7-1854? - 6-19-1941)
UMBERGER, Mary Jane Patterson- (3-27-1852 - 10-31-1927)
UMBERGER, Infant of C.A. & Mary J. Umberger (no dates)

WADDELL, Richard- (1863 - 1928){ H/O Dillie Kegley Waddell}
WADDELL, Dillie- (1866 - 1918) {D/O J.G & Esther Newberry Kegley)
WADDELL, Ella Miller- (5-21-1891 - 2-12-1975)(W/O Arthur, d/o Dr.
                       Daniel A. & Mary Elizabeth Newberry Miller}
WADDELL, William Arthur- (8-22-1885 - 10-25-1971){S/O Rich. & Dillie}
WADDELL, Willard- (3-19-1916 - 5-13-1989) {S/o Arthur & Ella)
WADDELL, Wanda- (2-1-1923 - 12-29-1978) {W/O Willard, nee Scott}
WADDELL, Alees- (1906 - 1939)
WADDLE, James- (no dates)
WADDLE, Infant of W.A. & Ella Waddle. (No dates)
WADDLE, Luther- (No dates)
WADDLE, Amanda (No dates)
WADDLE, Ina- (1919 - 1919)

WAGNER, Lennie William- (9-6-1906 -   ){S/o Emory Waggoner
WAGNER, Clara Stowers- (5-12-1903 - 2-18-1961){W/O Lennie}

WILLIAMS, Andrew Paul- (1918 - 1971) WW II
WILLIAMS, Rose Mary- (1925 - 1971)
WILLIAMS, Lela Jane- (5-13-1895 - 10-9-1954)
WILLIAMS, Kent- (8-15-1886 - 9-3-1948)
WILLIAMS, Andrew J.- (1847 - 1928) Age 81, Father
WILLIAMS, Matilda- (1856 - 1927) Wife of Andrew Williams.
WILLIAMS, Mamie T.- (2-8-1903 - 2-1-1945)
WILLIAMS, John A.- (11-5-1890 - 5-5-1964)

WILLIAMSON, F.R.- (1936 - 1986) {Newberry FHM}

WILSON, R. Grace- (9-3-1870 - 9-25-1950)
WILSON, A.P.L.- (7-4-1868 - 1-1-1926)
WILSON, William Wallace- (4-4-1904 - 2-27-1974)

YOUNG, Lula V.- (1-19-1896 - 3-11-1974)
YOUNG, Joseph E.- (9-8-1884 - 4-22-1966)
              { Numerous field stones and many that are illegible}

GREEN VALLEY METHODIST CHURCH CEMETERY
[On Wolf Creek in Bland County]

CHILDRESS, Taulby B.- (1-15-1901 - 8-2-1973)

FOX, Earl J.- (1-21-1907 - 1-26-1980) PFC US Army, WWI
FOX, Annie C.- (6-16-1838 - 6-23-1906)
FOX, Mathias A.- (7-28-1834 - 5-23-1909)
FOX, Bertha Kidd- (1885 - 1965)
FOX, Stephen Whitley- (1874 - 1930)

FRY, Allen P.- (7-10-1858 - 2-4-1907)

HEDRICK, (illegible dates) Infant dau of Wm. & Z.C. Hedrick.
HEDRICK, (died 11-3-1858) Infant son of Wm. & Z.C. Hedrick.

HEILMAN, Fred W.- (5-15-1876 - 7-14-1961)
HEILMAN, Fannie- (2-21-1889 - 7-6-1944)
HEILMAN, J. E. - (1-15-1929? - 8-?-1917)
HEILMAN, Maria C.- (2-2-1849 - 1-29-1921)
HEILMAN, Etta L.- (10-10-1880 _ 1-14-1949)
HEILMAN, Albert S.- (3-14-1879 - 5-11-1950)
HEILMAN, Fred "Ted"- (3-27-1909 - 3-18-1974)
HEILMAN, Olla B.- (6-7-1913 - 1991) Married Dec. 30, 1930
HEILMAN, Walter B.- (7-1-1907 - 3-28-1957)

HORTON, A. A.- (died 3-17-1911) age 68yrs 10mos 13das. W/o William.

IGO, Patrick Winton- (9-4-1886 - 7-2-1967)
IGO, N.J.- (1887-1955) W/o Patrick. D/o John & Julia Waggoner Smith.

KIDD, Vernie O.- (1884 - 1964)
KIDD, Ann H.- (1886 - 1965)
KIDD, J. Glenn- (1909 - 1984)
KIDD, Melvin Arthur- (7-8-1904 - 1-11-1984)
KIDD, Hazel Jean Heilman- (4-25-1912 - 10-4-1984)
KIDD, Edna M.- (10-24-1908 - 1-16-1963) Mother
KIDD, Clyde Wan- (Died April 25, 1994, age 77) S/o Vernin & Annie
    Heilman Kidd.

LOONEY, Robert Leon- (Died March 30, 1994, age 77) S/o Linkous &
        Mollie Igo Looney. (Obit)

O'FARRELL, Lawrence M.- (1918 - 1967)
O'FARRELL, Pearl K.- (1919 - living in 1987)

SMITH, Rev. John A.- (5-20-1832 - 9-7-1906)
SMITH, Julia A. (12-19-1839 - 6-14-1898) { W/o Rev. John Smith and
                        d/o Adam & Elizabeth Hutzell Waggoner.}
SMITH, Mary T.-(4-10-1875-1-8-1898) D/o John & Julia Waggoner Smith.
SMITH, Sarah J.-(11-26-1858-9-21-1863) D/o John & Julia W. Smith.

STOWERS, Elsie F.- (1905 - 1934)

GREEN VALLEY METHODIST CHURCH CEMETERY
[On Wolf Creek in Bland County]

STOWERS, Texas J.- (2-3-1895 - 4-13-1966)
STOWERS,- (Ed Hicks- (10-7-1893 - 1-3-1972)

WOLF, Whitley M.- (12-9-1973 - 8-30-1956)
WOLF, Texas M.- (7-27-1872 - 7-17-1906)
WOLFE, Emma Ann- (5-?-1905 - 7-30-1906
{ There are several unmarked graves and some with only fieldstones. }

FROM CROCKETT CEMETERY IN CROCKETT'S COVE IN WYTHE COUNTY VIRGINIA

PATTERSON, William, departed this life January 25, 1825, age about 81
            years. {He was the father of Annah, Louvisa and Matilda
            Patterson, who married the 3 Mustard brothers, William,
            John and Elisha. William's 2nd wife was Agnes Patton, d/o
            Capt. Henry Patton of Revolutionary War fame.

FROM OLD PATTERSON CEMETERY IN CROCKETTS COVE, WYTHE COUNTY VIRGINIA

PATTERSON, James- died July 15, 1850, aged 55 years & 7 days. {S/O
            William & Agnes Patton Patterson}
PATTERSON, Sarah-(2-5-1803 - 6-2-1884){W/O James, d/o Stephen Halsey}
PATTERSON, Calvin G.- (9-20-1833 - 9-14-1898) {Md. M. M. Patterson on
                                        8-16-1855}
PATTERSON, Margaret M.- died 1-2-1922. {W/O Calvin G. Patterson}
PATTERSON, John S.- (5-18-1837 - 1-19-1919)
PATTERSON, Margaret- (3-4-1839 - 8-9-1895) {W/O John S. Patterson}
PATTERSON, John Calvin- (5-25-1865 - 5-22-1926)
PATTERSON, Charles C.- (7-9-1849 - 8-31-1940)
PATTERSON, Eliza A.- (5-21-1849 - 10-6-1899)

{ These above names and dates from the old Crockett and Patterson
Cemeteries was given to me by Mr. Rush Crockett of Crockett's Cove in
Wythe County. He knew that I had been searching for documentation as
to the true name of my 5th generation grandfather. Some historians
have claimed that his name was "Isaac Patterson". Wythe County wills
and deed records prove that his name was William. His wife Agnes died
in Giles County about 1841. Many thanks to Mr. Rush Crockett for
proof of William's burial site and the pictures he made for me of the
grave stone. } Parke C. Bogle

GRAVES BEHIND CENTRAL CHURCH

Probably at one time there were more graves here. These stones are not old, so may have been put here much later than when the deaths occurred. Only four graves here at this time. June of 1997

BIRD, Charles R.- (1859 - 5-6-1931)
BIRD, Sarah Robertson , wife of Charles, (8-11-1861 - 11-13-1925)

HARMAN, Orsova C.- (1853 - 1930)
HARMAN, Mary A.- (1852 - 1924)

CEMETERY AT OLD SCHOOL HOUSE BETWEEN CENTRAL CHURCH AND ROUTE 42

HARMAN, Arista- (1882 -   )
HARMAN, Marcia Jane Hoge, (9-25-1894 - 6-30-1959) { Dau. of William
        Howe Hoge and Vicie Mustard Hoge. Wife of Arista Harman }
HARMAN, Verno- (10-24-1917 - 7-5-1980) Dau. of Arista and Marcia.

HOGE, William Howe- (7-18-1853 - 2-1910)
HOGE, Vicie J.- (6-18-1869 - 3-26-1957) { D/O James Harvey Mustard
        and Marcia Robinett Mustard}
HOGE, Ollie M.- 1st wife of William Howe Hoge, died May 24, 1888, age
        27 years and 25 days. (The top part of this stone was badly
        eroded, but the letters "OLL" were plain to see and the dates.
        Her maiden name was MAHOOD)
HOGE, Infant daughter of W.H. and Ollie Hoge, died 10-16-1885.
HOGE, Jamanah, daughter of W.H. & Ollie Hoge, 9-19-1887 - 8-11-1888)
        (I very carefully checked the spelling of this child's name.)

MUNSEY, Frank E.- (1858 - 1930)
MUNSEY, Mary Jane- (1858 -   )

MUSTARD, Ruby Agnes, (4-19-1885 - 1-13-1981) {D/o J.H. & Marcia M-}

THOMPSON, Lena Poca- (11-7-1868 - 2-12-1924) { D/O Joshua B.
        Thompson and Margaret Burton McCoy Thompson }
THOMPSON, Margaret E.- (2-5-1837 - 2-11-1919) {2nd w/o Joshua B. T--}

{ These two grave sites were copied in July of 1997 by Parke C. Bogle and Mrs. Garman Lester. If any one knows of others who may be buried here please let us know.

                          Mrs Garman Lester
                          85 Stafford Drive
                          Dublin, Va 24084
                                or
                          Parke C. Bogle
                          1117 High Street
                          Pulaski, VA 24301
                  Email- <parkebog@swva.net>

MUNCY CEMETERY

{ Cemetery is located about 2 miles east of Bland, to the left of
Route 42 across from G.C. Haven's farm.
[Copied in 1998 by Jo Ann Tickle Scott]

BAXLEY, Levi C..- (12-7-1880 - 1-5-1937)
BAXLEY, Minreva J.- (2-15-1896 - 1-2-1981)

BURTON, Miller T.- (5-16-1894 - 10-4-1918) {Killed in WW I }
BURTON, James George- (9-24-1902 - 7-5-1928)
BURTON, James Andrew- (1-17-1868 - 98-1943)
BURTON, J.J.- (2-18-1872 - 11-15-1930)

FANNON, Jasper N.- (10-18-1851 - 3-17-1909)
FANNON, Aclus- (5-10-1816 - 7-10-1881)

FISHER, Jesse J.- (10-21-1882 - 10-10-1947)

GRAVELLY, Peggy May- (5-23-1936)
GRAVELLY, James A.- (1-7-1915 - 4-3-1979)
GRAVELLY, Virginia N.- (3-7-1917 - 8-29-1995)

JOHNSON, Daisy G.- (10-19-1881 - 9-1-1934) {D/O J. Hoge Thompson}

KITTS, George W.- (5-19-1873 - 11-22-1921)
KITTS, Nannie B.- (8-13-1883 - 10-23-1946. {Married 1900}

MUNCY, Jacob- (5-19-1820 - 8-20-1888)
MUNCY, Martha- (10-7-1821 - 1-27-1901) {W/O Jacob}
MUNCY, John Gordon- (10-20-1856 - 9-28-1931)
MUNCY, Missouri Havens- (11-24-1856 - 3-4-1936)
MUNCY, Davis H.- (3-??-1849 - 6-25-1936)
MUNCY, Julia A. Stafford- (12-17-1850 - 7-27-1907) {W/O D.H. Muncy}

NELSON, Cecil W. Jr.- (4-10-1942 - 6-12-1993)
NELSON, Cecil W. Sr.- (4-11-1922 - 2-22-1994)
NELSON, Violet A.- (4-3-1925 -   ) {Married 11-3-1940}
NELSON, Edward Clinton- (1-13-1942 - 12-19-1972) "Our beloved son"

PEAK, Amanda V- (1863 - 1956)

STAFFORD, Esta Lee- (10-31-1902 - 5-11-1906) {D/O J.L. & M. Stafford}

THOMPSON, J. Hoge- (10-21-1851 - 11-15-1891)
THOMPSON, Rhoda Lou- (12-15-1849 - 3-10-1924) {W/O J.Hoge Thompson}
THOMPSON, Ossie F.- (12-2-1883 - 10-20-1964) {D/O J.Hoge & Rhoda}

{ 4 field stones in row 4}

GRAYSON CEMETERY
{ Cemetery is located on land now owned by Gerhart Schoenthal, south
of Bland Courthouse. It is at the very end of the road.}
[Copied in 1998 by Jo Ann Tickle Scott]

GRAYSON, A.J.- (8-28-1831 - 5-5-1910) {Capt. Co. F 45th Regiment, VA
                    Infantry from 1861-1865}
GRAYSON, Rosalie V.-(2-9-1838 - 3-25-1911) {D/O L.F. Johnson, W/O AJ}
GRAYSON, Andrew Jackson, Jr.- (1-8-1868 - 2-9-1868)
GRAYSON, Harriet Bell- (6-19-1863 - 1-29-1883)
GRAYSON, M.K.G.S.- (1864 - 1894) {D/O John J. & Mary Sinn}
GRAYSON, Virginia- (b.& d. 1-13-1869) {D/O A.J. & Rosalie J. Grayson}
{ One stone with "M.K.G" no dates}
{ One stone with "L.F.G" no dates}
{ A fieldstone between A.J. Jr and Harriet Bell Grayson}
{ A field stone on other side of Harriet Bell Grayson}

BURTON FAMILY CEMETERY
{ Copied in October of 1998 by Jo Ann Tickle Scott}

BURTON, Giles H.- (1859 - 1938)
BURTON, Callie D.- (1861 - 1935)
BURTON, Lorenza Dell- (1891 - 1963)
BURTON, Ada Hutzell- (1891 - 1976) {D/o Ira L. Tickle, W/o L. D.}
BURTON, Minnie S.- (4-23-1857 - 6-11-1929)
BURTON, Eliza E.- (11-27-1850 - 1-7-1948) {W/O Thomas Vaughn}

PAINTER, Steward G.- (6-3-1886 - 5-19-1928)

THOMPSON, Wade- (4-2-1900 - 12-17-1945)
THOMPSON, Fern- (8-18-1900 - 9-2-1992)
THOMPSON, Helen Fern- (10-7-1924 - 8-16-1928)
THOMPSON, Eleanor and Maxine, (b.&d. 1-8-1928) {twins of Kyle & Opal
                    Burton Thompson}

GRAVE SITE
{ This grave is up on a bank in a fence row between Tommy Mallory's
and Romano's land. It was formerly owned by Miller Dillow. Dillow was
overseer of the Poor House. According to Mildred Richardson, Dillow
buried this lady on his property. There is no marker. Nancy was a
servant woman who Parke Bogle remembers working in the home of Meek
Miller in the 1930's. Jo Ann Tickle Scott found this burial spot in
December of 1998. It is good to know that some one remembers the
resting places of these old people.}

RHINEHART, Nancy- (died in the 1930's) No stone for her here.

MUNSEY FAMILY CEMETERY
[Located on a hill south of Route 604, on Robert O. Munsey farm]
[Copied by Jo Ann Ticke Scott and Donna Distel]

HARMON, Infant- (b. & d. 11-8-1911) { S/O W.S & E.P. Harmon }

KITTS, Shuler Bruce- (3-30-1894 - 3-25-1950) { Pvt. US ARMY, WWI }
KITTS, M. Cathleen- (8-21-1931 - 4-13-1934) { D/O S.B. & Lena Kitts }

MUNSEY, Cecil W.- (5-14-1905 - 1-29-1944) (Brother }
MUNSEY, Olin M.- (9-15-1907 - 10-9-1981)
MUNSEY, Louise M.-(6-29-1912 -   ) { Nee McSpadden, W/O Olin }
MUNSEY, E. Marvin- (1-30-1878 - 1-31-1948) {S/O J.H. & Margaret H. }
MUNSEY, Lola F.- (9-23-1878 - 1-2-1964){Nee Foglesong, w/o E.Marvin }
MUNSEY, Margaret L.- (1-22-1842 - 11-18-1917){Nee Hutzell, w/o J.H.}
MUNSEY, James H.- (1-15-1830 - 3-6-1908){H/O Margaret Hutzell Munsey}
MUNSEY, Emily F.- (1871-1911) { Nee Kitts, 1st w/o Patton Munsey,
                and D/O Andrew & Nancy Kitts }
MUNSEY, Margaret Louise- (2-25-1925 - 2-27-1925)
MUNSEY, William Harry- (12-5-1928 - 6-19-1929)
MUNSEY, Infant- (b. & d. 2-3-1919) {Child of Bowman & Fannie Munsey}

ON A LARGE MUNSEY MONUMENT
{ These initials and dates }
EGM- (11-18-1898 - 5-18-1912)
NKM- (8-7-1890 - 7-12-1909)
RKM- (3-16-1906 - 4-23-1908)
HJM- (10-24-1862 - 7-21-1923)
CAKM- (1-12-1862 - 5-17-1943)
AMW- (12-14-1994)
ELM- (8-26-1888 - 12-23-1909)
The date "1923". (Unknown)

THESE NAMES ON FOOT STONES

Ruby Kate Munsey
Nora Kelly Munsey
Fayette Lee Munsey
Ettie G. Munsey
Annie Munsey Wyrick
Harvey J. Munsey

{ Cemetery is well kept. Need a 4x4 to reach it }

14

BLAND CEMETERY, BLAND COURTHOUSE, VIRGINIA
{ Also known as Temple Hill Cemetery }

ALLEN, George A.- (Feb. 19, 1893 - Aug. 18, 1954)
ALLEN, Ethel N. (March 7, 1897 - March 9, 1992)

ANDREWS, Amy N. Bogle, (Sept. 12, 1883 - Oct. 30, 1918), { Wife of
         L. Andrews. }
ANDREWS, Thomas Nye, (Aug. 1, 1905-Oct. 11, 1905) {Son of Amy & L.}

ASHBY, John- (March 12, 1916 - May 24, 1936)

ASHWORTH, Dewey- (Feb. 1, 1900 - Dec. 6, 1974)
ASHWORTH, Hugh T.- (March 24, 1902 - Jan. 22, 1975)
ASHWORTH, Sadie W.- (March 8, 1914 - May 12, 1973)
ASHWORTH, Angie Bird- (1890 - 1984)
ASHWORTH, James S.- (1874 - 1935)

BERGDOLL, John W.- May 13, 1906 - Sept. 24, 1958) (WW II)

BAKER, James C.- (April 27, 1896 - Dec. 27, 1973)
BAKER, Flora T.- (Feb.27, 1894 - Sept 13, 1975)
BAKER, Emmett [Roosevelt] - (1906 - 1990) { Funeral Home Marker
       gives his birth date as Oct. 1, 1904.}
BAKER, Beulah [French]- (Aug. 13, 1918- Oct. 27,1985)

BANKS, Annie K.- (May 27,1898-Nov. 10, 1899) Dau. B.C. & A.E. Banks.
BANKS, Infant of S.J. & Lizzie Banks- July 4, 1900.
BANKS, A.E.- (Nov. 18, 1835 - Jan. 13, 1921)
BANKS, Annie Eveline Green- (Dec. 3, 1867 - May 3, 1936)

BIRD, Ben Lee- (Feb. 25, 1895 - Dec. 2, 1971) Married July 7, 1920.
BIRD, Rosa Jones₋ (Sept. 26, 1901 - Feb. 24, 1990) Wife of Ben Lee.
BIRD, Harry Saunders- (Oct. 4, 1907 - April 22, 1976)
BIRD, Louisa Bernard- { wife of Harry S. }
BIRD, ? Roy, Sr.- (1903 - 1973)
BIRD, infant of Ben & Jane Barger Bird born & died Sept. 27, 1952.
BIRD, Jane Barger-(Jan. 5, 1937-Feb. 15, 1993) {W/O Ben Lee, Jr.}

BISSELL, Ruth E.- (July 15, 1897 - Jan. 1, 1983)

BLANKENSHIP, Charles K.- (Jan. 7, 1912-   )
BLANKENSHIP, Charlie H.- (June 28, 1882 - April 12, 1932)
BLANKENSHIP, Minnie L.- (April 19, 1893 - June 28, 1977)
BLANKENSHIP, J.N.- (1927 - 1988)

BOGLE, Randolph Dunn- (1859 - 1899) { Son of Lorenza Dow Bogle)

BOWMAN, Willie F.- (Jan. 13, 1864 - Nov. 6, 1886) Son of Rev. J.W.
         and S.A. Bowman.

BROWN, G.R. "Park" - (April 6, 1904 - Nov. 24, 1976)
BROWN, Ralph Wayne- (March 7, 1933 - July 14, 1966)
BROWN, Louella- (1876 - 1960)

BLAND CEMETERY, BLAND COURTHOUSE, VIRGINIA
{ Also known as Temple Hill Cemetery }

BROWN, Virginia Mae- (1892 - 1968)
BROWN, Robert Naff- (1883 - 1965)
BROWN, Anna Bird- (1892 - 1965)
BROWN, George R.- (April 19, 1869 - Jan. 30, 1941)
BROWN, Mary Shannon McGinnis- (March 6, 1871-July 17, 1912) { Wife
    of George R. Brown. On Shannon Plot. }
BROWN, Georgie- (Nov. 3, 1897-Oct. 6, 1897) { Dau. George R. & M.S.}
BROWN, Shirley S. [Shannon]- (Feb. 2, 1935 - Feb. 21, 1979)

BRUCE, Guy M.- (Oct 23, 1909 - June 30, 1997) {S/O Wm. J. & Amanda}
BRUCE, Cecil Robinett- (Dec. 26, 1900 - 1992) {Wife of Guy M.}
BRUCE, James Edward- (Jan. 18, 1849 - June 23, 1915)
BRUCE, Edna Harries- (May 5, 1860 - June 25, 1929)
BRUCE, Haynes Hoge- (1894 - 1944) {Son of James E. & Edna H. Bruce.}
BRUCE, Mitchell S.- (1851 - 1933)

BRYANT, Parley P.- (Feb. 8, 1910 - Dec. 3, 1990)
BRYANT, Mildred T.- (March 14, 1920 -   )

BURTON, Clifford M.- (1929 - 1968)
BURTON, Alex Kornick (died 1971)
BURTON, Samuel V.- (Oct. 8, 1896 - April 10, 1956)
BURTON, Robert L.- (July 11, 1901 -   )
BURTON, Annie L. - (Jan. 1, 1907 - Dec. 5, 1978)
BURTON, Varis- (1907 - 1976)
BURTON, James W.- (Aug. 10, 1869 - Aug. 5, 1931)
BURTON, Lola Painter, (Jan. 10, 1874-May 26, 1950) Wife of James W.
BURTON, G.R.- (Jan. 24, 1847-May 17, 1905) {Father}
BURTON, Virginia Caroline Kitts- July 27, 1840-Aug. 6, 1902) age 62
    years, 9 days. Wife of G.R. Burton.
BURTON, Samuel White- (Dec. 19, 1893 - April 14, 1944. (WW I)
BURTON, William C.- (May 2, 1902 - Dec. 1, 1855)
BURTON, Lena T.[hompson]- (Sept. 15, 1902 - Nov. 7, 1970)
BURTON, Junior Lee- (Sept. 20, 1925 - March 14, 1993) {US Navy WW II}
CARR, Mattie G. Straley, (Jan. 29, 1859 - Oct. 20, 1918) { Wife of
    John E. Carr }
CARR, John E.- (1857 - 1937)
CARR, Etta F.- (1881 - 1966)

CARTER, Catherine-(1901-1976) { On Repass plot. }

CARVER, James Daniel- (March 16, 1894 - July 1, 1975)
CARVER, Lillian Wynn- (Dec. 23, 1886 - Aug. 17, 1955)

CHANDLER, Charles F.- (1877 - 1957)
CHANDLER, Eliza J. - (1887 - 1965)
CHANDLER, C. Greever- (May 19, 1906 - March 15, 1979)
CHANDLER, Ruby B.- (June 23, 1916 -   )
CHANDLER, Micheal Scott- (1962 - 1963)
CHANDLER, Herman Brown- (born and died July 19, 1939)

CHANDLER, Eugene Ray- (born and died May 30, 1945)
CHANDLER, Clarence, Jr.(Sept. 17, 1937 - Sept. 18, 1937) Son of
       C.M. and Marie Chandler.
CHANDLER, Clarence M.- (June 13, 1913 - May 16,1963) { Father }
CHANDLER, Herman B.- (1904 - 1969) {Father}
CHANDLER, Willis D.- (1903 -   ) {Mother}
CHANDLER, John F.- (July 29, 1888 - Nov. 3, 1920)
CHANDLER, Bessie V.- (Dec. 18, 1881 - Feb. 7, 1944)
CHANDLER, George Milton- (April 10, 1880 - Aug. 8, 1954)
CHANDLER, William D.- (Oct. 23, 1902 - Sept. 16, 1920)
CHANDLER, Lusy E.- (March 9, 1900 - Sept. 23, 1918)
CHANDLER, Wallace S.- (Feb. 24, 1908 - May 5, 1993) {US Army WW II }

CLEMONS, William R.- (Aug. 19, 1920 - Married to Eva April 20, 1946
CLEMONS, Eva June- March 2, 1929 - March 21, 1984) wife of Wm. R.
CLEMONS, William R., Jr., (Nov. 2, 1947 - Nov. 6, 1947)

COLLINS, Robert "Buck"- Oct. 9, 1900 - March 29, 1982)
COLLINS, Joseph Sidney- (April 24, 1897 - June 23, 1983)

COMBS, Earl Lee- (June 18, 1899 - Dec. 9, 1944.
COMBS, Victor Harmey- (Oct. 18, 1880 - March 11, 1934)
COMBS, { Old stone, completely eroded, illegible }
COMBS, Addie Ella- (July 25, 1906 - Oct. 19, 1926)
COMBS, Sarah- (Feb. 23, 1870 - April 5, 1919)
COMBS, { Illegible, badly eroded } On Combs plot.

COMPTON, Arthur R.- (1928 - 1975)
COMPTON, Lawrence G.- (1894 - 1981)
COMPTON, Olvia M.- (1901 -   )
COMPTON, Blanche K.- (Jan. 21, 1921 -   ) { Nee Kinzer, w/o Joe B.}
COMPTON, Joe B.- (Sept. 27, 1914 - Dec. 2, 1990)

CRUMP, William B.-(July 16, 1848-July 16, 1870)S/o G.W. & S.J. Crump.

CURRY, Percy S.- (1895 - 1977)
CURRY, Anna Y.- (1908 - 1970)

DALTON, Ina K. - (1890 - 1979)
DALTON, Robert A.- (1894 - 1961)

DAMEWOOD, Willie F.- son of S.M. & S.E. Damewood (died Dec. 3, 1870,
       age 8 years, 4 mos. and 13 days.)
DAMEWOOD, Sallie E.- wife of S.M. Damewood, (died June 9, 1877, age
       37 years and 23 days.)
DAMEWOOD, Samuel M.- (Sept. 5, 1845 - Aug. 27, 1928)
DAMEWOOD, Elizabeth Botkins- (April 16, 1863 - June 19, 1913)
       { 2nd wife of S. M. Damewood }

DAVIDSON, Ethel Johnston- (1893 - 1988)

DAVIDSON, Eugene M.- (1885 - 1959)

DEHART, Richard F.- (Feb. 1, 1932 - Feb. 18, 1989)
DEHART, Bobbie Jo- (May 5, 1935 -   )
DETIMORE, Thomas- (8-7-1937 - 1-8-1995) {Pfc. US Marine Corps.}

DILLMAN, Ernest Wagoner- (Oct. 22, 1913 - Oct. 22, 1963)

DILLOW, Ina K.- (1890 - 1979)x
DILLOW, Robert A.- (1894 - 1961)x
DILLOW, Paul M.- (Feb. 10, 1918 -   ) { Md. Aug. 13, 1939 }
DILLOW, Alma (Harden)- (Sept. 23, 1918-Mar. 13, 1989) {W/O Paul M. }
DILLOW, Henry H.- (March 31, 1876 - April 5, 1957)
DILLOW, Miller Basil- (Feb. 10, 1918-   ) {Twin of Paul M.}
DILLOW, Anna Belle- (Sept. 23, 1918-   ) {Twin to Alma, w/o Basil}
DILLOW, Nannie Jane- (July 11, 1884 - Sept. 19, 1948)
DILLOW, Henry G. "Gordie" - (1922 - 1986)
DILLOW, Kate W.- (1923 -   )
DILLOW, Albert M.- (1897 - 1956)
DILLOW, Herbert R.- (Sept. 2, 1929 - Oct. 3, 1975) { Korean War }
DILLOW, Miller Allen- (March 11, 1890 - April 5, 1972)
DILLOW, Mary Davis- (April 4, 1887 - Dec. 16, 1965)
DILLOW, Rickey Allen- (March 5, 1956 - Dec. 10, 1991)
DILLOW, Luther A. "Eli"- (1922 - 1977)
DILLOW, Ruby Pauley- (no dates)
DILLOW, John Ambrose- (June 26, 1884 - Dec. 28, 1969)
DILLOW, Minnie Duncan- (July 19, 1890 - March 9, 1994){W/O John A. }
DILLOW, Jacob Nye- (1887 - 1945) { Dad }
DILLOW, Lena Stowers- (1895 - 1959) { Mom}
DILLOW, Nannie Grace- (Dec. 31, 1917 - Nov. 23, 1918) { Daughter }
DILLOW, Ralph Nye- (Aug. 14, 1927 - May 3, 1928) { Son }
DILLOW, Estel A.- (Oct. 2, 1910 - April 26, 1984) { WW II }
DILLOW, Myrtle P.- (Feb. 23, 1920 - April 29, 1990)
DILLOW, Everet G.- (July 10, 1917 - Feb. 21, 1919)
DILLOW, Eliza W.- (1881 - 1966)
DILLOW, Shannon F.- (Feb. 19, 1916 - July 1, 1922)
DILLOW, Robert Meek- (Nov. 1, 1877 - April 14, 1920)
DILLOW, Conley Trig- (Aug. 10, 1881 - July 19, 1933)
DILLOW, Conley Edward- (born & died Feb. 4, 1943)
DILLOW, Conley Talbert- (Nov. 30, 1921 - Dec. 21, 1947)
DILLOW, Della Tickle-(June 10, 1883 - March 23, 1973)
DILLOW, Frances Madelene- (Nov. 4, 1922 - Jan. 31, 1923)
DILLOW, Thomas G.- (Oct. 25, 1877 - Dec. 16, 1957)
DILLOW, Margaret Lou- (Sept. 3, 1875 - March 21, 1948)
DILLOW, Douglas Leon, Sr.- (Sept. 2, 1923 - June 26, 1982)
DILLOW, Mildred Ramsey- (July 29, 1929 - Oct. 19, 1996){W/O Douglas}
DILLOW, William C.- (1894 - 1963)
DILLOW, Mary H.- (1903 - 1974)
DILLOW, William A.- (Nov. 3, 1920 - March 12, 1984)
DILLOW, Betty Lee- (Aug. 7, 1946 -   )

DILLOW, D. Harold- (Feb. 3, 1923 -   )
DILLOW, Jamie M.- (Aug. 20, 1923 - Nov. 8, 1985)
DILLOW, Robert Grayson- (Sept. 29, 1912 - May 27, 1997) {S/O Bob Andy
                                    and Margaret Tickle Dillow }
DILLOW, Maggie (Parnell)- (Sept. 13, 1916 -   ) {W/O Robert G. }
DILLOW, Walter R.- March 16, 1911-June 4, 1996){S/o Miller & Mary }
DILLOW, Virginia Painter- (Dec. 21, 1918-Sept. 16, 1996) {W/O Walter}

DODD, Melinda- (Sept. 30, 1808 - April 7, 1881) { My mother }
DODD, Berkley- (June 13, 1808 - July 1, 1890)

DUNCAN, Allen T.- (died Nov. 5, 1932)
DUNCAN, Virginia Kitts, wife of Allen, (May 22, 1876-Jan. 19, 1952)
DUNCAN, Harvey E.- (1877 - 1966)
DUNCAN, Ananias- (Dec. 12, 1847 - Oct. 15, 1922)
DUNCAN, Eveline- (Sept. 25, 1845 - Jan. 18, 1922)

DUNN, Samuel B.- (1918 -   )
DUNN, Virginia M.-(1916 - 1972)
DUNN, Margaret Grayson Williams-(Feb. 19, 1876 - Feb. 9, 1958)
    { Wife of Joseph Bascom Dunn }
DUNN, Joseph Bascom- (Feb. 25, 1878 - Feb. 17, 1963)
DUNN, Emily Ruth- (June 4, 1893 - July 20, 1909)
DUNN, Mary Kate- (Aug. 1, 1890 - Oct. 16, 1973)
DUNN, Clarence Stanley- (Nov. 29, 1895 - Feb. 18, 1955)
DUNN, Helen Burkhard- (Feb. 18, 1902 - Mar. 19, 1966)
DUNN, Frank Lee- (Nov. 18, 1883 - April 25, 1959)
DUNN, William David- (March 10, 1916 - March 28, 1966)
DUNN, Mary Carson- (March 15, 1920 - March 8, 1981)
DUNN, Jackson Scherer- (Aug. 13, 1918 - May 14, 1987)
DUNN, Washington Scherer- (May 19, 1888 - July 30, 1964)
DUNN, Loetta Buck- (March 14, 1893-Aug. 21, 1945) Wife of W. Scherer.
DUNN, James T., Jr.- (Oct. 7, 1920 - May 12, 1991) { WW II }
DUNN, James Thomas, Sr.- (July 13, 1876 - Oct. 25, 1954)
DUNN, Annie Kegley- (Nov. 6, 1888 - May 12, 1977)
DUNN, Guy Brown- (May 2, 1886 - Nov. 10, 1954)
DUNN, Mary (Umbarger)- (Aug. 16, 1898-Dec. 14, 1992) {W/O Guy}
DUNN, Nora H.- (Jan. 7, 1894 - June 3, 1953)
DUNN, Roy Bryce- (Jan. 28, 1925-Sept. 26, 1948) { US Navy, WW II }
DUNN, E. Vance- (March 13, 1896 - Feb. 16, 1981) { WW I }
DUNN, Josephine B.- (d. Sept. 15, 1976)
DUNN, Jack S.- (1918 - 1974) { Air Force, WW II }
DUNN, Ruth Umbarger- (Oct. 13, 1909 - June 29, 1973) { WW II }
DUNN, Charles M.- (1894 - 1972)
DUNN, Lena T.- (died 1971)
DUNN, Ralph W.- (1906 - 1952)
DUNN, Mary R.- (1901 - 1990)
DUNN, E. Lorean- (May 17, 1931 - Oct. 14, 1971)
DUNN, Lucy May, dau. / D.W & C. Dunn, (Jan. 16, 1880-July 18, 1899)
DUNN, D.W.- (Nov. 27, 1846 - March 2, 1921)

BLAND CEMETERY, BLAND COURTHOUSE, VIRGINIA
{ Also known as Temple Hill Cemetery }

DUNN, Cynthia S. (Sept. 5, 1852 - June 1, 1919)
DUNN, Bettie Williams- (April 13,1865-Oct. 31, 1896) Wife, C.W. Dunn.
DUNN, Charlie W.- (Aug. 31, 1857 - Sept. 1, 1944)
DUNN, Ella Young- (Aug. 25, 1863 - Nov. 26, 1949)
DUNN, Joseph Young- (Sept. 4, 1904 - March 11, 1906)
DUNN, Sarah Effie- (Dec. 15, 1881 - Nov. 11, 1942)

EAGLE, William D.- (1868 - 1941)
EAGLE, Nannie J.- (1876 - 1927)

ENGLE, Morton A.- (July 29, 1918 -   )
ENGLE, Louise King- (Dec. 13, 1914 - Oct. 7, 1986)

ESTEP, Lettie Rose Wylie- (1915 - 1950) { Daughter, on Wiley plot}]
FELTY, Carl S.- (Nov. 28, 1934 - Feb. 6, 1990) { Md Jan. 27, 1960 }
FELTY, Janet S.- (Jan. 26, 1946 -   ) { Md Jan. 27, 1960 }

FINLEY, Thomas Nye- (Aug. 25, 1842 - May 28, 1917)
FINLEY, Loura Lester- (Oct. 24, 1868 - Feb. 22, 1918)
FINLEY, Thomas Nye, Jr., -(May 1, 1896 - Nov. 22, 1931)

GILLS, Pamela M.- (June 10, 1932 -   )
GILLS, Haven Howe, Jr.- (Sept. 5, 1932 - Oct. 3, 1957)
GILLS, Haven Howe, Sen.- (Nov. 27, 1890 - Sept. 3, 1968)
GILLS, Bessie King- (March 7, 1902 - Feb. 19, 1958)

GILLY, Victor Robert-(Nov. 30, 1915 - Sept. 30, 1976)
GILLY, Dorothy Shrader- (July 13, 1920 - Nov. 12, 1986)

GOINS, Ollie N.- (1916 -   )
GOINS, William J.- (1911 - 1969)
GOINS, Lillie B. Kelly- (March 23, 1888 - Aug. 6, 1965)
GOINS, James Franklin- (March 8, 1885 - Oct. 24, 1959)
GOINS, Victor R.- (Feb. 13, 1909 - March 5, 1990)
GOINS, Glada H.- (Nov. 7, 1920 -   )
GOINS, Dorothy May- (May 23, 1933 - March 31, 1934)

GORDON, Ella Julia- (1892 - 1992)
GORDON, L. Elizabeth- (1871 - 1959)
GORDON, J. Fulton- (1901 - 1920)
GORDON, Arthur- (1867 - 1937)
GORDON, J.S. Morton- (1898 - 1955)
GORDON, Buford W.S.- (1914 - 1990)

GRAHAM, Grace M.- (1906 - 1941)

GREEN, John Wiley- (Dec. 10, 1905 - Jan. 21, 1963)

GREEN, William Nye- (Oct. 15, 1909 - July 30, 1981)
GREEN, Callie Blevins- (Feb. 27, 1910 -   )

GREEN, Thomas Dunn- (Feb. 12, 1912 - April 1, 1988)
GREEN, Nina Marie- (March 30, 1917 - June 17, 1990)
GREEN, Hallie Naff- (Aug. 18, 1882 - Dec. 15, 1903)
GREEN, William Doan- (April 16, 1869 - May 21, 1949)
GREEN, Edith Pearl Green- (Feb. 23, 1877 - Feb. 24, 1910)
GREEN, Robert Crutchfield- (Oct. 9, 1836 - March 22, 1916)
GREEN, Robert C.- (1907 - 1983) { WW II }
GREEN, Mary Elizabeth- (Feb. 10, 1881 - Dec. 10, 1916)
GREEN, Bert Virginia Stowers- (Nov. 15, 1909-Aug. 15, 1994)
GREEN, Greg- (Oct. 22, 1955-Dec. 11, 1995){Adop. s/o Robt. & Mildred}

GREEVER, Martin Luther- (July 11, 1889 - May 12, 1964)
GREEVER, Mary Newberry- (Dec. 12, 1892 - April 6, 1974)

GROSSI, Emily King- (Oct. 16, 1957 - May 21, 1985)

GROUSE, Elizabeth K.- (Aug. 12, 1828 - July 12, 1910)

HAGY, William C.- (May 9, 1883 - Aug. 13, 1964)
HAGY, Ida King- (Oct. 28, 1881 - Jan. 17, 1962)

HALL, Herbert Kenneth, Jr., (Aug. 22, 1920 - June 19, 1961)
HALL, B.F. "Joe"- (1912 - 1992)
HALL, Wirt- (1897 - 1967)
HALL, Emily- (1896 - 1982)
HALL, Oren, son of N.W. Hall- No dates.
HALL, Henry Lee- (May 17,1892 -Jan. 1, 1900) Son of G.E.& B.B. Hall.
HALL, Gregory E.- (June 19, 1869 - Feb. 27, 1941)
HALL, Beatrix Snead- (Aug. 26, 1870 - April 29, 1967)
HALL, H. Kent- (Oct. 2, 1894 - Aug. 19, 1949)
HALL, Mary Neal- (Jan. 30, 1890 - July 11, 1973)
HALL,   A stone with no names or dates.
HALL, Wayne E., son of W.D & Alice, (1928-1929, age 14 months)
HALL, Alice May H.- (May 16, 1904 - Oct. 17, 1990)
HALL, Wayne Dorst- (Jan 10, 1900 - Oct. 3, 1983)
HALL, Samuel H.- (CSA stone- no dates.)

HAMBLIN, Margaret Pauley- (March 5, 1915 - March 2, 1941)

HAMILTON, Sena M.- (Nov. 26, 1879 - Sept. 11, 1943) { Sena was the
        daughter of William Thomas Hamilton and Rose Nye Hamilton.
        Hamilton was the clerk of the Bland County Court. The plot
        on which she is buried is marked by a huge stone with
        " HAMILTON-WYLIE" etched on it. }

HANCOCK, Charles E.- (Sept. 21, 1870 - March 12, 1939) { Father }
HANCOCK, Mary E.- (April 4, 1875 - March 5, 1945) { Mother }
HANCOCK, Jake W.- (1910 - 1973) { Father } Md. Oct. 22, 1938.
HANCOCK, Dorothy L.- (1922 - 1973) { Mother } Md. Oct. 22, 1938
HANCOCK, James E. Sr., (Nov. 30, 1943 - July 12, 1985)

BLAND CEMETERY, BLAND COURTHOUSE, VIRGINIA
{ Also known as Temple Hill Cemetery }

HANCOCK, Charles Walter- (March 18, 1942 - July 4, 1990) [FHM]
HANCOCK, C. Sheffie- (1901 - 1981)
HANCOCK, Lessie K.- (1905 - 1973)
HANCOCK, Ronald C.- (July 14, 1926 - Sept. 16, 1995)

HARDEN, David Morgan- (June 24, 1920 -   {Md. April 28, 1945 to Lois}
HARDEN, Lois Louise W.- (March 21, 1924 - June 26, 1985)
HARDEN, Denny Andrew- (Jan.1, 1952-Jan. 16, 1994) {S/O J.R. & Lois }
HARDEN, Rita Fowler- (Oct. 4, 1946 -   ) {2nd w/o Denny A. Harden}
HARDEN, Curtis S.- (March 1, 1930 - July 21, 1954)
HARDEN, Zelia Shelton- (April 13, 1903 - Jan. 31, 1939)

HARDY, Sam Leslie, Sr.- (Sept. 25, 1908 - Sept. 2, 1989)

HARMAN, Woodrow W.- (1915 - 1986)
HARMAN, Alberta M.- (1916 - 1967) (Dau of W.T & Narcie Mustard.)
HARMAN, Steven Howe- (Aug. 8, 1960-May 7, 1997){ S/O Mevo & Shirley }
HARMAN, Sharon (Goins)- (Feb. 22, 1957 -   ) { W/O Steven Howe }

HAVENS, Ida H.- (June 30, 1908 - May 27, 1983)
HAVENS, Walker- (July 28, 1898 - Dec. 28, 1911) { Son of Wylie and
        Victoria Havens. Age 13 years and 5 months. }
HAVENS, W.H.- April 26, 1873 - Oct. 30, 1934)
HAVENS, Victoria A.- (April 17, 1875 - May 4, 1941)
HAVENS, Lucy Rose- (June 9, 1940 - Feb. 9, 1968)
HAVENS, Martha Jean- (Jan. 28, 1948 - Dec. 20, 1971)
HAVENS, Gordon C. "Doc"- (Nov. 18, 1899 - Dec. 14, 1984)
HAVENS, Edith A. "Pete"- (Sept. 19, 1919 -   )

HEDRICK, Z.- (Aug. 24, 1829-Dec. 17, 1891) { Wife of W.M. Hedrick }

HEDRICKS, Maggie- (Feb. 20, 1868 - Feb. 22, 1872)
HEDRICKS, Willie Wise- (Aug. 13, 1887 - Sept. 18, 1888) { Son of
        W.C. and Ninnie H. Hedricks }
HEDRICKS, Mary Dean- (July 11, 1889 - July 9, 1900) { Dau of W.C. &
        Ninnie H. Hendricks }
HEDRICKS, Ninnie Bird- (June 21, 1864 - July 5, 1891)
HEDRICKS, a stone so badly eroded, it is illegible.

HIPPS, Euna Pruitt Dilow- (Aug. 16, 1931 - Oct. 13, 1981)

HUBBLE, Reba Slusher- (1892 - 1979)
HUBBLE, Harman Brown- (1887 - 1961) { WW I }

HUNNICUTT, Estelle Repass- (1898 - 1985) Buried on Repass plot.]

HUTCHINSON, Arnold Scott- (Dec. 11, 1914 - Dec. 15, 1983) { WW I }
HUTCHINSON, Emily Pauline- (Nov. 27, 1918 - Aug. 13, 1985)

HYLTON, Robert Sherman- (Sept. 4, 1909 - Oct. 1, 1982)

BLAND CEMETERY, BLAND COURTHOUSE, VIRGINIA
{ Also known as Temple Hill Cemetery }

HYLTON, Bertha Marie- (July 1, 1911 - Jan. 10, 1983)

JONES, Josie Tickle- (Oct. 30, 1896- Nov. 7, 1995){D/O Geo. & Ellen
        Pegram Tickle. W/O Ira Lozier Tickle, Jim Gulliam & L.A. Jones}

KEGLEY, Eloise M.- (1890 - 1983)
KEGLEY, Benjamin H.- (1890 - 1960)
KEGLEY, J. Muncy- (1915 - 1944)

KELLEY, Jas. Willie- (Nov. 14, 1894 - Feb. 20, 1911)
KELLEY, J.G.- (May 15, 1886-Dec. 14, 1909) { Son of J.D. & Rebecca
        T. Kelley, age 23 years, 6 months, and 29 days. }
KELLEY, James D.- (Aug. 2, 1863 - March 12, 1956)
KELLEY, Rebecca Cox- (July 4, 1857 - Jan. 4, 1930)
KELLEY, W. Peirce- (Jan. 16, 1910 - Nov. 21, 1915) { Son of John }
KELLEY, Elizabeth Repass- (No dates)

KIDD, John W.- (July 2, 1941 - Dec. 7, 1983)
KIDD, Rosie K.- (March 20, 1943 -   ) { W/O John W. Kidd }
KIDD, Ira S.- (Jan. 19, 1895 - May 14, 1971)
KIDD, Mildred N.- (May 21, 1906 - May 30, 1997) {W/O Ira S. Kidd }
KIDD, Emma Florence- (Aug. 20, 1894 - April 9, 1964)
KIDD, Sam W.- (1902 - 1977)
KIDD, Roy C.- (Dec. 19, 1896 - March 4, 1984) { Md April 18, 1932 }
KIDD, Mattie H.- (Oct. 23, 1910 -   ){ Wife of Roy C. }
KIDD, David N.-(Sept. 5, 1924-Nov. 9, 1993) { S/O Ira & Mildred
                        Newberry Kidd and W/O Dorothy Sparks }

KIMBERLING, L.B. Jr., - (Sept. 2, 1928 - Sept. 11, 1928)
KIMBERLING, Infant son of L.B. & N.J., March 12, 1929.
KIMBERLING, Lessie B.- (Sept. 1901 - May 17, 1981) Father
KIMBERLING, Pinkie T.- (Oct. 24, 1899 - March 17,1998) Mother.

KING, Howard N.- (Feb. 14, 1926 - March 10, 1963)
KING, Elizabeth B.- (Dec. 30, 1924 -   )
KING, Danny C.- (July 21, 1942 - Dec. 13, 1989)
KING, Willie Kitts- (April 5, 1912 - Feb. 22, 1962)
KING, Dorothy E.- (1920 - 1946)
KING, Texie M.- (1899 - 1985) Mother
KING, Edgar Palmer- (May 29, 1895 - Jan. 2, 1958) Father { WW I }
KING, Rebecca Sue- (March 24, 1941 - March 25, 1941) Infant of
        Helen and Wm. King.
KING, William P.- (Oct. 7, 1914 - Aug. 4, 1964)
KING, John Davidson- (Aug. 12, 1909 - March 24, 1993)
KING, Clara Sarver- (Dec. 3, 1916 -   ) {W/O John Davidson }
KING, Will Keith- (Aug. 23, 1904 - Feb. 14, 1981)
KING, Nannie Dillow- (Nov. 13, 1918 -   )
KING, Lacy P.- (March 10, 1889 - Oct. 19, 1956) Son
KING, E. Terry- (April 29, 1894 - May 10, 1953)
KING, Frances G.- (April 29, 1863 - Oct. 6, 1944)

BLAND CEMETERY, BLAND COURTHOUSE, VIRGINIA
{ Also known as Temple Hill Cemetery }

KING, Harvey N.-(Aug. 22, 1860 - Dec. 3, 1928)
KING, Susan E.- (June 15, 1864 - Nov. 1, 1938)
KING, Pete- (Sept. 15, 1905 - April 17, 1966)
KING, Charles- (1930 - 1931)
KING, Fred- (died 1934, age 21 days.)
KING, Arthur J. Sr.- (May 29, 1895 - Aug. 19, 1952)
KING, Lucy Butcher- (May 30, 1906 - June 6, 1976)
KING, Infants of Mr. & Mrs. A.J. King, May 3, 1962, age 4 days 10 hrs.
KING, Elwood- (March 13, 1932 - Nov. 6, 1941){ Son of Henry & Ida.}
KING, Henry S.- (1907 - 1959)
KING, Ida H.- (1913 -   )
KING, Dorothy Ann- (1960) Infant.
KING, David Allen- (May 31, 1949-Oct. 21, 1993) {US Navy WW II }
KING, Wanda Christine (Puckett)- April 6, 1932-Dec. 9, 1998)
        { W/O Garland and D/O Milford & Cansada Puckett }

KITTS, James Andrew- (1886 - 1965)
KITTS, Mrs. Andrew- (1896 - 1956)
KITTS, Miller W.- (Jan. 17, 1866 - May 4, 1956)
KITTS, Emma J.- (Dec. 19, 1877 - July 22, 1960)
KITTS, Ida Sexton- (1897 - 1974)
KITTS, N. Finley- (Sept. 14, 1908 - April 13, 1983)
KITTS, Elizabeth N.- March 28, 1918 - Oct. 19, 1991)
KITTS, Eli Dale- (Aug. 30, 1873 - March 1, 1946)
KITTS, Ida Lou Burton- (April 7, 1898 - May 13, 1984)
KITTS, Allison Hallie- (June 5, 1895 - May 28, 1978)
KITTS, Andrew W.- (Feb. 19, 1918 -   )
KITTS, Claudine R.- (Jan. 15, 1920 -   )

KOREN, Albert T.- (1911 - 1978)

LAMBERT, Elizabeth H.- (Oct. 8, 1927 - April 26, 1976)
LAMBERT, Dell Purkey- (June 21, 1899 - Aug. 6, 1968)
LAMBERT, Tilden Scott- (Nov. 15, 1894 - March 2, 1987)
LAMBERT, Thursa Lindamood- (Nov. 29, 1874 - Feb. 22, 1958)

LESTER, Garman L.- (June 26, 1922 - July 7, 1985)
LESTER, Elsie M.- (June 30, 1926 - Feb. 17, 1985) {W/O Garman Lester}

LINDAMOOD, Chloe- (March 16, 1909 - Sept. 8, 1975)
LINDAMOOD, Beulah- (April 30, 1912 - April 26, 1997){W/O Chloe}
LINDAMOOD, William M.- (April 30, 1905 - May 8, 1970)
LINDAMOOD, Florene S.- (Oct. 23, 1908 -   )

LOGAN, James P.- (March 27, 1886 - Dec. 13, 1957)

MALLORY, James Thomas- (born & died Oct. 9, 1967)

MANN, Allen Thompson- (July 25, 1920 -   )
MANN, Rosa C. Bird- (April 20, 1921 - Feb. 21, 19??)

BLAND CEMETERY, BLAND COURTHOUSE, VIRGINIA
{ Also known as Temple Hill Cemetery }

MANN, Allen T. Jr.- (March 22, 1945 - May 16, 1953)

MCLEAR, Josephine D.- (April 10, 1902 - Oct. 17, 1963)

MCPEAKE, Paul Hoover- (June 30, 1928 - May 1, 1985)
MCPEAKE, Rosalee H.- (Sept. 3, 1926 -   )

MILLER, June M.- (1932 -   )
MILLER, Rev. Earl M.- (1914 - 1983)

MILLIRONS, Mosie- (Sept. 15, 1908 - Aug. 19, 1938)
MILLIRONS, Frances- (Sept. 15, 1906 - April 19, 1993) {W/O Mosie}
MILLIRONS, Delphene- (April 17, 1932 -   ){D/o Mosie & Frances}

MOORE, Imogene Martin- (Jan. 7, 1935 - Aug. 18, 1969)
MOORE, Joe Ed- (April 20, 1935 - Feb. 7, 1991)
MOORE, Carolyn T.- (Aug. 12, 1941 -   )

MOREHEAD, Annie H.- (Nov. 8, 1902 - Nov. 24, 1985)
MOREHEAD, Eugene M.- (March 14, 1898 - Jan. 30, 1981)
MOREHEAD, Fannie L.- (Oct. 18, 1910 - Nov. 24, 1954)
MOREHEAD, Glen K.- (Dec. 18, 1901 - Oct. 15, 1976)

MUNCY, James B. Sr.- (Feb. 24, 1907 - Oct. 5, 1953){S/O C.P.& M.E}
MUNCY, Charles Peery, Jr.- (Feb. 10, 1906 - Aug. 2, 1952)
MUNCY, Mary Elizabeth H.- (Feb. 8, 1911 -   )
MUNCY, Joseph Hounshell "Jo-Boy"- (Sept. 6, 1939 - Aug. 22, 1952)
MUNCY, Gratton Mustard- (Sept. 17, 1898 - April 19, 1962) Father
MUNCY, Mary E. McNutt- (Feb. 7, 1898 - Feb. 12, 1948) Mother.
MUNCY, Sarah Elizabeth- (1891 - 1965)
MUNCY, Charles Peery- (June 14, 1854 - Aug. 18, 1908)
MUNCY, Mary Ella- (Jan. 13, 1868 - Oct. 5, 1954)
MUNCY, Anna Josephine- (Nov. 3, 1895-Sept. 30, 1986)School teacher.
MUNCY, Nannie Rose- (Feb. 10, 1904 - 10-11-1993) School teacher
MUNCY, Minor- (July 4, 1892 - May 4, 1962) { WW I }
MUNCY, Cynthia D.- (Jan. 13, 1928 - Nov. 7, 1965)
MUNCY, Bess Repass- (Nov. 15, 1894 - Feb. 21, 1992) {W/O Minor }
MUNCY, Hilary S.- (Oct. 3, 1928 - Sept. 12, 1984) { Korean War }
MUNCY, Gilbert Carter- (Dec. 4,1929-April 28, 1992){S/O Minor & Bess}
MUNCY, Patricia R.- (March 17, 1925-Sept. 28, 1992) {D/Minor & Bess}
MUNCY, Thomas J.- (April 2, 1864 - May 7, 1922)
MUNCY, Hope LaMoore- (died June 2, 1966)
MUNCY, Andrew N.- (Aug. 5, 1900 - Nov. 27, 1986)Md Sept. 8, 1924.
MUNCY, Merle V.- Nov. 13, 1903 - April 21, 1986) Md. Sept. 8, 1924.
MUNCY, William M.- (Oct. 31, 1938-Dec. 12, 1994) {S/O Andrew & Merle}

MUSTARD, Rosebud Martin- (Aug. 17, 1940-March 14, 1988){W/O Jacob A.}
MUSTARD, Jacob Andrew- (June 15, 1922 -   ) {S/OJohn C. & Effie}
MUSTARD, John C.- (1867 - 1947) {S/O J.H.& Marcia Robinett Mustard}

BLAND CEMETERY, BLAND COURTHOUSE, VIRGINIA
{ Also known as Temple Hill Cemetery }

MUSTARD, Effie W.- (1884 - 1975) {D/O Dr. J.A. Wagner}

NEAL, Barnett A.- (Feb. 18, 1885 - July 31, 1957)
NEAL, Nellie Tickle- (Aug. 4, 1895 - Aug. 10, 1984)
NEAL, Ray Andrew- (1902 - 1983)
NEAL, Roxie Lee- (1904 - 1988)

NEEL, Nannie J.- (Nov. 25, 1849 - March 7, 1929)

NESTER, Virginia D.- (1882 - 1933)
NESTER, Luther Clarence- (Aug. 8, 1910 - Nov. 19, 1910)
        { Son of J.H & V.D. Nester. }
NESTER, Dugless- (July 21, 1920 - Nov. 17, 1920) Son of V.C. & S.J.
NESTER, Ethel Goins- (April 21, 1911 -   )

NEWBERRY, Henry Stuart- (Aug. 25, 1918 - Sept. 19, 1970)
NEWBERRY, Walter Stephen- (July 16, 1880 - June 21, 1964)
NEWBERRY, Cynthia Stuart- (Dec. 8, 1885 - April 19, 1973)
NEWBERRY, William M.- (Aug. 26, 1910 - April 10, 1972)
NEWBERRY, Kemp G.- (April 21, 1888 - July 2, 1957){W/O Lawrence N }
NEWBERRY, Edgar A.- (Jan. 31, 1921-May 22,1997){S/O Walter & Cynthia}
NEWBERRY, Lorene D.-(July 13, 1927-   ) {W/O Edgar, nee Dillow}
NEWBERRY, Dianna L.- (May 23, 1951 -   ) {D/O Edgar & Lorene}
NEWBERRY, Robert G.- (Sept. 22, 1925-   ) {S/O Walter & Cynthia}
NEWBERRY, Naomi U.- (Dec. 17, 1926-May 6, 1996){ D/O Harlow Umbarger
                                    and W/O Robert G. Newberry }
NICEWANDER, Burl- (1895 - 1968)
NICEWANDER, Faye A.- (1903 - 1978)

OTT, Eugene Page- (June 1, 1924 -   )
OTT, Lois Porterfield- (Jan. 29, 1922 -   )

PAINTER, Zebulon L.- (July 3, 1892 - May 28, 1973) { WW I }
PAINTER, Kate B.- (died Aug. 18, 1983)
PAINTER, Alice B.- (March 18, 1887 - Feb. 26, 1975)
PAINTER, Sharla H.- (Sept. 10, 1991 - Sept. 28, 1986)
PAINTER, Hezekiah G.- (July 7, 1890 - June 8, 1954)
PAINTER, Elizabeth Tickle- (Sept. 24, 1848 - Jan. 12, 1947)
PAINTER, George D.- (May 15, 1854 - May 16, 1932)
PAINTER, Irene M. Chandler, wife of J.G. Painter, (Feb. 27, 1882 -
        Dec. 1, 1908) Age 26 years, 9 months, 4 days.
PAINTER, Joseph G.- (March 20, 1870 - Dec. 13, 1932)
PAINTER, Cynthia P.- (Nov. 27, 1866 - Aug. 6, 1936)

PATTERSON, J.F. "Dixie"- (March 16, 1903 - Feb. 28, 1992)
PATTERSON, Annie Miller- (Nov. 9, 1896 - Jan. 28, 1987)
PATTERSON, George S.- (April 7, 1900 - March 15, 1987)
PATTERSON, Pearl S.- (Sept. 15, 1905 - Feb. 11, 1983)

PAULEY, Albert- (1902 - 1984)

BLAND CEMETERY, BLAND COURTHOUSE, VIRGINIA
{ Also known as Temple Hill Cemetery }

PAULEY, Paul R.- (March 10, 1916- ?-1998) {H/O Dora Belle Ramsey}
PAULEY, Dora Belle- (Sept. 26, 1923-Sept. 20, 1996) {D/O Otho Ramsey}
PAULEY, Ruby- (1909 -   )
PAULEY, Perry- (Dec. 6, 1911 -   )
PAULEY, "Bud" William G.- (June 15, 1887 - April 1, 1953)
PAULEY, Freelove Hancock- (May 31, 1891 - May 18, 1967)
PAULEY, Isaac W.- (1907 - 1961)
PAULEY, Walker B.- (May 22, 1905 - March 11, 1965) Wife of Paul
PAULEY, Cornelia- (Nov. 17, 1917 - Oct. 6, 1992)
PAULEY, Josephine Tickle- (July 17, 1920 - April 16, 1965)
PAULEY, Paul Lake- (Oct. 16, 1917- Oct.6, 1992){H/O Josephine Tickle}
PAULEY, Ward L.- (April 30, 1903 - March 20, 1961)
PAULEY, Dow, (Dec. 27, 1918 - Jan. 26, 1972) { WW II }
PAULEY, Myrtle N.- (Feb. 22, 1891 - May 25, 1959)
PAULEY, Harmon W.- (Feb. 2, 1892 - Dec. 13, 1956)
PAULEY, Carl H.- (May 5, 1883 - Feb. 28-1956) { Father }
PAULEY, Sheffie M.- (Feb. 5, 1887 - May 4, 1978)   { Mother }
PAULEY, Milli℮ Johnson- (May 12, 1945 -   )
PAULEY, Ralph Wayne- (May 15, 1934 - May 27, 1981)
PAULEY, Ella H.- (March 18, 1915 -Feb. 3, 1998) { Nee Hancock, w/o
                    Chaffin K. Pauley and Charles Blankenship.}
PAULEY, Chaffin K.- (June 5, 1899 - March 26, 1964)
PAULEY, Rosa M.- (Oct. 3, 1890 - May 10, 1986)
PAULEY, Daniel C.- (July 15, 1888 - Dec. 11, 1963) { Father }
PAULEY, Bertha L.- (Feb. 8, 1895 - Aug. 26, 1972) { Mother }
PAULEY, Albert S.- (1895 - 1965)   { Father }
PAULEY, Ethel K.- (1902 - 1966)   { Mother }
PAULEY, Earl G.- (Aug. 31, 1924-Feb.18, 1944){Killed in Italy, WW II}
PAULEY, Elmer Frazier- (April 29, 1923 - Sept. 28, 1986) { WW II }
PAULEY, Isaac G.- (Aug. 18, 1825 - July 9, 1907) age 81 yrs, 21 das
PAULEY, Jerry Rae- (March 10, 1959 - March 13, 1959)
PAULEY, Charlie G.- (1893 - 1967)
PAULEY, Gertrude Baker- (1898 - 1982)
PAULEY, Julia M.- (Jan 11, 1866 - Sept. 3, 1946)
PAULEY, Nancy Lee- (April 11, 1950 - July 19, 1950)
PAULEY, Garnett C.- (Aug. 12, 1910 -   )
PAULEY, Charlie- (Jan. 12, 1915 - July 26, 1988)
PAULEY, Virgie Mae- (Sept. 21, 1921 -   )
PAULEY, George M.- June 18, 1957 - Aug. 10, 1990)
PAULEY, Harvey Hiram- (Feb. 21, 1886 - March 7, 1952)
PAULEY, Gratton G.- (Oct. 3, 1855 - Jan. 22, 1927)
PAULEY, Mary Geneva Kitts- (Feb. 8, 1860-Jan. 26, 1930) Wife of Grat.
PAULEY, Jane Ella- (July 30, 1930 - May 20, 1991)
PAULEY, Walter T.- (Oct. 24, 1910 -   ){ Md Mar. 12, 1934 }
PAULEY, Ruby K.- (July 8, 1915-March 10, 1985) { Md Mar. 12, 1934 }
PAULEY, Ward Clifton- (May 7, 1964 - Sept. 18, 1993){S/O Ward, Jr.
                    and Geneva Carrol Pauley.}
PAULEY, Julia Hancock- (March 7, 1883 - May 15, 1952)
PAULEY, Harve B.- (June 28, 1876 - Oct. 5, 1951)
PAULEY, Pauline- (Oct. 16, 1917 - Oct. 22, 1917)

BLAND CEMETERY, BLAND COURTHOUSE, VIRGINIA
{ Also known as Temple Hill Cemetery }

PAULEY, Pinkie J.- (Aug. 16, 1901 - Aug. 28, 1901)
PAULEY, Virgie Mae- (May 21, 1921-Feb. 6, 1993)

PEAK, James F. "Boss"- (1879 - Jan. 4, 1959)
PEAK, Allie- (-Feb. 28, 1953   )

PEARSON, Grace S.- (Oct. 10, 1892 - Jan. 18, 1982) { Shannon Plot }

PEERY, Minnie Wayne McColgan- (March 4, 1895 - Sept. 18, 1970)

PENLEY, Merle R.- (Aug. 14, 1907 - Aug. 12, 1965)
PENLEY, Alfred M.- (Jan. 28, 1906 - Dec. 26, 1981) { Husband }
PENLEY, Mary W.- (Feb. 11, 1913 - Sept. 27, 1987) { Wife }
PENLEY, Sandra Suzette- (Oct. 10, 1956 - March 15, 1961)
PENLEY, John S.- (May 25, 1910 - Oct. 23, 1992) S/O Way & Agnes
PENLEY, Margaret E.T.- (July 7, 1911 - Nov. 30, 1965) { Daughter of
    Miller Hoge Thompson and Mollie Kate Ashworth Thompson. She
    married John S. "Buddy" Penley, June 21, 1940. }

PORTERFIELD, Mary Virginia- (1918 - 1979)
PORTERFIELD, Arthur Roland- (March 29, 1875 - March 18, 1924)
PORTERFIELD, Cynthia G. Brown- (May 21, 1893 - May 22, 1941) {
          { Arthur and Cynthia were married Sept. 26, 1916 }
PORTERFIELD, James H.- (Sept. 7, 1878 - Feb. 22, 1936)

POWLEY, Ed- (1883 - 1906) [Probably is "Pauley" misspelled]

PUCKETT, Milford- (Feb. 7, 1905 -   )
PUCKETT, Cansada- (June 12, 1907 - Feb. 15, 1978)

RATCLIFF, James E.- (1848 - 1930) { Bailey Funeral Home Marker }
RATCLIFF, Maggie I. Painter, wife of J.E. Ratcliff, (Sept. 20, 1848-
          Feb. 1, 1907) age 55 yrs 1 month & 11 days.
RATCLIFF, Virginia Bower- (July 29, 1850 - July 27, 1922)

REPASS, David E.- (May 23, 1917 - Dec. 13,1964)
REPASS, Hazel Bruce- (1898 - 1962)
REPASS, Gilbert Raymond- (1893 - 1960)
REPASS, James C.- (Aug. 29, 1903 - July 31, 1976)
REPASS, Zola M.- (Oct. 28, 1905 -Oct. 16, 1994) { W/O Jim Repass and
                    d/o Lee Kyle & Emmarilla Miller Morehead }
REPASS, Everette Fulton- (1908 - 1978)
REPASS, Mary Belle D.- (1909-1998) {W/O Everette "B" Repass & d/o
                    John & Minnie Dillow}
REPASS, S. Roy- (April 16, 1906 - Dec. 29, 1973)
REPASS, Lucy D.- (Nov. 3, 1906 - March 4, 1946) { Wife of Roy }
REPASS, Robert G.- (June 15, 1900 - May 23, 1988)
REPASS, Raymond C.- (Oct. 5, 1860 - Feb. 19, 1928)
REPASS, Juliet E.- (Aug. 27, 1871 - Sept. 2, 1940)

BLAND CEMETERY, BLAND COURTHOUSE, VIRGINIA
{ Also known as Temple Hill Cemetery }

RICHARDSON, C.P. "Bud"- (June 7, 1899 - July 19, 1987)
RICHARDSON, Ruth P.- (April 15, 1926 -   )
RICHARDSON, Hubert G.- (Feb. 17, 1905 - May 9, 1972)
RICHARDSON, Clara D.- (Feb. 22, 1906 - June 2, 1991)
RICHARDSON, Charles N.- (April 9, 1887 - Sept. 13, 1968)
RICHARDSON, Alice B.- (1900 - 1986)
RICHARDSON, Edith- (1915 - 1967)
RICHARDSON, John- (1910 - 1954)
RICHARDSON, Infant of Charles and Alice, born & died Nov. 5, 1935.
RICHARDSON, Stuart S.- (June 25, 1901 - Dec. 8, 1971) { Father }
RICHARDSON, Artie K.- (Aug. 5, 1900 - May 28, 1990) { Mother }
RICHARDSON, Tom Lewis- (April 17, 1935 - July 1, 1940)
            { Son of Hubert and Clara Richardson }
RICHARDSON, Lavada J.- (July 23, 1897 - May 4, 1920)
RICHARDSON, Jefferson J.- (July 3, 1892 - Nov. 10, 1970)
RICHARDSON, Etta E. Neal- (Aug. 4, 1905-June 26, 1926) Wife of J.J.
RICHARDSON, Garnette-(June 2, 1926-July 25, 1926) Dau. of J.J.& E.E
RICHARDSON, C.A.J.- (Aug. 5, 1862 - Dec. 27, 1952)
RICHARDSON, Alice V.- (March 30, 1864 - Oct. 2, 1946)
RICHARDSON, Everette Shanon- (Feb. 20, 1891 - Oct. 22, 1906) { Son
            of C.A.J. and Alice V. Richardson }
RICHARDSON, Walker P.- (Oct. 13, 1894-March 18, 1918) { Pvt, WW I }
            { Son of C.A.J. and Alice V. Richardson }

ROSKA, Lelia Rose T.- (April 12, 1912 - Aug. 11, 1983)

SADLER, Kermit Paul- (Sept. 8, 1912 - July 3, 1976) { WW II }

SARVER, Clyde- (1911 - 1985)
SARVER, Mary- (1919 - 1991)

SCHWONKE, William A.- (Dec. 11, 1925-April 10, 1997)
SCHWONKE, Glorena H.- (July 6,1929-   ) {W/O Wm. A. & d/o Sheffie &
                                          Lessie Hancock }

SCOTT, Ritchie W.- (Dec. 20, 1944 - May 6, 1973)
SCOTT, John M.- (Oct. 16, 1875 - Sept. 28, 1923)
SCOTT, Cynthia Bogle- (Nov.11, 1878 - Nov. 19, 1979)
SCOTT, Charlotte Virginia- (Aug. 16, 1912-May 10, 1993) {D/O John M.
                            and Cynthia Bogle Scott }
SCOTT, Everett- (Sept. 27, 1907-June 6, 1909) Son of John & Cynthia
SCOTT, Walter Russell- (Feb. 3, 1903 - July 13, 1985)
SCOTT, Polly W.- (Jan. 6, 1908-Sept. 20,1984) {Md April 21, 1928}
SCOTT, Carl W. Sr.- (May 16, 1905-Feb. 11, 1991){Md April 21, 1928}
SCOTT, Patsy Ann- (Oct. 27, 1930 - Sept. 26,1932) Dau/ Carl & Polly
SCOTT, John Kenneth- (June 14, 1910 - March 7, 1987)
SCOTT, Anna Laura N.- (May 8, 1914 - April 22, 1987) Wife\ Kenneth.
SCOTT, Kathleen Gayle- Sept. 27, 1935- Aug. 21, 1995) {W/O Carl
                Scott, Jr. and d/o Andrew & Merle Vanhoose Muncy.}

BLAND CEMETERY, BLAND COURTHOUSE, VIRGINIA
{ Also known as Temple Hill Cemetery }

SHANNON, Edgar Earl- (Nov. 8, 1903 - Aug. 21, 1970)

SHAW, William Robert- (1878 - 1963)

SHEWEY, Claude D.- (Aug. 11, 1911 -   ){ Md May 12, 1928 }
SHEWEY, Hazel D.- (March 5, 1906 - Feb. 1, 1978) { Wife of Claude }

SIFFORD, Robert Gordon- (May 26, 1907 - May 14, 1966) { Son }
SIFFORD, Vernie Munsey- (Dec. 18, 1882 - July 17, 1936) { Mother }
SIFFORD, James Gordon- (Dec. 27, 1883 - Sept. 4, 1951) { Father }
SIFFORD, Anna Foley- (Dec. 26, 1902 - Jan. 14, 1988)

SIX, Roy Virgil, Jr.- (Aug. 24, 1948 - Nov. 17, 1963)

SOUTH, Charles M.- (1932 - 1969)
SOUTH, Walter G.- (1894 - 1976)
SOUTH, Bessie Dunn- (1896 - 1968)

SPARKS, Verlie L.- (Jan. 14, 1910 - Feb. 5, 1972)
SPARKS, Ezra- (May 12, 1909 - Sept. 22, 1936)

SPENCE, Mary J.- (1908 - 1985) { Funeral Home Marker }

STACY, Geraldine- (1929 - 1930)

STAFFORD, John R.- (May 29, 1891 - Jan. 4, 1959)
STAFFORD, Virginia O.- (Feb. 6, 1910 - June 28, 1988)

STOWERS, Claude Swanson- (March 18, 1908-Jan. 7, 1981) { Teacher }
STOWERS, Josephine Mustard- (Sept. 14, 1918-   ){ W/O Claude. }
STOWERS, Randolph Carl- (June 4, 1913 - March 9, 1967) { He died at
          St. Joseph, Montana. }
STOWERS, Bessie Robinett- (Aug. 17, 1892 - Feb. 10, 1972)
STOWERS, Emma Green- (Aug. 14, 1872 - July 23, 1956)

STROUPE, Faye Pauley- (March 14, 1933 - Feb. 9, 1990)

STROUSE, Leona B.- (June 5, 1905-April 21, 1996) {D/O Giles & Callie
               Kitts Burton and w/o Archie Strouse }
STROUSE, James A.- (1884 - 1957)

SUITER, Albert W.- (July 27, 1882 - Oct. 23, 1956)
SUITER, Samuel Davis- (1884 - 1960)
SUITER, Cornelia Dutton- (1881 - 1962)

SURRATT, Jimmie- (1795 - 1915) age 120.
          { Two blank stones near the Surratt grave }

SUTPHIN, Arlie J.- (Dec. 18, 1931 - Aug. 10, 1988)
SUTPHIN, Peggy H.- (July 5, 1937 -   )

TAYLOR, Eric Brian- (Jan. 14, 1968 - April 7, 1988)
TAYLOR, Joe- (1881 - 1961)
TAYLOR, Cora- (1892 - 1954)
TAYLOR, Ben Jesse- (March 7, 1914 - June 10, 1954)   { WW II }
TAYLOR, Mary Lou- (June 11, 1912 - July 6, 1992) { Nee Thompson }
TAYLOR, John H.- (Aug. 22, 1917 - Feb. 25, 1989)
TAYLOR, Stella N.- (Dec. 10, 1926 -   )
TAYLOR, Enoch E.- (1901 -   )
TAYLOR, Della B.- (1901 - 1983)

THOMPSON, Cynthia Mae- (Oct. 28, 1920 - July 27, 1978)
THOMPSON, Everett W. Sr.- (Jan. 16, 1926 - July 19, 1986) { WW II }
THOMPSON, George A.-   (Feb. 4, 1929 - Nov. 5, 1972)
THOMPSON, Hatcher- (Jan. 14, 1892 - May 17, 1968)
THOMPSON, Grey Virginia- (April 16, 1897 - June 6, 1964)
THOMPSON, Robert Johnson- (Oct. 19, 1913 - July 9, 1979)
THOMPSON, Lillian Malcomb- (Dec. 29, 1921 -   ) W/o Robert
THOMPSON, Thomas Cicero- (Dec. 12, 1881 - June 9, 1965)
THOMPSON, Ada Miller- (Oct. 23, 1888 - March 22, 1987)
THOMPSON, Kyle- (1895 - 1978)
THOMPSON, Opal- (1894 - 1971)
THOMPSON, Lakie F.- (1901 - 1973)
THOMPSON, Joseph T.- (1929 - 1981) { Korean War }
THOMPSON, Arista C.- (Nov. 11, 1886 - Feb. 22, 1949)
THOMPSON, Effie R.- (Dec. 22, 1893 - Dec. 20, 1979)
THOMPSON, Alice Telie- (1877 - 1958) { "Alice Telie" is all that is
         visible on this stone, but since it was at the Thompson
         plot, I have assumed that her last name was Thompson. }
THOMPSON, Ira Kelly- (1890 -1978) { Md Dec. 29, 1913 }
THOMPSON, Ira Woodrow- (1-8-1914 - 8-12-1995)
THOMPSON, Juanita Shaw- (4-2-1917 - 7-25-1993) {Md. Ira, 7-7-1936}
THOMPSON, Eliza Agnes- (1897-1945){ Md Dec. 29, 1913 } Wife of Ira.
THOMPSON, Everett R.- (Feb. 13, 1916 - April 7, 1952)
THOMPSON, Edgar J.- (1917 - 1969)
THOMPSON, Eva Fern- (1923 -   )
THOMPSON, Brian Shockley- (March 7, 1969 - March 8, 1969)
THOMPSON, G.W.- Aug. 13, 1862 - Sept. 8, 1934)
THOMPSON, Mattie Fox- (Jan. 24, 1863 - Nov. 26, 1937)
THOMPSON, J. Grat- (Dec. 10, 1883 - Dec. 15, 1963)
THOMPSON, Geneva A.- (May 11, 1868 - April 19, 1926)
THOMPSON, Rachel- (1863 - 1930)
THOMPSON, Eddie Hoge- (Sept. 6, 1943 - Oct. 31, 1943)
THOMPSON, Edward- (1867 - 1950)
THOMPSON, Hatcher G. Jr.- (April 22, 1924 - Sept. 21, 1925)
THOMPSON, Betsy- (April 8, 1832 - March 21, 1916) { Nee Melvin }

TIBBS, Baby boy- (July 5, 1982)

TICKLE, Lizzie M. Hancock- (May 18, 1888 - Feb. 21, 1983)
TICKLE, William Nye- (May 28, 1885 - Dec. 19, 1960)

BLAND CEMETERY, BLAND COURTHOUSE, VIRGINIA
{ Also known as Temple Hill Cemetery }

TICKLE, Jesse B.- (March 12, 1922 - May 6, 1986)
TICKLE, Lemuel H.- (1887 - 1971)
TICKLE, Ida Lou- (1888 - 1957)
TICKLE, Claude W.- (July 24, 1916 - Jan. 17, 1984)
TICKLE, Nannie M. Burton- (Aug. 12, 1889 - Feb. 14, 1963)
TICKLE, Kelly Foster- (Aug. 28, 1890 - Dec. 3, 1969)
TICKLE, Robert H.- (1915 - 1969)
TICKLE, Mary D.- (1918-1992) {W/O Robert H, d/o John & Rose S. Davis}
TICKLE, Eula A.- (April 19, 1892 - May 9, 1985)
TICKLE, Howard N.- (June 6, 1899 - June 25, 1985)
TICKLE, Eugene C.- (June 28, 1903 - Nov. 13, 1970)
TICKLE, Pinkie C.- (Sept. 14, 1910 -   )
TICKLE, Mary Katheryne- (Sept. 13, 1946 - Jan. 7, 1947)
TICKLE, Mozell- (March 15, 1917 - Dec. 3, 1919)
TICKLE, Fred L.- (May 6, 1915 - April 8, 1950)
TICKLE, Fred L. Jr.- (May 7, 1945 - Dec. 19, 1986)
TICKLE, John N.- (Feb. 16, 1892 - Jan. 26, 1919)
TICKLE, Mary A. Wagoner- (Aug. 7, 1852 - Oct. 18, 1944)
TICKLE, Mary Lou- (Oct. 17, 1911 - July 25, 1938)
TICKLE, Charles Anthony- (Nov. 13, 1961 - Nov. 14, 1961)
          { Son of Mr. and Mrs. Charles Gordon Tickle }
TICKLE, Eugene C.- (1930 - 1934)
TICKLE, Patricia A.- (1937 - 1937)
TICKLE, Jenetta L.- (1910 - 1941)
TICKLE, Gordon H.- (Sept. 12, 1850 - Aug. 5, 1940)
TICKLE, Christina G.- (July 11, 1863 - Dec. 3, 1934)
TICKLE, Gracie Hounshell- (July 10, 1911 - Jan. 22, 1944)
TICKLE, E. Mason- (Aug. 30, 1908 - Jan. 23, 1978)

TOLBERT, Kemp G.- (April 13, 1909 - April 9, 1958
TOLBERT, Clarence D.- (Aug. 10, 1904 - March 25, 1984)
TOLBERT, W.S.- (a concrete marker, no dates on it)

TRINKLE, Nora L.- (Oct. 5, 1898 - Aug. 9, 1900)

UMBARGER, Everett- (1914 - 1973)
UMBARGER, Marie M.- (1910 - 1980) {W/O Everett, nee Mustard}

WADDELL, Gilbert C.- (Jan. 22, 1898 - July 5, 1978)
WADDELL, Claribelle- (Oct. 26, 1913 -   )
WADDELL, Charles A.- (Aug. 23, 1856 - June 24, 1929)
WADDELL, Angeline- (Jan. 28, 1853 - Sept. 24, 1934)

WADDLE, Ollie G. "Kitt"- (Nov. 14, 1884 - May 4, 1958)

WAGNER, Naomi J.- (1882 - 1957)
WAGNER, Jacob A.- (1861 - 1941) {Beloved physician of Bland Co.}
WAGNER, Josephine M.- (1858 - 1933) {W/O Dr. Jacob Wagner, and d/o
          Dr. Lorenza John Miller }

BLAND CEMETERY, BLAND COURTHOUSE, VIRGINIA
{ Also known as Temple Hill Cemetery }

WALKER, Bertie Olivia Green- (no dates)
WALKER, Dr. Jasper Newton- (1866 - 1938)

WALLS, Willie- (April 5, 1900 - Feb. 16, 1964)

WILLIAMS, Charles Carrington- (Dec. 20, 1924 - April 20, 1925)
WILLIAMS, Brook Grayson- (Sept. 18, 1921 - Feb. 6, 1922)
WILLIAMS, Brooke L.- (Jan. 16, 1927 -   )
WILLIAMS, James David- (Sept. 10, 1957 - Sept. 11, 1957)

WILSON, Clarence Vernon- (Aug. 13, 1911 - Feb. 2, 1987){Korean War}
WILSON, Bynum E.- (March 30, 1903 - Sept. 25, 1989)

WIMMER, Hebert Harold- (May 22, 1924 - Sept. 25, 1989)
WIMMER, Lois H.- (Sept. 23, 1924 -   )
WIMMER, Archie A.- (1902 - 1976)
WIMMER, ZAda Kidd- (1899 - 1967)
WIMMER, Jason Allen- (Oct. 18, 1983 - Oct. 19, 1983)

WOLFE, Kathy- (Nov. 18, 1953 - Nov. 19, 1953)
WOLFE, Charles Sammy- (Jan. 26, 1953 - June 7, 1980)
WOLFE, June Dillow- (1931   ) { Mother of Sammy & Cathy}
        { The name "WOLFE" is not on June's stone, but it is on the
            WOLFE plot. June married a WOLFE.}

WRIGHT, Frank James- (1895 - 1967)
WRIGHT, Sally L.- (1897 - 1983)
WRIGHT, Carl Reid- (April 20, 1921 -   )
WRIGHT, Ethel Meadows- (Sept. 20, 1921 -   )
WRIGHT, Vicki Lynn- (Sept. 20, 1963 - Sept. 22, 1963)

WYATT, Anna D.- (Aug. 7, 1908 - Aug. 23, 1979)
WYATT, Albert P.- (Nov. 27, 1912 - Nov. 20, 1982)

WYLIE, Edgar Nye- (Aug. 17, 1888 - Oct. 28, 1943)
WYLIE, Robert- (April 19, 1840 - May 29, 1886)
WYLIE, Rose C.- (March 8, 1857 - Oct. 22, 1934) { 2nd w/o William
        Thomas Hamilton, md. 2nd to Robert Wylie. Wylie graves are on
        the "HAMILTON-WYLIE" plot.}

WYNN, Infants of A.J. & Julia Wynn- (No dates)
WYNN, Julia M. Hughes- (Feb. 1, 1857 - March 30, 1921) { W/O A.J. }
WYNN, Andrew Jackson- (Sept.25, 1863 - May 27, 1937)
WYNN, Nannie S. Wall- (April 16, 1868 - Dec. 3, 1952)

{ This cemetery was copied on September the 2nd and 3rd of 1992. We
ask your indulgence when you find a mistake that we have made in
copying the dates or in typing them. Please call it to our attention
so that we may correct it on the master disk. } Jo Ann Tickle Scott
reviewed it in November of 1998 and supplied many new death dates.}

BLAND CEMETERY, BLAND COURTHOUSE, VIRGINIA
{ Also known as Temple Hill Cemetery }

Those who copied this cemetery are:
        Mrs. Garman Lester, 82 Stafford Drive, Dublin, VA 24084
                                and
                         Parke C. Bogle
                         1117 High Stree
                         Pulaski, VA 24301
                  Email<parkebog@swva.net>

{All death dates after September of 1992 were copied by Jo Ann Scott}
                    Jo Ann Tickle Scott
                    R.F.D. Bland, VA.
                  Email- <jotickle@naxs.com>

RAMSEY CEMETERY
[A fairly new cemetery, located on top of a hill on Route 631, south
of Route 633, to the right of Kimberling Creek Road. One will need a
4x4 to reach it. It is in excellent condition.]
            { Copied by Jo Ann Tickle Scott }

RAMSEY, Vance- (10-7-1913 - 11-21-1993)
RAMSEY, Ina K.- (11-28-1916 -   ) {Md. Vance, 11-27-1937}

CLARK CEMETERY
[These two graves are on top of a hill south of Route 633, on Pinch
Creek Road. The road is to the right of Kimberling Creek Road]
            { Copied by Jo Ann Tickle Scott }

CLARK, Bernard M.- (1918 - 1977)
HYLTON, William Darrell- (10-9-1938 - 8-2-1995)

FINLEY CEMETERY
[This cemetery is beyond restoration. There were several indentations
in the ground. It is located on a road just past the former house of
Porch Helvey and up on a hill. The graves are down a bank. I capoid
it in 1989 and there have been no burials here since then.
            { Copied by Parke C. Bogle }

FINLEY, J.W.(Jackson Weaver)- (2-13-1838 - 11-22-1919) { S/O James &
            Rebecca Dunn Finley, who were married in Wythe County,
            11-17-1836 by Rev. John Bogle.}
FINLEY, Nannie Neel- (11-11-1844 - 4-3-1922) {D/O Hiram & Nancy
                            Neel and w/o Jackson Weaver Finley }
FRENCH, Infant son (3-9-1925)
MILLER, Lorenza Meek- (1865) { S/O Dr. L.J. Miller. He died in 1952}
MILLER, Rebecca May- (1869-1947) { W/O Lorenza Meek. D/O J.W & Nannie
                            Neel Finley.
SPANGLER, Leona Finley- (4-22-1899 - 2-2-1915) {W/O W.R. Spangler and
                            d/o Frank & Caroline Kyle Ramsey)

BIRD CEMETERY

{ Cemetery is located on the Woodrow D. Bird farm on Route 42 about 2
and 1/2 miles east of Bland. Copied by Jo Ann Tickle Scott in 1998}

ASHWORTH, E. Lee- (6-28-1864 - 10-6-1928)
ASHWORTH, Geneva Bird- (9-11-1868 - 2-9-1945)
ASHWORTH, Arthur M.- (1894 - 1962)
ASHWORTH, Thomas Newton- (7-8-1867 - 2-4-1925)
ASHWORTH, Martha S.- (1874 - 1957)
ASHWORTH, Rev. Armstead A.- (5-23-1818 - 11-19-1910) {A Minister}
ASHWORTH, Parthena Dobbins- (10-18-1827 - 4-1-1918) {W/O Armstead A.}
ASHWORTH, Herman- (8-8-1889 -   ) {W/O Joseph Ashworth. Nee Stuart}
{ A broken stone illegible. Probably Joseph Ashworth }

BIRD, P.H.M.- (9-27-1811 - 6-11-1913)
BIRD, Sarah Francis Noble- (2-25-1839 - 10-21-1909) {W/O P.H.M. Bird}
BIRD, Benj. V.- (1-7-1845 - 5-9-1864) {Killed, Battle of Cloyd's Mt.}
BIRD, Daniel Woodrow- (7-6-1912 - 11-16-1995) {S/O George T. Bird}
BIRD, Elizabeth Dunn- (8-14-1916 -   ) {W/O Daniel Woodrow }
BIRD, George Thomas- (10-9-1865 - 8-12-1945)
BIRD, Carrie Burton- (6-17-1871 - 12-19-1930) {W/O George T. Bird }
BIRD, Benjamin V.- (2-18-1814 - 4-11-1836)
BIRD, Katherine C. Saunders- (3-20-1824 - 3-31-1908) {W/O Benj. V. }
BIRD, Margaret Angie- 12-9-1862 - 1-24-1886) {D/o B.V & K.C. }
BIRD, Infant of Benjamin V. & Katherine Saunders Bird. (No dates)
BIRD, Joseph S.- 9-14-1850 - 5-3-1857) {S/O B.V. & K.C. Bird}
BIRD, William W.- (3-18-1853 - 11-24-1898)
BIRD, Mamie K.- (9-17-1892 - 11-4-1913)
BIRD, Bertha L.- (10-18-1897 - 12-20-1913)
BIRD, Nannie Burton Grayson- (8-26-1874 - 6-11-1922)
BIRD, Infant S/O Vance Lamont & Lucindie Margurite,(b.& d. 1-15-1918)

KINCHLOE, Joan Elizabeth- (1-16-1936 - 11-23-1937) {D/O Joe & Eliz.}

THOMPSON, Amos (@1782 - @1875)
THOMPSON, Andrew- (1750 - 1840) { Soldier of the Revolution. Marker
        placed here by the Count Pulaski Daughters of the Revolution.}
THOMPSON, Ann- (1755 - 1840) {W/O Andrwew Thompson} { Marker placed
                here by Count Pulaski Daughters of The Revolution}

{ 2 field stones in row 2 }
{ 1 field stone in row 3 }
{ 2 field stones in row 5 }
{ 6 field stones in row 6}

CEMETERY IN FIELD EAST OF INTERSTATE 77
{Can be seen on right of road as one approaches Bland after leaving
the Walkers Mountain Tunnel from Wytheville }
[Copied in 1992 by Parke Bogle and Alma N. Waddell]

KEGLEY, J.G. (James Gordon)- (Aug. 3, 1838 - July 1, 1913) Son of
    Isaac Kegley and his wife, Prudence Devor Kegley. He was
    first married to Hester Ann Newberry, daughter of Allen
    Taylor and Elizabeth Bogle Newberry. By Hester he had two
    children, Edward Harman Kegley and Dillie Kegley who married
    Richard Waddle.
KEGLEY, Hester Ann Newberry- (April 6, 1836 - June 30, 1872)
    { D/O Allen Taylor and Elizabeth Bogle Newberry. There is no
    stone for her grave. The dates I have entered were taken from
    the Newberry genealogy, by John A. Newberry. Alma N. Waddle
    assured me that Hester was buried here. The other child of
    Hester and J.G. Kegley was, Dillie Kegley who married Richard
    Waddle and is buried in Bethany Cemetery.}
KEGLEY, Edward Harman- (Nov. 29, 1861 - died in 1887) He was shot
    and killed by a man named Terry because Edward was riding his
    horse on the sidewalk at Bland and refused to move. He was
    unmarried. He is buried here but no stone has survived.
KEGLEY, George E.- (9-20-1883 - 6-25-1884) {S/O J.G.& Fannie }
    { Only fieldstones mark these graves.}
KEGLEY, Fannie- (Aug. 7, 1847 - May 13, 1914) Second wife of James
    Gordon Kegley. Nee Bird.
{ There are about eight graves visible at this time but there are no
  markers to identify those who are buried here. There are two graves
  with plain fieldstones with no markings on them. }
                ORIGINAL SITE OF NEWBERRY CHAPEL
        [On land now owned by the late Carl Rudder]
        {Copied in 1992 by Alma N. Waddell and Parke C. Bogle}
{ Newberry's Chapel was built in 1849 and abandoned in 1950. A red
granite marker placed there by Robert G. Newberry and Allen Taylor
Newberry, III, marks the spot where it once stood. Both Newberrys are
descendants of Rev. Sanuel Newberry who was ordained to preach in
1812, at the Nicewander Meeting House at Crandon.
  There are two small fenced in areas near the red granite marker. In
one area is buried,
REBECCA WOODS, wife of A.T. DUNCAN. (1843 - 1907)
        {Inside the larger area are the following graves}
RUDDER, Jesse Adams- (Nov. 27, 1886 - May 20, 1969)
RUDDER, Minnie Lucille- (March 22, 1898 - 1993?) {Nee Havens }
RUDDER, Charles M.- (1834 - 1918)
RUDDER, Louvisa J.- (1854 - 1938) { 2nd w/o Charles M. Rudder and
daughter of William P. Mustard and his wife Louisa Robinett.}
{Jane Wohlford Raines, 1st wife of C.M Rudder. No stone here for her}
RUDDER, Willie Lou (1881 - 1883) {D/O Charles & Louvisa)
{ In the Archives of the Virginia State Library is listed an unnamed
male child of Charles and Louvisa Rudder as dying on Oct. 29, 1893 at
the age of one month and seven days, from Bold Hives. } There was no
visible sign of another small grave. }
RUDDER, Karl- (5-22-1931 - 7-10-1996) {S/O Jesse & Lucille}

SHRADER'S CHAPEL CEMETERY
[Copied by Jo Ann Tickle Scott in October of 1998]
{ Cemetery located, North side of Route 601, East of the Church }

BROWN, Stuart N.- (10-18-1915) {VA Pvt 155 Depot Brig}

COLLINS, Frank Estol- (5-24-1922 - 4-28-1988)

DEAN, Ocie E.- (5-3-1913 - 6-21-1962) {W/O Herbert Dean, nee Hancock}

HANCOCK, Rosie Collins- (6-3-1910 - 1-16-1985)
HANCOCK, Ellen J.- (4-27-1918 - 7-21-1990)
HANCOCK, Robert L.- (4-21-1915 - 5-2-1978)
HANCOCK, Mabel Irene- (6-8-1932 - 6-10-1932)
HANCOCK, Baby Lucille D.- (9-3-1933 - 10-24-1933)
HANCOCK, Thelma Jane- (6-10-1912 - 1-8-1960) {W/O Clarence Hancock}
HANCOCK, Sanders H.- (12-30-1892 - 9-24-1963)
HANCOCK, Carrie Louise- (7-17-1892 - 4-21-1962) {W/O Sanders H. }
HANCOCK, Ruby Ella- (9-29-1918 - 9-24-1940) { Our darling}
HANCOCK, Buster Lee- (8-2-1928 - 2-8-1929)
HANCOCK, Carl C. "Jack"- (10-21-1927 - 3-21-1981)
HANCOCK, John- (1894 - 1978)
HANCOCK, Sherman Russell- (6-24-1914 - 9-22-1928) {Broken stone.}
HANCOCK, Beatrice R.- (11-8-1918 -   )
HANCOCK, Houston S.- (12-14-1916 - 11-30-1995)
HANCOCK, Noah H.- (7-28-1922 - 8-18-1976)
HANCOCK, Fred Ralph, Sr.- (2-14-1930 - 4-26-1993) {Pvt. US Army}
HANCOCK, Annabel Virginia- (8-12-1932 -   ) {Md. 4-28-1950)
HANCOCK, J.E.- (1-15-1889 - 2-28-1940)
HANCOCK, Lila May- (2-8-1890 - 10-8-1969)
HANCOCK, Mason E.- (5-22-1916 - 9-25-1965}
HANCOCK, M. Walker- (1855 - 1929)

JACKSON, Clara W.- (1904 - 1966)

KING, Eva H.- (1892 - 1931)
KING, G.W.- (1883 - 1958)

ODHAM, Fredia D.- (4-2-1934 - 6-20-1982)

PAULEY, William H.- (12-2-1894 - 5-21-1922) {Father}

ROGERS, Willard B.- (11-5-1924 - 3-24-1986)
ROGERS, Hazel Hancock- (9-29-1931 - 5-22-1983)

SHELOR, Nina F.- (11-27-1935 - 8-7-1988)

TERRY, May Hancock- (- d. 1931
TERRY, Benjamin Franklin- (1869 - 1945)

3 wooden crosses and field stones, 4 wooden crosses, no names,
1 field stone and wooden cross, 1 field stone,
1 field stone, 3 field stones and 3 wooden crosses.

```
BECKLEHEIMER              &              STUART
  Herbert Lee                            J. Wesley
  5-12-1920                              7-28-1928
  8-28-1935                              3-17-1930
                    Infant Daughter
                    Rebecca Marie
                    Oct. 24, 1936
                    Asleep in Jesus
[ The above three names are all on one stone as above stated ]
```

ASBURY, Thomas William- (7-9-1861 - 4-19-1931)

ATWELL, " Little Bunny " (3-17-1916 - 10-3-1917)
ATWELL, Cora Lee- (8-6-1878 - 1-1-1944) (Mother)
ATWELL, Fitzhugh Lee- (3-26-1885 - 2-15-1950)(Father)
ATWELL, Herbert Lee- (3-1-1910 - 5-4-1986)
------- 2 infants near Atwell plot, no names or dates.

AUSTIN, William G. Confederate War Stone- no dates.
AUSTIN, Elizabeth Nester- (1832 - 1923)

BEAMER, Nancy S.- (4-6-1905 - 3-4-1976)
BEAMER, Ben V.- (10-5-1907 - 4-12-1994)

BERRY, Amy Beth- (1-6-1975 -   )
BERRY, Matthew Jason- (11-27-1972)

BLANKENSHIP, Bessie Radford- (12-29-1888 - 1-23-1963)
BLANKENSHIP, Millard Fillmore - (3-11-1878 - 11-22-1927)
BLANKENSHIP, Marvin P.- (8-27-1924 - 5-1-1990)
BLANKENSHIP, Charles R.- (1876 - 1950)
BLANKENSHIP, Flora G.- (1894 - 1986)
BLANKENSHIP, Jenny Bell- (8-9-1895 - 10-23-1877 -)
BLANKENSHIP, Walter Brown- (6-23-1877 - 12-15-1965)
BLANKENSHIP, Curtis D.- (1915 - 1972)
BLANKENSHIP, Ruth W.- (1920 -   )
BLANKENSHIP, Joseph Curtis- (1985 - 1985)
BLANKENSHIP, Earnest C.- (1922 - 1978)
BLANKENSHIP, Pearl W.- (1924 - 1981)
BLANKENSHIP, W. Vance- (1907 - 1973)
BLANKENSHIP, V. Mae- (1907 -   )
BLANKENSHIP, John W.- (7-8-1928 - 3-16-1981)
BLANKENSHIP, Artie B.- (12-22-1931 - 6-5-1976)
BLANKENSHIP, John H.- (5-21-1905 - 5-26-1986)
BLANKENSHIP, Maudie R.- (2-15-1904 - 2-29-1973) {Md. 7-1-1925.}
BLANKENSHIP, Curley J.- 4-12-1936 - 6-22-1971)

BOKSA, Lawrence R.- (4-11-1943 - 4-12-1975) US Army

BRADSHAW, Frank, Jr.- (7-31-1928 - 8-15-1989)

SHILOH METHODIST CHURCH CEMETERY

BRADSHAW, Elizabeth W.- (2-7-1927 -   )
BRADSHAW, George- (11-28-1933 - 2-23-1959)
BRADSHAW, [No given name] 1971 - 1971) FHM
BRADSHAW, Amos E.- (3-7-1946 - 11-2-1969)
BRADSHAW, Frank- (11-12-1907 - 1-20-1993)
BRADSHAW, Barbara Cooper- (10-8-1907 -   )
BRADSHAW, Anita Kay- (Infant of Shannon & Bea Bradshaw- no dates)
BRADSHAW, Fred A.- (1927 - 1998) {Father }
BRADSHAW, Reba M.- (1932 -   ) { Mother }

BRANHAM, George W.- (8-7-1905 - 11-5-1995) {US Army WW II }

BROWN, John A.- (4-24-1831 - 12-26-1915?)
BROWN, Timothy Tad and Anthony Todd- (1979 - 1979)
BROWN, Connie Wright- (1950 - 1992)

BURTON, Elizabeth J.-(11-22-1850 - 3-30-1921)
BURTON, Madella J.- (8-5-1868 - 11-6-1906) (D/O F.F. Repass)
BURTON, Charlotte Blanche - (7-14-1901 - 2-11-1903)
BURTON, Pendleton - (2-1-1836 - 12-5-1919)
BURTON, Josephine R.- (10-14-1880 - 8-29-1930)
BURTON, John W.- (12-30-1868 - 7-6-1952)
BURTON, Ethel Iola - (3-12-1904)
BURTON, Frederick Hash- (2-29-1904 - 11-9-1982)
BURTON, Arland D. - (2-5-1894 - 7-3-1967) {US Army, WW I }
BURTON, Callie Mae Sarver - (8-1-1897 - 1-26-1943) { W\o Arland }
BURTON, Mason E.- (12-19-1897 - 6-29-1969)
BURTON, Gladys E. - (5-15-1907 - 4-21-1961) {Nee Morehead, w/o Mason}
BURTON, Mildred L. - (2-19-1928 - 6-14-1929)
BURTON, Evelyn T.- (8-18-1932 - 4-29-1979) {Mother}
BURTON, Evelyn Elizabeth- (born & died 11-20-1950)
BURTON, William K.- (10-29-1929 - 10-6-1967) {Father}
BURTON, Robert E. - (1930 - 1954)
BURTON, Robert W. _ (4-20-1871 - 2-28-1937)
BURTON, Emory W. - (6-14-1939 - 1-31-1988)
BURTON, James H. - (2-18-1870 - 4-9-1958)
BURTON, Daisey- (2-10-1876 - 11-15-1953) {Nee Mitchell, w/o James H.}
BURTON, Charles R. _ (1-26-1876 - 11-10-1960)
BURTON, Ressie Mae Dunagan- (10-7-1886 - 2-15-1946) { W/O Charles }
BURTON, Wilburn P.- (2-19-1921 - 7-11-1963)
BURTON, Marge L. - (2-17-1937 - 1-1-1940) D\o Mr.& Mrs.F.H.Burton.
BURTON, Fred H.- (1910 - 1956)
BURTON, Maggie L. -(2-17-1937 - 3-1-1940)
BURTON, Mattie J.- (9-23-1906 - 3-3-1931)
BURTON, Dora J.- (9-25-1908 - 12-22-1933)
BURTON, James D.- (6-7-1913 - 11-15-1934)

BYRD, James O.- (1903 - 1987)
BYRD, Zetta C.- (1911 - 1994)

CAMPBELL, John Daniel- (12-2-1920 - 3-29-1996){Father US Navy WW II}

SHILOH METHODIST CHURCH CEMETERY

CAMPBELL, Phyllis Burton- (8-5-1932 -   ) {Mother}{W/O John D.}

CARNER, Permelia- (3-21-1895 - 3-9-1938)

CHANDLER, Walter Bowman- (9-21-1907 - 5-20-1987)
CHANDLER, Elsie Drummond- (11-29-1910 - 11-9-1982)
CHANDLER, Lester N.- (1881 - 1944)
CHANDLER Nina J.- (1884 - 1970)

CLARK, Meek P.- (4-12-1888 - 12-27-1961)
CLARK, Della M.- (4-15-1891 - 12-2-1971)
CLARK, Clovis E.- (1899 - 1976)
CLARK, Belle Sarver- (1893 - 1973)

CLEMONS, Frank C.- (1914 - 1967)_
CLEMONS Mary F.- (1914 -   )

COMPTON, Ruth Alice- (11-23-1925 - 10-19-1971)

CONLEY, Minnie Radford- (11-9-1907 - 1-5-1986)
CONLEY, Charlie Ernest- (9-10-1925 - 2-4-1988){ US Navy Korean War }
CONLEY, James A.- (1931 - 1974)
CONLEY, Ila G.- (1-31-1918 - 1-29-1999){W/O Rudolph, md. 12-24-1936}
CONLEY, H. Rudolph- (6-28-1916 - 8-16-1995) { Md. 12-24-1936}

DALTON, Julia E.- (1900 -   )
DALTON, Clyde R.- (1889 - 1964)
DALTON, Cecil F. Wolfe- (1-8-1901 - 3-7-1941) { W/O Clyde Dalton }
DALTON, Alfred- (only date legible-8-31-1931) S/o C.F.& C.R. Dalton
DALTON, Ballard- (2-19-1865 - 1-23-1933)
DALTON, G. Odell- (8-13-1927 - 5-6-1994) {US Army WW II }

DAVIS, Mary Wolfe- (10-31-1912 -   ) Md. 12-20-1933.
DAVIS, Fayette F.- (9-21-1908 - 8-15-1972) Md. 12-20-1933.

DEHART, Isaac Franklin- (9-20-1878 - 4-19-1952)
DEHART, Kizzie Strock- (9-12-1875 - 6-21-1955)
DEHART, Ora May- (2-28-1902 - 12-28-1985)
DEHART, Infant- (B&D 9-12-1939) {Child of R.W. & Josephine}
DEHART, J.S.- (11-1-1875 - 2-13-1963)
DEHART, Carrie M.- (9-5-1885 - 5-2-1954)
DEHART,Carl M.- (11-5-1907 - 11-7-1988)
DEHART, Dorotha Ramsey- (9-5-1911 - 7-9-1989)
DEHART, Raymond S.- (11-6-1937 - 2-23-1987)
DEHART, Roy William- (11-21-1911 - 7-7-1995)
DEHART, Doris Lee- (9-21-1921 -   )
DEHART, Robert V.- (1934-1994)
DEHART, Emogene- (1934-   ) {Md. 1-1-1963 }

DUNAGAN, Queenie- (died 2-11-1970, age 71.)

SHILOH METHODIST CHURCH CEMETERY

ENGLAND, Annibell- (1-14-1923 - 12-21-1992) {Mother}

ESTEPP, Martha- (1870 - 1956)

FARLOW, Carl R.- (6-28-1908 - 10-8-1985)
FARLOW, Edna Mae- (3-13-1906 - 1-6-1975)

FAULKNER, George A.- (4-8-1862 - 11-29-1941)
FAULKNER, Laura Ellen Wright (4-11-1868 - 4-6-1947) Wife of George.
FAULKNER, Clemmie Grace- (3-19-1901 - 1-15-1988)
FAULKNER, Clyda L.- (1895 - 1976)
FAULKNER, Archie H.- (1925 - 1942) {S/O Clyde & Clara Faulkner}
FAULKNER, William Lee- (1-14-1915 - 4-27-1954)
FAULKNER, Joe B.- (7-7-1930 - 6-26-1970)
FAULKNER, Robert E.- (7-31-1925 - 1-8-1969)
FAULKNER, William M.- (4-21-1897 - 4-27-1954)
FAULKNER, Mamie K.- (9-26-1893 - 12-10-1974) {Nee Kitts}
FAULKNER, Fayette- (1907 - 1973) { H/O Irene Vest}
FAULKNER, Irene V.- (1909 -   ) { D/O A. Vest & Julia Warner}
FAULKNER, William M.- (8-1-1920 - 3-4-1998) {US Army WW II }
FAULKNER, Anna Sue- (1930 -   ) { Md. 1948}
FAULKNER, C. Ray- (1928 -   )
FAULKNER, Zella B.- (1930 _   )
FAULKNER, Clara C.- (1902 - 1982)
FAULKNER, Frankie May- (5-23-1913 - 11-7-1927)

FINLEY, Tyler J.- (2-15-1915 - 3-29-1993)
FINLEY, Jessie H.- (4-9-1921 -   ) { W/O Tyler J. }
FINLEY, Wilmarine- (8-9-1947 - 12-17-1951)
FINLEY, John Dunn- (7-7-1883 - 3-11-1967)
FINLEY, Carrie S.- (5-4-1881 - 12-4-1949)

FLICK, George W.- (9-19-1896 - 6-2-1951) {US Army WW I}
FLICK, Flossie M.- (6-7-1897 - 10-27-1962) [Nee Morehead]

FRANCIS, Samuel R.- (8-15-1912 - 1-16-1961)
FRANCIS, Fay Ramsey- (1-14-1913 - 10-19-1977)

FRAZIER, Ruby Lee- (1926 -   )
FRAZIER, Arnold Lee- (1925 - 1972)

FRENCH, Mabel B.- (3-13-1925 -   )
FRENCH, Guy D. - (9-24-1912 - 3-6-1981)
FRENCH, Dolly McNiel- (5-10-1872 - 7-16-1940)
FRENCH, John C.- (4-20-1849 - 1-16-1933)
FRENCH, Busch P.- (10-16-1906 - 3-7-1924)
FRENCH, Miller L.- (2-2-1872 - 6-9-1951)
FRENCH, Alley B.- (3-20-1874 - 5-16-1950)
FRENCH, Turner Ashby- (3-2-1910 - 4-20-1972)
FRENCH, Tyler Frazier- (7-16-1903 - 8-3-1942)
FRENCH, Elizabeth- (4-7-1870 - 2-2-1948)

FRENCH, John D.- (6-26-1859 - 1-13-1941)
FRENCH, Miller D.- (5-28-1911 -   )
FRENCH, Mary Alice- (9-4-1930 - 6-3-1987)
FRENCH Robert F.- (1908 - 1979)
FRENCH, Goldie B.- (1906 -   )

FULFORD, Estal W.- (12-3-1923 - 3-2-1971)

GILLESPIE, Mattie- (7-17-1917 - 7-17-1996}

GLICK, William Gerald- (11-6-1948 - 11-24-1997)

GREY, James Daniel- (FHM- dates missing)

GRIFFITH, Clara King- (7-22-1898 - 6-21-1972)

GUSLER, William E.- (9-20-1891 - 11-19-1972)
GUSLER, Sarah Ethel Morehead- (1888 - 1952) {W/O William E. Gusler}
GUSLER, James Gordon- (1913 - 1976)
GUSLER, Nellie C.- (2-6-1911 - 1-18-1991)
GUSLER, Ollie Evelyn- (1917 - 1991)
GUSLER, D. Clayborn- (1915 - 1987)
GUSLER, A. Beatrice- (1921 -   )
GUSLER, Daniel Paul- (4-10-1940 - 6-12-1980)

HAGER, Roger Dale- (8-31-1950 - 11-11-1970)
HAGER, Micheal Wayne- (1962 - 1963)
HAGER, Elizabeth May- (1-2-1925 - 2-7-1948)
HAGER, Clyde- (1907 - 1969)
HAGER, Troy Lee- (11-2-1959 - 7-4-1982)
HAGER, Betty M.- (10-9-1930 - 11-1-1986)
HAGER, Paul P.- (2-2-1928   )
HAGER, Sharon Kay- d. 7-11-1965.
HAGER, Barry Ray- d. 7-11-1965.

HAMILTON, Ada B.- (4-20-1878 - 11-26-1939)
HAMILTON, Wiley R.- (9-28-1904 - 4-14-1958)
HAMILTON, Ida Sarver- (4-6-1898 - 1-25-1940)

HARMAN, Scott M.- (2-12-1903 - 12-25-1965)
HARMAN, Scott McKinley, Jr.- (1925 - 1994)
HARMAN, Annie St. Clair- (12-5-1916 - 10-21-1995)

HARRIS, David Allen- (10-31-1955 - 2-4-1978)

HART, George N. (son) (1887 - 1911)
HART, William R.- (1861 - 1939)
HART, Marih V.- (1858 - 1937)
HART, Agnes Vanblaricom- (1916 - 1936) { 1st W/O Shuler P. Hart }
HART, Shuler P.- (12-4-1913 - 8-14-1995)
HART, Velma V.- (4-28-1920 -   ) {2nd W/O Schuler P. Hart }

HART, Robert Wagner- (8-29-1936) {Infant}
HART, { Two wooden crosses with no names or dates, by Hart plot.}
HART, John H.- (1892 - 1970)
HART, Lena Sarver- (1891 - 1941)
HART, Bethel- (6-14-1912 - 8-18-1912) { age 2 months}
HART, Shannon A.- (1911 - 1942)
HART, William P.- (10-26-1888 - 5-19-1953)
HART, Minnie V.- (12-7-1891 - 1-5-1984)
HART, Roger B.- (1928 -   )
HART, Lois S.- (1930 -   )
HART, Herbert W.- (5-17-1919 - 11-2-1954) [WWII stone]
HART, Margaret M.- (5-4-1921 - 3-5-1977)

HAVENS, Effie N.- (1899 - 1937)
HAVENS, William E.- (1896 - 1957)
HAVENS, Robert A.- (6-8-1913 - 12-31-1981)
HAVENS, Thelma W.- (10-31-1915 -   )
HAVENS, Robin Aaron- (6-26-1947 - 9-28-1987) [USAF, Viet Nam.]
HAVENS, Billie G.- (6-7-1940 - 7-3-1945) Dau.,of Robert & Thelma.
HAVENS, Garnette Kidd- (9-8-1917 - 10-5-1985) [Mom]
HAVENS, Rebecca Dawn- (11-14-1960 - 11-26-1960)
HAVENS, Rufus William- (1911 - 1997)
HAVENS, Lida- (1910 -   ) {Md. 5-29-1930}

HELVEY, Eudora B.- (10-13-1886 - 11-9-1910)
HELVEY, T.P. "Port"- (11-6-1886 - 11-4-1966) { Tyler Porterfield }
HELVEY, Mozelle F.- (6-7-1885 - 10-15-1977) { W/O T.P. Nee Finley }

HOWERY, Ruth F. Hager- (1906 - 1986) [Mother] {Sis/o Clyde Hager}

HUBBLE, Infant, b. & d. 11-28-1964

HUGHES, Virginia Austin- (9-7-1871 - 4-8-1950)

HUNTER, Cynthia- (1867 - 1924) { Wife of L.D. Hunter }
   "   Lloyd M.- (8-29-1893 - 2-12-1919)

JOHNSON, Regenia Gayle- (1-4-1963 - 9-17-1988)
JOHNSON, George R.- (11-13-1922 - 5-29-1978)
JOHNSON, Eleanor B.- (5-21-1923 -   )

LAMBERT, Donald O.- (10-6-1926 - 12-26-1976) {PFC US Army WW II }

LANE, Johnny M.- (10-12-1925 - 5-16-1983)

LAWRENCE, William A.- (11-18-1847 - 9-21-1930)
   "   Catherine- (9-14-1845 - 9-10-1920) { Wife of William A. }

LOGAN, Amanda Austin- (1882 - 1917) Wife of J.P. Logan

LONG, Jerry R.- (2-7-1942 -   )   ·

LONG, Karen D.- (2-7-1946 -   )

LOVE, Merita Ramsey- (9-19-1942 -   )
LOVE, Thomas Watha- (1-18-1937 - 2-7-1997) {Pfc. US Army }

LYONS, Randy Scott- (5-18-1967 - 5-26-1990)
LYONS, Donald Ray - (7-8-1960 - 9-13-1965)

MAHAFFEY, Anna Mae- (5-20-1930 - 5-20-1967)

MCGINLEY, Janet Allene- (12-25-1942 - 7-24-1988) {W/O Homer K.M. }
MCGINLEY, Homer Kedrick Ramsey- (11-28-1927 - 10-1-1989)
MCGINLEY, Clarence M.- (5-6-1914 - 1-2-1967)
MCGINLEY, Ercell Ramsey- (9-24-1915 - 1-1-1986)

MEADOWS, Charles L.- (7-14-1886 - 7-22-1948)
MEADOWS, Ressie K. Ramsey- (8-29-1900 - 1-11-1933) Wife of Charles

MILLER, Albert Lee- (3-7-1906 - 7-4-1994)
MILLER, Edna Ruth DeHart- (5-11-1906 - 7-26-1990) {W/O Albert Lee }
MILLER, Two infant daughters of Albert & Ruth Miller.
MILLER, D. Stafford- 1896 - 1972)
MILLER, Clara W.- (1900 - 1970)
MILLER, Robert Wayne- (12-18-1906 - 10-7-1996)

MOREHEAD, Infant of J.M. & E.K. Morehead b. & d. 2-6-1908
MOREHEAD, Robert McKinley- (5-1-1889? - 7-2-1899)
MOREHEAD, Thomas R.- (7-24-1890 - 2-16-1914)
MOREHEAD, Sallie J.- (3-28-1866 - 10-26-1900)
MOREHEAD, John M. - (1-23-1862 - 11-9-1926)
MOREHEAD, Edna K.- (10-5-1874 - 5-18-1961)
MOREHEAD, Francis A. -(1903 - 1957)
MOREHEAD, Mamie S.- (9-3-1905)
MOREHEAD, Jeff Troy- (2-26-1924 - 10-3-1944)
MOREHEAD, Mollie Dunagan- (5-6-1901 -   )
MOREHEAD, Lake DeWitt- (4-22-1895 - 3-6-1971)
MOREHEAD, Kate Burton- (7-8-1898 - 2-4-1942) Wife of Lake D.
MOREHEAD, Baxter- (5-28-1851 - 5-22-1916)
MOREHEAD, Ida- (11-27-1876 - 9-9-1930)
MOREHEAD, Robert- (8-11-1902 - 12-8-1921)
MOREHEAD, James M.- (7-31-1856 - 1-25-1912) (Father)
MOREHEAD, Elizabeth- (5-23-1827 - 8-16-1896) [Lettering eroded.]
MOREHEAD, Daniel F.- (9-13-1817 - 9-14-1899) Age 82 yrs. & 1 day.
MOREHEAD, John N.- (5-29-1889 - 9-9-1964) Md.- 11-21-1917
MOREHEAD, Allie Lee- (9-10-1893 - 12-19-1965){ Md. 11-21-1917 }
MOREHEAD, Harold F.- (8-20-1926 - 1-29-1986) WWII stone.
MOREHEAD, Mary E.- (1923 -   )
MOREHEAD, Andrew D.- (1918 - 1984)
MOREHEAD, Vicki Lynn- (6-22-1952 - 5-2-1963)
MOREHEAD, William Bunyon- (8-5-1885 - 9-1-1962)
MOREHEAD, Cora S.- (9-29-1890 - 3-20-1979)

SHILOH METHODIST CHURCH CEMETERY

MOREHEAD, Alton P.- (1904 - 1962)
MOREHEAD, Ruth B.- (1911 -   )
MOREHEAD, Willie Sue- (8-15-1913 -   )
MOREHEAD, Zeb W.- (10-28-1905 - 3-3-1963)
MOREHEAD, Robert L.- (5-11-1892 - 11-20-1961)
MOREHEAD, Eula D.- (5-18-1894 - 5-21-1967)

MOSER, Ruby B.- (1925 - 1971)

MULLINS, Sharon Lynn- (1975 - 1975)

MYERS, Kelley D., Sr.- (4-25-1924 - 6-9-1983)
MYERS, William Elmer- (5-16-1894 - 11-30-1973)
MYERS, Minnie Lee- (5-18-1898 - 11-2-1972)
MYERS, Ernest C.- (5-4-1915 - 9-30-1969) WWII marker.
MYERS, Lisa M., Reida R., and Joseph V.- (1976 - 1976)

NOWLIN, Charlie Sherman- (12-25-1864 - no death date)
NOWLIN, Virgie Radford- (2-12-1891 - 2-17-1956)

NUNN, Cynthia R.- (1877 - 1964)
NUNN, Doc Lee- (1870 - 1959)
NUNN, Sallie V.- (1900 - 1970)

OREY, James W.- (10-30-1931 - 7-17-1980)

PFFIFFER, Ann Wright- (1912 -   )
PFFIFFER, A. Rowland- (1904 - 1973)

PARNELL, Robert E.- (5-19-1944 - 11-26-1984) [US Navy]
PARNELL, Brenda B.- (5-23-1944 -   )

POFF, Billy- (1935 - 1935) { Near the HART plot }

PRESCOTT Elsie B.- (6-8-1899 - 1-23-1985){D/O James & Daisey
                                        Mitchell Burton }
PRESCOTT, Leslie L.- (8-21-1872 - 8-21-1957) {H/O Elsie Burton }
PRESCOTT, Edward C.- (4-30-1925 - 10-25-1980)
PRESCOTT, Ester F.- (1-9-1918 -   )

PRUETT, Eva- (1912 -   )
PRUETT, Henry H.- (1907 - 1964)

RADFORD, Jessie Gertrude- (2-7-1914 - 3-29-1918)
RADFORD, Lillian Arlene- (6-2-1916 - 3-30-1918)
RADFORD, Charles P.- (2-22-1891 - 1-13-1964)
RADFORD, Lucy E. Hunter- (9-14-1896? - 11-6-1945)
RADFORD, Charles Anthony- (6-5-1970) {Son of Charles & Barbara.}
RADFORD, Montague S.- (11-24-1901 - 11-30-1948){Bro/O Minnie Conley}
RADFORD, Sarah E.- (2-5-1872 - 9-19-1938)
RADFORD, F. M. - { Francis Marion } (11-29-1935 - 2-5-1935)

RADFORD, George William-(10-18-1928 - 2-21-1930)
RADFORD, William Goebel- (10-24-1899 - 1-13-1976)
RADFORD, Emma Conner- (12-8-1903 - 9-26-1976) {D/O Geo. & Jennie
                                      Mustard Conner (Corner) }

RAMSEY, Nina Ann- (4-6-1898 - 5-10-1960)
RAMSEY, Inf. dau. of Loranza & Leona Ramsey- (b.& d. 3-20-1925)
RAMSEY, Hobert Emmett, son of Tony & Viola (3-9-1928- 4-20-1928)
RAMSEY, Claude H.- (11-24-1910 - 11-26-1944)
RAMSEY, Thomas R.- (6-5-1870 - 3-14-1958)
RAMSEY, Carline F.- (11-30-1872 - 3-21-1952)
RAMSEY, Viola B.- (3-31-1907 -   )
RAMSEY, Tony L.- (11-4-1898 - 2-19-1960)
RAMSEY, Three stones with no names or dates.
RAMSEY, Herman Edward- (5-25-1919 - 12-8-1987)
RAMSEY, Alice Semones- (3-12-1915 - 1-27-1980) Wife of Ira W.
RAMSEY, Ira Weston- (7-7-1914 -   )
RAMSEY, James O.- (4-28-1916 - 3-8-1944)
RAMSEY, Leona Adeline Miller- (9-14-1887 - 1-20-1980) {W/O Loranza}
RAMSEY, Loranza Naff- (3-18-1885 - 1-23-1957)
RAMSEY, Leon Kenneth- (9-26-1923 - 8-21-1989)
RAMSEY, Michael Leon- (4-17-1954 - 1-20-1975) S\o Edith & Kenneth.
RAMSEY, Byron F.- (4-16-1919 - 5-26-1946)
RAMSEY, Macie M.- (2-20-1896 - 3-15-1960)
RAMSEY, Shuler- (1-18-1894 - 4-9-1966)
RAMSEY, Velma Neel- (9-3-1919 - 1-23-1943)
RAMSEY, James Bell- (5-1-1887 - 8-26-1968)
RAMSEY, Etta C. Faulkner- (11-12-1894 - 10-2-1993)
RAMSEY, Dallas- (1894-1942) Dates underground. {Jo Tickle got them}
RAMSEY, Ray Mitchell- (10-17-1902 -   )
RAMSEY, Janie Wright- (3-16-1919 - 3-26-1972){ D/O J.R. Wright }
RAMSEY, Charles James- (4-26-1876 - 10-29-1958)
RAMSEY, Ida Spangler- (2-2-1879 - 9-3-1963)
RAMSEY, William B.- (12-3-1902 - 10-19-1963)
RAMSEY, Sylva Alice- (4-19-1931 - 12-25-1949)
RAMSEY, Cora Lee- (9-25-1910 - 3-9-1966)
RAMSEY, William L.- (5-5-1901 - 4-30-1958)
RAMSEY, Hazel Short- (8-31-1909 - 3-7-1982)
RAMSEY, Almeda- (8-12-1880 - 3-6-1963)
RAMSEY, Charles Harman- (1875 - 1940)
RAMSEY, Homer Kedrick- (1927 - 1985)
RAMSEY, Charles Anthony- (B.& D. 6-25-1970) {S/O Charles & Barbara.}
RAMSEY, Name illegible,(FHM) only date showing is D. 1976.

RASNICK, Charlie- (1895 - 1984)
RASNICK, Lenora- (1899 - 1972)

REPASS, Frederick F.- (10-15-1831 - 1-23-1913)
REPASS, Mattie Wheeler - (2-18-1862 - 11-26-1938)

ROBERTSON, Lodeska Blankenship- (10-1-1902 - 1-6-1982)

ROBINETTE, William Henry- (2-22-1895 - 5-27-1963)
ROBINETTE, Ollie Wolfe- (6-22-1896 - 8-8-1955)

SANDERS, M.- (10-15-1798 - 12-11-1881) [Macajiah Saunders]

SARVER, Ada G.?- (3-24-1890 - 8-28-1959)
SARVER, John Orc?- (11-10-1894 - 5-1933)
SARVER, Dora B.- (9-10-1893 - 7-17-1920)
SARVER, Ina L.- (12-3-1924 - 8-20-1925)
SARVER, Edith L.- (7-12-1926 - 9-21-1929) Our baby.
SARVER, Della M.- (1903 - 1936)
SARVER, William R.- (1899 - 1969)
SARVER, Louise V.- (1901 - 1973)
SARVER, M. B.- (10-19-1862 - 6- " letters underground "
SARVER, S. E. - (5-10-1859 - 7-11-1946)
SARVER, Glen C.- (5-6-1934 - 12-22-1941)
SARVER, T. Wade- (5-31-1932 - 6-11-1989)
SARVER, Emory E.- (4-4-1942 - 8-12-1996)
SARVER, Gladys R.- (1905 -   )
SARVER, M. Lester- (1900 - 1969)
SARVER, John K. - (9-11-1901 - 10-1-1977)
SARVER, Lena Barger- (5-24-1871)
SARVER, James Henry- (9-7-1908 - 2-5-1982)
SARVER, Helen Nelson- (1919 - 1990) FHM { W/O James Henry }
SARVER, John Berry- (2-29-1868 - 11-6-1945)

SHAWVER, Alice F.- (4-22-1905 - 10-12-1987) { "Coonie" Nee Faulkner}
SHAWVER, Walker D.- (7-4-1903 - 12-23-1973) {H/O Alice "Coonie" }
SHAWVER, Edward Hicks- (9-12-1936 - 11-4-1954) USAF
SHAWVER, Regena Dodd- (2-22-1942 - 2-22-1942)

SHELTON, Mary E.- (11-8-1922 - 12-11-1978)

SHRADER, S. Annie- (1875 - 1951)

SPANGLER, Joseph H.- (9-1-1876 - 8-2-1944)
SPANGLER, Bertha R.- (2-28-1884 - 4-30-1963)

STANLEY, Franklin- (5-28-1944 - 12-2-1987) Married, 3-9-1963
STANLEY, Janie- (2-16-1944) Married, 3-9-1963 { Nee Wright }
STANLEY, Roger Lee- (8-7-1942 - 5-11-1960)
STANLEY, Lillie E.- (2-24-1892 - 6-5-1958) { Nee Dalton }
STANLEY, Ervin Henry- (9-23-1940 - 1-16-1941) Son of Mr.&Mrs. W.H.
STANLEY, Ballard D.- (5-8-1923 -   )
STANLEY, Mamie Ruth- (4-21-1923 - 11-1-1991) {D/O Mason and Gladys
                    Morehead Burton and wife of Daniel Stanley }
                    Married Daniel Stanley, Jan. 7, 1942. }
STANLEY, C.W.- (b. & d. 19???) { Plaque on a wooden cross }

STARLING, Emily Ann- (b. & d. 5-6-1991)

STEELE, H.W.- (3-9-1849 - 12-7-1927)
STEELE, V.J.- (6-6-1852 - 1-26-1934)

STOWERS, Wallace H.- (10-22-1933 - 12-25-1971) WEWII
STOWERS, Perry Hatcher- (10-27-1878 - 11-23-1955)
STOWERS, Stella Steele- (8-5-1891 - 1-2-1974)
STOWERS, Perry Wayne- (8-4-1919 - 3-18-1989)
STOWERS, Iola Burton- (8-7-1925 - 3-29-1995)

TABOR, Large family stone, no dates or names.
TABOR, Jackson H.- (5-22-1891 _ 9-3-1946)
TABOR, Alvin Eugene- (1914 - 1986)

THOMPSON, W.H.- (1-29-1859 - 5-2-1916)

TOLBERT, Earl H.- (1915 - 1975)
TOLBERT, Vernice- (1921 - 1968)
TOLBERT, Jonathan Mark- (1970 -   )

WALKER, Brenda Gail- (1953 - 1998) FHM

WETZEL, Otis Burle- (4-23-1932 - 9-29-1932) { Son of Karl & Eugie }

WHEELER, Pierce P.- (3-25-1884 - 9-27-1920)

WHITTAKER, Wavie D.- (8-11-1909 - 9-28-1909)

WILBURN, Clovis Carr- 8-20-1931 - 12-3-1983) { US Army WW II }

WILLIAMS, Sherry Y.- (11-11-1961 - 11-14-1961)
WILLIAMS, Lillian P.- (8-23-1909 - 1-31-1981)
WILLIAMS, Blake E.- (10-15-1905 - 2-20-1988)
WILLIAMS, Jack Ward- (8-24-1931 - 8-1-1946)
WILLIAMS, Eugene P.- (1873 - 1956)
WILLIAMS, Lovie L.- (1879 - 1957)
WILLIAMS, Edward J.- (10-6-1910 - 7-7-1983)
WILLIAMS, Minnie S.- (7-7-1910 -   )
WILLIAMS, M. Clair- (12-3-1905 - 2-1-1965)
WILLIAMS, James H.- (12-17-1904 - 12-15-1971)
WILLIAMS, Don Mandel- (3-21-1958 - 7-4-1982)
WILLIAMS, Wilma Yvonne- (1938 - 1939)
WILLIAMS, Edwin R.- (3-14-1941 -   ) { Father }
WILLIAMS, Emma Jane- (9-13-1940 - 12-7-1994) { Mother }
WILLIAMS, Yvonne- (1938 - 1939) { Our baby }

WOLFE, George, son of E.C. & Nannie, d. 1930 age 2 mos. 20 days.
WOLFE, Everette C.- (1894 - 1959)
WOLFE, Nannie Shrader- (1899 - 1971)
WOLFE, Kelley W.- (12-31-1915 - 2-6-1976)
WOLFE Ward- (10-9-1910 - 11-30-1983)
WOLFE, Viola- (8-10-1913 -   ) { D/O Rush Mustard, W/O Ward }

WOLFE, Gaye Ann- (1978 - 1978) { D/o Albert & Barbara. On back of
WOLFE, stone, are names, Faye Ann, Maria, Wendy Albert, Jr. & Sondra.
WOLFE, Walter Ward- (12-4-1968 - 3-12-1969) Son of Wm. & Judy.

WRIGHT, James Elbert- (1967 - 1971)
WRIGHT, Lucille Gusler- (5-15-1946 - 12-5-1970)
WRIGHT, Robert F.- (1901 - 1963)
WRIGHT, Lucy E.- (1905 - 1951)
WRIGHT, Chester Earl- (3-7-1918 - 3-13-1920)
WRIGHT, Wilma May Cox- (7-13-1948 - 8-3-1975) Wife of Ned Wright.
WRIGHT, Fairly Clifford- (7-15-1945 - 8-25-1974)
WRIGHT, Minnie Edith Ramsey- (10-31-1909 - 4-18-1975)
WRIGHT, Eugene Wellington- (3-25-1907 - 6-16-1996 }
WRIGHT, Macie Spangler- (5-5-1881 - 2-11-1922) { W/O W.G. Wright }
WRIGHT, William G.- (7-25-1875 - 3-5-1959)
WRIGHT, David Oliver- (2-15-1842 - 9-28-1910) CSA marker
WRIGHT, Stones on both sides of David Oliver, no names or dates.
WRIGHT, Jonathan K.- (11-3-1982 - 12-10-1982)
WRIGHT, A. Elwood- (3-31-1904 - 7-15-1980) { Dad }
WRIGHT, Verrena R.- (4-23-1910 -   ) { Mom }
WRIGHT, Arthur C.- (10-29-1938 - 8-22-1986) USA
WRIGHT, George A.- 9-30-1916 -   )
WRIGHT, Edna J.- (1-22-1920 - 2-1-1989) { Nee Gusler }
WRIGHT, Hallie Lawrence- (4-20-1904 - 2-8-1965)
WRIGHT, Charles H.- (2-24-1897 - 6-2-1972)
WRIGHT, James W.- (5-16-1921 - 10-17-1969) WWII
WRIGHT, Alma Lois- (1929 - 1969)
WRIGHT, Grover C.- (7-6-1893 - 12-30-1971)
WRIGHT, Nellie R.- (9-1-1895 - 11-7-1966)
WRIGHT, Lila J.- (10-26-1888 - 11-16-1951)
WRIGHT, John B.- (11-17-1886 - 9-20-1961)
WRIGHT, William Lee- (1-14-1915 - 4-27-1954)
WRIGHT, Irene Meadows- (10-30-1922 - 4-26-1993)
WRIGHT, Micky D.- (1941 - 1994) { S/O Agnes Wright Strock }

WYRICK, Louise Hunter- (2-6-1875 - 1-25-1954)
WYRICK, Henry Asa- (2-26-1878 - 10-21-1935)
WYRICK, David Earl- (5-16-1904 - 3-4-1958)
WYRICK, Cules B.- (7-1-1909 - 3-20-1970)
WYRICK, Datura E.- (7-13-1900 - 2-4-1972)
WYRICK, Leather Nathan- (11-10-1916 - 7-15-1981) { US Army WW II }

{ We apologize for any mistakes we may have made in copying these old
grave stones. To err is human, and some of the stones are hard to
read. We will appreciate any corrections that any one can offer.
Please send corrections or additions to this list to your Bland
County Historical Society, Mrs. Garman Lester, Dublin, VA, Mrs.
Parke C. Bogle, Pulaski, VA. Email- <parkebog@swva.net> } or Jo Ann
Tickle Scott, Bland, VA Email- <jotickle@naxs.com>
    Dates were copied in 1993 by Parke Bogle and Mrs. Garman Lester. It
was checked again in 1998 by Jo Ann Tickle Scott. }

KIDD CEMETERY
[On Wolf Creek, above the Wolf Creek Golf Club]
{ Copied in 1991 by Parke C. Bogle }

KIDD, John T.- (May 19, 1889 - Nov. 18, 1949)

KIDD, N.J.{ Nettie Jerushia}- (June 29, 1875 - 1-27-1931)-Mother
   [Grand daughter of Mark Reed Bogle. Daughter of Jerushia Bogle
     and John Blessing.]

KIDD, I.C.- { Isaac Columbus Kidd } (Nov. 17, 1869 - June 25, 1913)
         Father { Husband of Nettie Jerushia Blessing }

KIDD, A.T.{Archibald Thompson}- Dec. 13, 1846 - April 20, 1901)

KIDD, Rhoda J. - (Mar. 10, 1852-Aug. 3, 1920) Wife of A.T. Kidd and
      dau of Isaac and Phebe Hedrick Repass.

KIDD, Earl H.-(Oct.10, 1905-Aug.25, 1953) [S/o Rachael Smith Kidd]

KIDD, Marie - (April 21, 1917-   ) Wife of Earl. Living 1987

KIDD, E. Ray - (1874 - 1938)

KIDD, Julia C- (1881-1908)

KIDD, Mason- (1918 - 1980)

KIDD, Tobe Thompson- (June 6, 1903 - Jan. 8, 1948)

KIDD, Archie Stephen- (Dec. 25, 1905 - Nov. 12, 1941)

KIDD, Julias William- (Mar. 7, 1874 - Dec. 17, 1940)

KIDD, Susan Jeanette- (Jan. 24, 1881 - Aug. 20, 1962)

KIDD, Arthur Conrad- (Nov. 25, 1900 - April 28, 1962)

KIDD, Calvin Leatis- (Dec. 10, 1910 - Oct. 5, 1971)

KIDD, Emory Walter- (Feb. 7, 1908 - June 21, 1973)

KIDD, Alfred Robert- (March 25, 1923 -   )

KIDD, Gwendolyn C.- (July 13, 1921 - Feb. 26, 1994)
      { Wife of Alfred Robert Kidd }
KIDD, Nancy J.- (April 20, 1894 - April 2, 1990)
      One stone so badly eroded it cannot be read.

KIDD, Claude- (March 9, 1914 - Sept. 23, 1935)
   [This cemetery is in a good state of repair. It is clean, and
     appears to be mowed often. It is near a camping ground above the
     road. It was checked again in 1998 by Jo Ann Tickle Scott]

OLD BOGLE CEMETERY ON WOLF CREEK, BLAND COUNTY VIRGINIA
[On land once owned by Mark Reed Bogle, now owned by Looney family]
{Copied in 1987 by Parke C. Bogle and Elene Endress, a Bogle
 descendant from Moses Lake, Washington.}

BLESSING, Stella M.- (2-2-1884 - 8-8-1934) {W/O of J.H. Blessing}
        [Stella was daughter of Issac Columbus Kidd.]
BLESSING, John H.- (6-12-1876-3-23-1914) S/o Jerushia Bogle and
        John Blessing.
BLESSING, E. J.- [Elizabeth Jerushia Bogle] (1-1-1846-3-8-1916)
        [D/o Mark Reed Bogle and Jane Newberry Bogle. She was the
        widow of John H. Blessing, who disappeared soon after the
        births of Jerushia's two children, John H. Jr. who
        married Stella Kidd, and Nettie Jerushia who married
        Isaac Columbus Kidd.]
BLESSING, Robert Clay- (9-25-1908 - 7-9-1965)

BOGLE, Mark Reed- (3-4-1809 - 6-19-1890) {Youngest child of Robert
        H. Bogle and his first wife, Rachael Dunn Bogle.}
BOGLE, Jane- (6-9-1813-7-18?-1890) [D/o Rev. Sam Newberry and
        Eunice Powers Newberry, and wife of Mark Reed Bogle]
BOGLE, James Buchanan- (3-10-1818- 9-1898) S/o Ralph Bogle, Jr. and
        Margaret Hutzell Bogle. He was married three times and had
        children by all three wives. His first wife was Jane Munsey, a
        daughter of Old Zazhariah Munsey. His 2nd wife was Susan
        Raulston, to whom he was married in Blount Co. TN. His 3rd
        wife was Annie Pauley. There are no stones here for any of his
        wives. It is said that his 2nd wife, Susan Raulston is buried
        somewhere on Kimberling. It is not known when his 3rd wife
        died or where she is buried.
BOGLE, F. C.- [Freeling Clay Bogle] CSA stone with no dates.
        [He was the son of James Buchanan Bogle and his first wife,
        Jane Munsey Bogle. He married Martha Jane Bogle, daughter of
        Mark Reed and Jane Newberry Bogle. There is no stone for her
        grave here. Martha Jane was a daughter of her groom's uncle.
        She died in September of 1918.] [How they did intermarry!]

CHILDRESS, Leuna E.- (1-30-1918 - 11-30-1941) {Jo says, d. 1-22-1919}
CHILDRESS, Infant girl- (born and died 3-26-1921)

DURETT, Earl- (1908 - 1994)
DURETT, Julia- (1899 - 1991)

EAGLE, Etta M.- (9-3-1862 - 9-26-1914) { Nee Maxwell }
EAGLE, John H.- (2-6-1860 - 12-30-1950){ H/O Etta Maxwell Eagle}

IGO, James W.- (12-16-1859 - 10-25-1924)
IGO, Mary Isobel- (12-19-1860 - 11-19-1918)
IGO, Carl Thompson- (6-21-1902 - 11-14-1918)

KIDD, Roy Dewayne- (7-29-1939 - 8-13-1941) S/o Roy and Agnes Kidd.

LOONEY, Mollie Igo- (8-3-1897 - 3-22-1918) {Mother}

OLD BOGLE CEMETERY ON WOLF CREEK, BLAND COUNTY VIRGINIA
[On land once owned by Mark Reed Bogle, now owned by Looney family]
{Copied in 1987 by Parke C. Bogle and Elene Endress, a Bogle
 descendant from Moses Lake, Washington.}

LOONEY, Linkous- (4-28-1894 - 11-30-1941) {Father}
LOONEY, Ruby Kidd- (10-31-1910 - 1-4-1997) {Mother}
LOONEY, Erby- (11-10-1909 - 9-5-1981) {Father}
LOONEY, Lousinda- (6-4-1892 - 5-3-1973)
LOONEY, Hicks S.- (12-28-1869 - 5-26-1956)
LOONEY, Ira- (7-30-1896 - 12-4-1969)
LOONEY, Chloe M.- (6-10-1915 - 10-11-1977) {Mother}
LOONEY, Corbet- (1-17-1912 - 9-7-1998) {Father} {Jo got death date}
LOONEY, Paris- (1898 - 1972)
LOONEY, Lena K.- (1898 - 1969){W/O Paris}
LOONEY, Beverly Gay- (9-10-1953 - 12-19-1953)
LOONEY, Vicie Stiltner- (1-22-1870 - 4-2-1955)
LOONEY, Marlene S.- (6-15-1929 - 6-1-1989) {Husband}
LOONEY, E. Margaret- (11-8-1919 -   ) {Wife}
LOONEY, Linkous- (4-25-1894 - 11-23-1941)
LOONEY, Mollie Igo- (8-30-1897 - 3-22-1980)

MAXWELL, J.E. (James Edward)- (6-9-1837 - 9-15-1894) Father
             [Husband of Rachael Ann Bogle, dau. of Mark Reed Bogle.]
MAXWELL, Rachael Ann- (9-26-1835 - 9-8-1917) {D/O Mark R. Bogle}

STOWERS, William S.- (born & died 11-29-1950) Son of W.F. Stowers.

 [This cemetery is excellent condition, considering the age of some
   of the stones. It is my understanding that some of the Blessing
   descendants help with the upkeep of this old grave yard.]
   We will appreciate any corrections or additions to the names
   copied here. There are several graves with no markers, so if you
   know of any one else who is buried here, please let us know and we
   will add the names to our list.]
 { This cemetery was checked again in 1998 by Jo Ann Tickle Scott and
   she has added several new graves and death dates. Jo says there
   are 2 adult graves with badly eroded stones and 1 child's grave
   with no stone.}

HUTZELL CEMETERY
[On Bob Munsey's farm on Route 604 about 6 miles east of Bland, VA]
{ Copied by Donna Distel and given to Jo Ann Tickle Scott}

HUTZELL, J.A.- (11-16-1782 - 12-8-1856) { Nee Cooley, D/O Thaddeus
                    Cooley and W/O Michael Hutzell.
HUTZELL, M.- (d. 5-22-1859) Age 74. { Michael Hutzell was born about
                            1783, the son of Lewis Hutzell, Sr.}
HUTZELL, W.G.- (d. 11-17-1845) {Age 25yrs. 10 mos. & 2 days.
                {Probably the son of Michael & Julia Cooley Hutzell}

{ 4 field stones in Row 1}
{ 8 field stones in row 2 }
{ 5 field stones in row 3 }
{ 2 field stones and 2 indentations in row 4 }
{ 1 stone and 4 indentations in row 5 }

OLD UNKNOWN BURYING GROUND
{ Located on top of a hill where Skidmore Munsey once lived and now
  owned by Robert O. Munsey. Copied by Jo Ann Tickle Scott}

THOMPSON, William H.- (1-11-1836 - 5-9-1864)

{ A stone with the letters "P H" and a date of possible April 21 1856
  age 22}
        { Approxmately 30 graves with stones barely visible.}

CHILDRESS CEMETERY
{ Cemetery is on land owned by a Mr. Webb, on route 614 about 4 miles
                    from State Route 52.
    { Copied by Jo Ann Tickle Scott in October of 1998.}

CHILDRESS, Nancy V.- (4-7-1841 - 3-5-1927) { W/O William}
CHILDRESS, William- (1-28-1839 - 6-21-1927} { 6th VA Cav. CSA}
CHILDRESS, William J.- (11-26-1878 - 5-25-1926)

LESTER, Charlie- (1-19-1777 - 7-5-1829}

PAULEY CEMETERY

{ Cemetery is located on the Hiram Pauley home place near the Bowen property. According to family history, Hiram's parents, John and Margaret Meadows Pauley are also buried here. There is no information on these stones. The dates comes from marriage records. A 4x4 is necessary to reach the cemetery. It was copied in 1998 by Donna Distel and Jo An Tickle Scott. Thanks to Thomas, H.G, Jr. and Mildred Wilson Richardson for taking us to these graves.}

PAULEY, Hiram- (1818 - 4-9-1895) { Co. F 8th VA Cav. CSA}
PAULEY, Nancy Havens- (@1827-   ) {W/O Hiram, md. 6-10-1850}

HARMAN CEMETERY NEAR HIGH ROCK

{ Cemetery is located on route 608 at the Penley farm now owned by Mollie Ellen Penley Thompson. The cemetery in a small flat place on the side of a hill behind their house. Mollie Thompson is the daughter of the late John S. "Buddy" Penley and Margaret Thompson Penley and a grand daughter of Way and Agnes Wohlford Penley There is no record of how many more people that may be buried here.}
[Cemetery was copied by Jo Ann Tickle Scott in November of 1998 }

HARMAN, "Big" Daniel- (1797 - 11-6-1845)
HARMAN, Rhoda- (3-3-1796 - 9-24-1845) {W/O "Big" Daniel Harman and
        also his 1st cousin. She was a twin to Susanna Harman.}
HARMAN, Sidney- (d. 1845)
HARMAN, Ephriam- (d. 1845)
HARMAN, Juliet- (d. 1845)
{ The last three were children of "Big" Daniel and Rhoda. They all died in 1845 from Typhoid.

GROSS CEMETERY

{ Cemetery is located on a hill north of the Gross home, which is north of State Route 52, between Bastain and Interstate 77. One needs a 4x4 or walk to the site.
        [Copied in 1998 by Jo Ann Tickle Scott]

GROSS, Harvey J.- (1-7-1907 - 2-15-1988) {Father}
GROSS, Alma B.- (9-8-1903 - 2-12-1997) {Mother{ {Nee Billups}
GROSS, Harvey G.- (1-1-1829 - 3-12-1905) {Co.F 8h VA Cav. CSA}
GROSS, Mary E.- (10-15-1833 - 10-3-1916) {W/O Harvey G.}
GROSS, Joseph- (1866 - 1934) {Father}
GROSS, Bettie B.- (1870 - 1944) {Mother}
GROSS, Miss Clara Stewart- (9-14-1896 - 1-26-1960){D/O Jos. & Bettie}

BEASLEY, Georgia Edith- (6-17-1914 - 6-18-1914)
BEASLEY, Jackson- (7-19-1921 - 12-21-1940)
BEASLEY, Edner S.- (8-27-1890 - No death date)
BEASLEY, Mary G.- (1-29-1890 - 6-5-1950) {Nee Gross}

SHUFFLEBARGER CEMETERY

{ Cemetery is located on a hill north of State Route 52, west of the home of Billie Jean Carty, granddaughter of Harvey & Margaret Shufflebager. Billie told this compiler that there were only two graves at this spot. One must walk to reach the site.}
[Compiled by Jo Ann Tickle Scott, with thanks to Billy Jean Carty]

SHUFFLEBARGER, Harvey Boston- (8-31-1863 - 9-21-1923) { S/O Newton S. and Ann Wygal Shufflebarger. He was born in Pulaski County and died at Hicksville in Bland County}
SHUFFLEBARGER, Margaret "Maggie"Louise- (4-7-1870 - 7-3-1955) {D/O David Fleming Thompson and Cathering Young Munsey Waggoner Thompson. Born in Kimberling Valley, died at Hicksville in Bland County.

NUNN CEMETERY

{Cemetery located Southwest of where Kimberling Road (612) enters State Route 606, upon a hill. The fence can be seen from the road. One needs a 4x4 to drive to the site. Thanks to Donald Helvey for his help showing me the colation of this cemetery. }
[Copied by Jo Ann Tickle Scott in November 1998.]

HOLLINS, Effie M.- (10-22-1892 - 11-27-1960)

MILLER, Jasper W.- (4-20-1850 - 5-4-1928)
MILLER, Rhoda E.- (5-15-1857 - 6-15-1949) {Nee Helvey, W/O Jasper W.}

NUNN, Herbert Wayne- (5-30-1910 - 8-1998)
NUNN, Maudie Ella Elkins- (4-4-1908 - 8-27-1991) {W/O Herbert Wayne }
NUNN, Jimmie- (b. & d. 2-7-1936) {S/O Maudie & Herbert Wayne Nunn}
NUNN, Argle P.- (8-17-1942 - 3-3-1979)
NUNN, Henry P.- (5-31-1910 -   )
NUNN, Mae Norris- (3-13-1915 - 9-26-1977)
NUNN, Louella- (4-15-1875 - 6-20-1910)
NUNN, Thomas- (illegible dates on plain field stone)
NUNN, Ethel- (1905 - 4-14-1923) { On field stone}
NUNN, Herschel- (d. 7-2-1923) {On field stone}
NUNN, Gilbert W.- (1906 -   )
NUNN, Francis M.- (1905 - 1989)
NUNN, Dwayne Lewis- (1965 - 1982)

UNKNOWN, Roxie- (died 4-19-1923) {Unable to read it all. All on a plain field stone.}

{Field stone with no markings}

LEVITT FAMILY CEMETERY
{ Located north of route 614 on an old dirt road just east of the
Grapefield Church Of God. It is well kept and fenced with a huge
holly tree in the center. The road forks at the top of the hill and
the site is at the end of the left fork. Need a 4x4 to drive to it}
[Copied in October 1998 by Jo Ann Tickle Scott]

BURRESS, Dorothy V.- (12-8-1930 - 1-21-1931)
BURRESS, Ruby P.- (10-12-1925 - 9-30-1998){D/O Sallie & Silvey B--}
BURRESS, Sallie M.- (2-2-1902 - 12-3-1961) {W/O Silvey M.}
BURRESS, Silvey M.- (5-16-1902 - 7-28-1992)

CARTER, Emory Ray, Jr.- (7-23-1949 - 7-24-1949)
CARTER, Harman G.- (3-28-1882 - 8-16-1960)
CARTER, Minnie L.- (4-15-1900 - 11-30-1974) {W/O Harman G. Burress}
CARTER, Ida Gertrude- (10-24-1886 - 7-29-1966) {Sister}
CARTER, Mary Alice- (4-1-1918 - 10-5-1920)
CARTER, Ollie May- (6-1914) {Infant}

HAMM, Coy- (2-15-1935 - 2-14-1937) {S/O Mr. & Mrs I.O Hamm}
HAMM, Isaac Oscar- (7-22-1887 - 3-5-1953)

KIDD, Herbert A.- (10-12-1894 - 1-28-1966) {Father}
KIDD, Bertie, (6-7-1896 - 5-14-1975) {Mother}
KIDD, Lewis H.- (8-27-1931 - 12-28-1978) {Brother}
KIDD, Arnold S.- (8-16-1926 - 2-14-1979) {Brother}
KIDD, Ollie V.- (1-2-1880 - 7-4-1932) {W/O Henley H. Kidd}
KIDD, Henley H.- (1-6-1879 - 4-9-1958)
KIDD, Gladys K.- (1-25-1911 - 9-16-1969) {Mother}
KIDD, Kermit- (12-5-1909 - 10-6-1970) {Father}
KIDD, Archiable C.- (7-11-1882 - 10-31-1953)
KIDD, Archie N.- (4-16-1913) {Our baby}
KIDD, A.R.- (3-2-1844 - 6-11-1911)
KIDD, Missouri A.- (10-16-1867 - 8-31-1945){D/O Charlotte & A.R Kidd}
KIDD, Charlotte R.- (12-12-1847 - 12-16-1935) {D/O Isaac & Phebe
                      Repass, W/O Absolem Ray Kidd}
KIDD, S.S.- (8-3-1878 - 1-17-1920)
KIDD, Cynthia L.- (7-24-1875 - 2-3-1948)
KIDD, Nancy D.- (12-11-1956 - 12-18-1946)
KIDD, Alice V.- (1-2-1880 - 7-4-1932) {W/O Henley H. Kidd}
KIDD, Charles Albert- (5-15-1945 - 7-4-1945)
KIDD, D.W.- (9-9-1865 - 6-19-1958)
KIDD, M.C.- (1854 - 1939)
{ 8 small homemade markers, M.Kidd, R. Levitt, A. Kidd, N. Kidd }

LEVITT, Charles H.- (9-17-1925 - 3-2-1982)
LEVITT, Geneva L.- (12-9-1927 - 7-7-1973) {W/O Charles H. Levitt}
LEVITT, Clara Dell- (6-26-1903 - 10-8-1953) {W/O George R. Levitt}
LEVITT, George R.- (1-19-1900 - 2-7-1969)
LEVITT, John E.- (4-22-1907 - 8-17-1952)
LEVITT, Laura Bell- (3-19-1886 - 9-8-1965) {Wife}

THOMPSON, Edith A.- (4-5-1932) and Tad B.- (7-11-1933) {Infants}

JUSTICE FAMILY CEMETERY
{ Located north on route 614 past Kegley Manor Nursing Home and behind some double-wide mobil homes. It is in sad condition. At one time a large cemetery but now the stones are broken and badly eroded}
[Copied in November of 1998 by Jo Ann Tickle Scott]

BLANKENSHIP, Martha B. Johnston- (9-20-1874 - 8-27-1943)
        A field stone by Martha'a grave, no markings.

JOHNSTON, Geneva Elizabeth- (9-25-1849 - 3-1-1907) {W/O J. Newton}
JOHNSTON, J. Newton- (7-10-1847 - 4-2-1903)
JOHNSTON, John P.- (11-24-1846 - 11-4-1898) {Father}
JOHNSTON, Sallie J.- (10-27-1849 - no date) {Mother, W/O John P.}
JOHNSTON, C. Ida- (d. 10-5-1891){Age 12yrs11mos &14das; D/O J.P&S.J.}

JUSTICE, Jessie- (5-31-1817 -   ) {S/O John & Mary}
JUSTICE, John N.- (12-17-1771 - 12-13-1829)
JUSTICE, Mary- (12-20-1777 - 3-10-1851) {W/O John N.}

PENLEY FAMILY CEMETERY
{ Cemetery is in very bad condition. Located upon a hill on the former John "Buddy" Penley farm on the north side of Route 608.}

PENLEY, Agnes W.- (8-7-1880 - 11-19-1956) {D/O Gordon Wohlford & W/O
                                 Way Penley }
PENLEY, Way- (10-27-1875 - 12-10-1948) {S/O G.W. & Adeline Robinett
                                 Penley.}
PENLEY, G. Gordon- (9-7-1908 - 2-2-1921) {S/O Way & Agnes}

UMBARGER, Crate (Lucretia)- (1873 - 1942) {D/O G.W. Penley & Adeline}
UMBARGER, Keithly- (1896 - 1927) {S/O Crate and Umbarger husband}
UMBARGER, George- (1906 - 1991) {S/O Crate Penley Umbarger)
UMBARGER, Dane- (1898 - 1900) {S/O Crate Penley Umbarger}

Three cement rectangles with sunken spots inside, containing no stones or other infromation. According to family records, George Washington Penley and his wife Adeline Robinett and a child are buried in these sunken rectangles.
There four plain field stones and one other indentation.
Cemetery data compiled by Jo Ann Tickle Scott, R.F. D. Bland, VA..
                Email- <jotickle@naxs.com>

HOGE'S CHAPEL CEMETERY
[Located on State Route 42, 1/2 mile east of Point Pleasant in Bland
County, Virginia. On land now owned by David Morehead.]

ASHWORTH, William B.- (1845 - 1921) Pvt. VA. Co F. 45 Inf. CSA
ASHWORTH, Martha Ellen Compton- (11-18-1844 - 3-29-1922)

BAILEY, Maude N.-(10-11-1884 - 8-4-1934)D/o Wm & Mary Bogle Dunagan.

BIRD, Sarah- (5-8-1831 - 3-9-1855) Consort of Daniel H. Bird.

BOGLE, James Raulston-(10-20-1860 - 5-3-1949) { S/o James B. Bogle }
BOGLE, M.J. (Nee Pruitt)- (4-23-1865 - no date) 1st w/o James R.
BOGLE, Mary Wagner- (8-27-1866 - 6-8-1946) {2nd w/o James R. Bogle}.

CALDWELL, W. Marvin- (1915 - 1987)
CALDWELL, Mary M.- (1925 -   ) {W/o Marvin, md. 6-10-1944 }
                      { Nee Morehead }
CARROLL, Millard Randolph- (9-12-1933 - 9-15-1933) S/o H.L. & L.E. C-

CARVER, Martha J.- (10-17-1876 - 4-23-1958)
CARVER, Sam D.- (3-19-1873 - 7-6-1930)

CHEWNING, Arbie H.- (1911 - 1993) {Mother} {Nee Hamlin}
CHEWNING, Robert F.- (1908 - 1968) { Father }
CHEWNING, Donald R.- (3-14-1936 - 3-12-1962) { S/O Robt. & Arbie }
CHEWNING, 3 infants in Chewning section
CHEWNING, Gilbert Wallace- (8-16-1934 - 10-28-1935)
CHEWNING, Willie Edmond- (4-2-1933 - 9-17-1962)
CHEWNING, Fred Brammer- (1945-1973) { S/o Orson & Leona)
CHEWNING, Orson W.- (1902 - 1976) {S/o Abner & Florence}
CHEWNING, Maggie Leona- (1905-1994) {W/O Orson, nee Hamlin }
CHEWNING, Trubie L.- (11-1-1905 - 2-16-1988)
CHEWNING, Doris S.- (3-29-1927 -   ) {Nee Spickard, W/O Trubie}
CHEWNING, Abner W.- (3-29-1889 - 9-16-1963)
CHEWNING, Florence G.- (6-20-1886 - 9-4-1953) { Nee Hamilton }
CHEWNING, William W.- (12-2-1906 - 2-2-1907)
CHEWNING, Gilbert E.- (8-29-1913 - 1-2-1913)

DUNAGAN, Mary Bogle- (10-28-1857 - 3-19-1916) { D/o Andrew & Mariah
          Cubine Bogle }
DUNAGAN, William- (9-2-1851 - 12-5-1928) H/o Mary Bogle Dunagan.
DUNAGAN, Emory, (2-18-1895 - 5-21-1924) S/o Wm. & Mary Bogle Dunagan
DUNAGAN, Snow Mitchell, (6-7-1880 - 9-21-1928) S/o Wm.& Mary Dunagan.
DUNAGAN, Mabry [William M.]-(7-22-1889 - 2-10-1950) S/o Wm & Mary
DUNAGAN, Ella- (1872 - 1933)
DUNAGAN, Enoch- (1865 - 1915)
DUNAGAN, Robert E.- (10-2-1911 - 9-29-1973) US Army, Cpl WWII
DUNAGAN, Elbert Sherrill- (2-5-1892 - 9-30-1972) Pvt US Army WWI
DUNAGAN, Willie L.- (8-23-1902 - 6-12-1899) S/o Enoch & Ella.

FANNING, Cynthia Mary- (12-27-1838 - 8-1-1899)
FANNING, Mollie Robinett- (1854 - 1928) D/o Jezreal Robinett.

HOGE'S CHAPEL CEMETERY

[Located on State Route 42, 1/2 mile east of Point Pleasant in Bland County, Virginia. On land now owned by David Morehead.]

FANNING, Hugh C.- (4-22-1843 - 4-24-1900) { S/o Joseph & Jane Bogle
      Fanning and husband of Mollie Robinett Fanning.}

FOLEY, Emmet- (6-5-1882 - 3-2-1956)
FOLEY, Josephine M.-(2-19-1892 - 3-30-1971) { Nee Munsey }

HAMILTON, Kelly H.- (7-20-1890 - 7-9-1925)

HARMAN, Sgt. John W.- (Co. F 8 Va. Cav. CSA (No dates)
HARMAN, Glenn S.- (1893 - 1943)
HARMAN, Kate Bogle- (8-26-1870 - 12-13-1958) W/o Otto V. Harman.
HARMAN, Otto V.- (1-7-1876 - 3-13-1851)
HARMAN, Oakley A.-(11-12-1904 - 7-20-1964) S/o Otto & Kate B. Harman
HARMAN, June D.- (10-24-1923 -   ) {W/O Oakley, nee Durham}
HARMAN, Addison- (11-14-1829 - 11-13-1887)
HARMAN, S.E.- (Sarah Ellis) (3-16-1834 - 2-21-1886) { D/o Garland
      and Julia Mustard Ellis and wife of Addison Harman.}
HARMAN, Eliza J.- (12-25-1868 - 12-27-1889) D/o Addison & Sarah.
HARMAN, G.W.- (6-10-1857 - 4-18-1878) S/o Addison & Sarah E. Harman
HARMAN, Daniel Levi-(6-4-1874 - 7-12-1934) S/o Addison & Sarah E. H--
HARMAN, Cynthia Virginia- (7-24-1875 - 8-6-1935)
HARMAN, Ward S.- (5-3-1883 - 7-5-1947)
HARMAN, Pearl Munsey- (6-1-1884 - 10-22-1969) W/o Ward S. Harman.
HARMAN, Mevo- (5-15-1916 - 11-5-1983) S/o Arista & Marcia Hoge Harman
HARMAN, Shirley W.-(9-9-1936 -   ) W/o Mevo and d/o Floyd &
      Bert Walker.

HAVENS, Luther Brown- (5-15-1878 - 7-23-1962)
HAVENS, Cynthia F.- (6-6-1907 - 2-16-1980) Nee Fanning
HAVENS, Alfred J.- (6-18-1918 - 4-5-1996)
HAVENS, Emma Morehead- (1-20-1917 - 9-22-1996)

HELVEY, Etta Mae Chewning-(4-25-1904 - 1-16-1987) D/o Abner Chewning.
HELVEY, William Archie- (9-9-1888 - 6-26-1973) 2nd h/o Etta Mae.

HERRON, Elizabeth J.- (3-8-1831 - 10-18-1929) {AKA "Hearn", Md 1st
               George Eli Waggoner, 2nd Wm. Hearn}

JONES, Bannie Townley- (1-2-1915 - 12-1-1988)

KIRBY, John C.- (12-2-1904 - 6-8-1986)
KIRBY, Annette C.- (5-11-1912 - 5-2-1984)

KITTS, S.B.- (11-11-1858 - 11-13-1920)

LEFEW, Willie Frances Carroll- (7-6-1920 - 11-4-1943) W/o James C.
      LeFew. D/o H.L. & L.E. Carroll. Killed by train in Pulaski, VA

MEADOWS, John Trenton- (6-24-1913 - 11-23-1994)

HOGE'S CHAPEL CEMETERY
[Located on State Route 42, 1/2 mile east of Point Pleasant in Bland
County, Virginia. On land now owned by David Morehead.]

MEADOWS, Lovenia Brunk- (6-17-1920 -   )

MELVIN, Harvey A. (Andrew)- (3-7-1907 - 1-15-1981)
MELVIN, Kate Fanning, (3-13-1905 - 4-17-1942) 1st w/o Harvey Andrew
MELVIN, Irene K. (Kirby)- (11-14-1913 -   ) 2nd w/o Harvey Andrew
MELVIN, Wallace Brown- (10-23-1931 - 1-17-1993) {S/O Andrew & Kate}
                       { Sgt. US Air Force, Korea & Vietnam }
MELVIN, Donald Wayne- (4-9-1941 - 12-11-1991) {S/O Andrew & Kate }
MELVIN, Burl E. "Bun"- (5-24-1914 - 11-22-1996) {S/O John & Julia}
MELVIN, Hazel Carroll- (2-17-1921 -   ) {W/O Burl }
MELVIN, Burl E. "Bun"- (5-24-1914 - 11-22-1996){ S/O John Melvin
                       and Julia Ella Mustard Melvin }

MILLIRONS, Linda J.- (7-30-1953 - 10-25-1972)
MILLIRONS, James M.- (7-5-1965 - 7-9-1965)
MILLIRONS, Randolph D.- (7-16-1955 - 6-24-1956)

MOREHEAD, A.E. "Aussie" - (3-17-1882 - 10-8-1935)
MOREHEAD, Ella M.- (1884 - 1970) W/o Otto G. Morehead. (Nee Miller)
MOREHEAD, Otto G.- (1877 - 1957)
MOREHEAD, James O.- (6-30-1915 - 4-23-1989) S/o Otto & Ella Morehead.
MOREHEAD, James Ward- (1879 - 1971)
MOREHEAD, Bessie (Mae) Helvey- (1888 - 1980)
MOREHEAD, Emory- (8-28-1888 - 11-20-1978)
MOREHEAD, Vera Dell Wagner- (1890 - 1920) {1st W/O Emory }
MOREHEAD, Nannie B. (Burton)- (8-28-1899 - 2-17-1978){2nd W/O Emory}

MUNCY, Alma L.- (1902 - 1959) {Sister of Pearl & Josie Foley Munsey}.

MUNSEY, Joseph P. (Patton)- (1871 - 1961)
MUNSEY, Willie Sue- (1891 - 1965) {Nee Morehead}

PEAKE, John A.- (9-6-1909 - 9-5-1967)
PEAKE, Elizabeth G.- (B.& D. 10-31-1946)
{ 2 stones near Peake plot illegible }

PENLEY, Paul C.- (4-28-1901 - 3-13-1956)
PENLEY, Harry S.- (11-15-1907 - 6-27-1990) { Was deaf and mute }

PRUITT, Mattie- (1909 - 1979) {FHM}
PRUITT, Charlie- (3-1911 - 5-1991) {FHM}

RATLIFF, Patsy Jean- (2-13-1935 - 11-14-1935)

ROBERTS, George W. (1859 - 1904)
ROBERTS, Nannie E.- (1865 - 1941)

SLUSS, Brenda C.- (10-22-1950 - 3-23-1951)

HOGE'S CHAPEL CEMETERY
[Located on State Route 42, 1/2 mile east of Point Pleasant in Bland
  County, Virginia. On land now owned by David Morehead.]

SMITH, Obediah- (1-23-1839 - 1-25-1911)
SMITH, Louise- (1928-1991){Nee Wolfe, w/o Jack Smith, md. 10-23-1948}
SMITH, Edward Jackson "Jack"- (7-2-1924 -   )
SMITH, a grave with fieldstones. No name or dates.}

STOUT, Geneva Peake- (6-25-1950 - 8-3-1995)

TAYLOR, Joseph Purver- (6-13-1889 - 4-3-1966)
TAYLOR, Lena Mable- (3-2-1912 - 12-21-1963)
TAYLOR, Virginia Thompson- (4-9-1893 - 3-15-1969)

THOMPSON, Mollie Kate- (8-7-1870 - 5-22-1922) W/o Miller H. Thompson,
          dau of Wm. B. & Martha Ellen Compton Ashworth.
THOMPSON, Miller Hoge- (1-2-1873 - 6-19-1930)
THOMPSON, H. Wayne- (5-21-1906 - 9-15-1963) S/o Miller H. & Mollie.
THOMPSON, J. Woodson- (8-1-1904 - 7-14-1961)S/o Miller H. & Mollie.
THOMPSON, Margaret L.-(1922 - 1967)
THOMPSON, Paris E.- (11-10-1888 - 3-3-1973)
THOMPSON, Nannie L.- (6-16-1892 - 3-14-1974)
THOMPSON, Comey E.- (7-17-1867 - 2-28-1944)
THOMPSON, Willie E.- (7-1958 - 3-1959)
THOMPSON, Harold Francis- (2-23-1953 - 3-24-1955)
THOMPSON, Ballard Preston- (No dates) {Co. F, VA INF CSA}
THOMPSON, Margaret H.- (5-15-1871 - 5-12-1956)

TICKLE, Lillie Belle- (1877 - 1958) {Nee Harman} W/o Robert L.
TICKLE, Robert L.- (1875 - 1945) S/o Daniel Lineberry and Polly
          Bogle Tickle. Polly Bogle, d/o George and Jane Ray Bogle.
TICKLE, John D.- (4-6-1911 - 2-25-1990) Md. Ruby M. 6-24-1936.
TICKLE, Ruby M.- (11-28-1912 - 3-9-1983) { Nee Morehead, Md. John D.
          Tickle 6-24-1936}
TICKLE, Meek Bogle- (2-3-1871 - 10-7-1957) S/o Dan'l. L. & Polly
          Bogle Tickle. Md Palmyra Harman, 6-30-1898.
TICKLE, Palmyra Harman- (9-20-1873 - 5-13-1957) D/o John W. & his
          2nd wife, Martha Burton Harman. George W. Harman was s/o
          Addison and Sarah Ellis Harman. Sarah Ellis was d/o Garland &
          Julia Mustard Ellis.
TICKLE, L. Clara- (8-28-1899 - 6-15-1982)

TOWNLEY, Cecil Wagner- (6-12-1902 - 2-23-1962)
TOWNLEY, Elvira Davis- (10-24-1901 - 3-24-1947)
TOWNLEY, Herman E.- (2-9-1933 - 4-27-1963) Military data on stone.
TOWNLEY, John Hubert- (1-16-1907 - 12-22-1978)
TOWNLEY, Mellicue S.- (6-30-1917 - 12-28-1987) Md Meryln 10-17-1936
TOWNLEY, Meryln W.- (10-26-1881 - 6-2-1984) Md Mellicue, 10-17-1936
TOWNLEY, Samuel Mellicue- (5-15-1874 - 8-2-1943)
TOWNLEY, Rebecca Alice- (8-26-1881 - 8-2-1943.
TOWNLEY, William Frank- (10-11-1899 - 4-7-1961)
TOWNLEY, Barbara- (1942 - 1950) " Our daughter "

HOGE'S CHAPEL CEMETERY
[Located on State Route 42, 1/2 mile east of Point Pleasant in Bland
County, Virginia. On land now owned by David Morehead.]

TOWNLEY, Rev. Leonard S.- (9-1-1930 - 12-3-1970)
TOWNLEY, Mae McPeak Carroll- (5-16-1900 -   )
TOWNLEY, Beulah G.- (4-26-1928 - 6-15-1996)Affectionately called TOM.
TOWNLEY, Trovia Dale- (8-22-1937 - 7-18-1998)
TOWNLEY, Edna H.- (7-5-1908 - 3-25-1991)
TOWNLEY, R. Blaine- (3-14-1935 -   )
TOWNLEY, Alice V.- (11-11-1942 - 8-28-1996) {W/O Blaine, nee Vest }

WAGNER, William Foster- (5-5-1860 - 2-1-1946) H/o Octavia V. Munsey
                        {S/O George E. & Mollie Hearn Wagner }
WAGNER, Octavia Victory Munsey- 3-14-1860 - 8-9-1933) W/o Wm. Foster
WAGNER, Emory H.- (4-4-1882 - 2-23-1965) S/o Foster & Victory Wagner.
WAGNER, Mollie E.- (3-1-1884 - 1-28-1954){Nee Morehead 1st W/o Emory}

WOLFE, Willie K.- (1902-1975) { Nee Kirby, w/o Vernie Wolfe.}
WOLFE, Vernie E.- (1907 - 10-11-1975) { Md. Willie, 10-12-1927 }

    There are at least 20 graves here with no markers. Some graves have
only funeral home markers. Some of these markers are minus the name
cards which contain the birth and death dates. I would appreciate
hearing from anyone who has loved ones buried here and can help fill
in the names on the unmarked graves. Parke Bogle
{ Jo Ann Tickle Scott went over this cemetery again in October of
1998 and added some names and dates that I did not have.}

OLD BOGLE CEMETERY ON WALKERS CREEK
[Until 1861, in Giles County. Now lies about 1/4 mile across the
Bland County line and slightly southwest of Mount Zion Church.]
Copied by Parke C. Bogle in 1979.]

1- R. FLETCHER, d. June 24, 1849. [On hand carved field stone. Only
   the death date given.] H/o Jane Moore, d/o Enos Moore & Polly
   Bogle Moore.
2- B.P. STAFFORD, (May 11, 1835 - Nov. 7, 1910) S/o Ralph Stafford
   & Margaret Orr Stafford.
3- MARY J. STAFFORD, w/o B.P. Stafford. (1836 - 1916) D/o John &
   Betsy Henderson. B.P. md. Mary J. in 1855 in Giles County.
4- SALLY WYGAL, (dates illegible) Believed to be Sarah, daughter of
   Joshua & Elizabeth Davis Mustard, who married T. B. Wygal. }
5- RALPH STAFFORD, (died Jan. 24, 1879, age 84 yrs.) (Married in
   Giles County by bond issued Oct. 13, 1814, to Margaret Orr.
6- MARGARET STAFFORD, (Nee Orr) died Sept. 28, 1880, age 88 years.
7- C.M. WRIGHT, (Nov. 11, 1849-May 8, 1921) H/o Cecilia S. Bussey.
8- SAMUEL T. LEFLER, (Feb. 9, 1903-Feb. 3, 1906)
9- NANNIE RUTH LEFLER, (July 11, 1907-July { #'s 8 & 9, children of
   H.S. & D.A. LEFLER } Graves inside a neat wrought iron fence.
10- HIRAM STINSON, (1815 - 1888) H/o RUTH BOGLE. S/o JACOB & POLLY
    SIMPKINS STINSON.
11- RUTH A. BOGLE, wife of Hiram Stinson, died Feb. 3, 1879, age 68.
    { Dau of John Bogle, Sr. and Margaret ???.}
12- EMMA B. FERGUSON, (1887 - Oct. 6, 1896) D/o W.M. & M.S. Ferguson.
13- EMMA BOGLE, (Oct. 20, 1860-1887) D/o John & Julia Brawley Bogle.
14- LULA CATHERINE BOGLE, (Feb. 14, 1862-May 30, 1890) D/o John &
    Julia Brawley Bogle. Buried in her wedding gown.
15- JOSEPH BOGLE, (Nov. 30, 1809-Dec. 18, 1877) S/o John & Margaret
    (MNU) Bogle. Unmarried.
16- J.L. (JOSEPH LONGSREET) BOGLE, (1864-March 6, 1900) S/o John &
    Julia Brawley Bogle. H/o Roxie Pauley Bogle .
17- JOHN BOGLE, (JR) died April 6, 1872, age 57 yrs 1 mo 27 days.
18- MARGARET BOGLE, (1813-1889) D/o John & Margaret (MNU) Bogle.
19- NANCY DAVIS, (age 83 years) No other dates. Believed to be
    Nancy Baynes Davis widow of George Baynes and 2nd wife of William
    Davis. She was 62 in 1860. She died in 1881.
20- JAMES D.,(July 31, 1878-Oct. 7, 1881) S/o J.N. & M.E. MUSTARD.
21- PRISCILLA LEFEW, (April 20, 1862-Oct. 17, 1921) {Nee Fletcher }

OLD BOGLE CEMETERY ON WALKERS CREEK
[Until 1861, in Giles County. Now lies about 1/4 mile across the
Bland County line and slightly southwest of Mount Zion Church.]

PEOPLE ASSUMED TO BE BURIED HERE WITH NO MARKERS ARE,

22- JOHN BOGLE, SR., died Aug. 17, 1859, age 84 yrs. 5 mos. & 20
days. Born in Pennsylvania. (Death record, Giles County.)
23- MARGARET BOGLE, w/o John Sr., Maiden name unknown.
24- MARGARET SUSANNA BOGLE FERGUSON, (June 19, 1858-July 28, 1900)
D/o John & Julia Brawley Bogle. W/o Wm. Mitch Ferguson. (Known to
be buried here per her obituary notice.)
25- JULIANN BRAWLEY BOGLE, died 1916. W/o John Bogle, Jr. D/o Anslem
Brawley of Wythe County. (Will & probate record, Bland Co. Va.)
26- JAMES BOGLE, the early settler and ancestor of all others here.
Believed to have died before between 1816 and 1817.
27- MARY "POLLY" BOGLE, wife of JAMES. Believed to be buried here.
28- MARY "POLLY" BOGLE MOORE, died July 18, 1860, age 89 yrs, 6 mos.
{D/O James and Polly Bogle & wife of Enos Moore. Born Maryland }
29- ENOS MOORE, H/o POLLY BOGLE MOORE, died between 1860 and 1870.
Was age 85 in 1860 Giles County Census. He was born in Maryland.
30- SARAH "SALLY" BOGLE, D/o James & Polly Bogle. born abt. 1779.
She died before 1870. Was age 81 in 1860 Giles County Census.
31- JAMES BOGLE, (born abt. 1804, died 1872, married Susanna
Kennison.)
32- MADISON ALLEN BOGLE, born abt 1835, son of James and Susanna
Kennison Bogle, killed in battle near Princeton, W.VA, during
Civil War. He married Sarah Patterson.
33- CATHERINE BOGLE, born abt 1803, died before 1870. Listed in the
home of her brother, John and his wife, Julia, in 1860, age 57.
Daughter of John & Margaret (MNU) Bogle.
34- JANE MOORE FLETCHER, wife of R. (Rowland) Fletcher died about
1880. She was the daughter of Enos Moore and Polly Bogle Moore.
She was born in Sciota County Ohio about 1797. This leaves
research to be done in that county. Evidently the old James Bogle
at one time lived in Ohio, which at an early date was in
Virginia.

There is space for forty or fifty graves in this old cemetery, with
few empty places. There are many graves with no markers of any kind.
There are several with unmarked fieldstones. Though this cemetery is
now in Bland County, those who are interred here came to Southwest
Virginia while Giles was still in Montgomery County. I copied the
names and dates in 1979. I returned again in 1992, to find that the
cemetery had deteriorated very much since my first visit. In a very
short while it will be beyond restoration. These people who lived so
long ago will be completely forgotten, as if they had never lived.

[Please send any additions or corrections to,
Parke C. Bogle
1117 High Street
Pulaski, Va 24301
EMAIL address- <parkebog@swva.net>

[On old route 42, east of Mechanicsburg, Bland County, Virginia]
Cemetery is well kept and easily accessed. Copied in 1992 by Parke
Bogle and Melissa Lester. Reviewed in 1998 by Jo Ann Tickle Scott.]

ALLEN, Delia Mae Mustard- (11-28-1894 - 6-29-1918){W/O M.S. Allen}
ALLEN, John Madison (7-11-1881 - 3-3-1934)
ALLEN, Maude Fanning (2-16-1882 - 11-13-1951)

ANDERSEN, Jane Miller West, (1902 - 1979) (ashes) d/o D.A. Miller

ASBURY, Maudie Mae- (1908 - 1995) {D/O J.R. & ellie Shrader Wright}

ATKINSON, Sarah Ellen- (1925 - 1997) {D/O Rob & Clanie Bird Mustard}

ATWELL, Adrien Stewart- (4-18-1961 - 4-19-1961) {S\O John & Eleanor}
ATWELL, Bernard Cadet (9-25-1937 - 11-28-1985){S/O Ruth & Cadet}
ATWELL, P. Cadet (1900 - 1966)
ATWELL, Ruth B. (1911 - 1997) { D/O S.H. Bernard, w/o Cadet Atwell }
ATWELL, Samuel Berlin (6-12-1944 - 6-14-1944) { S/O Cadet & Ruth}

BAKER, Ora Myrtle (5-6-1903 - 12-20-1970){ D/O Rev. Neal Baker}

BANE, Robert Asa (1896 - 1989) {H/O Hazel Stafford}
BANE, Hazel Stafford (1908 - 1995) {D/O W.H. & Emma Wright Stafford}

BERNARD, Elliot Oscar (8-4-1872 - 8-8-1922)
BERNARD, S. Paul, Sr. (5-3-1915 -   )
BERNARD, Blanche W.   (12-15-1913 - 5-7-1988)
BERNARD, John S. (9-17-1878 - 4-20-1933)
BERNARD, Eula G. (1-4-1889 - 5-2-1956) D/o Francis M & Ellen Gordon
BERNARD, S. H. (3-11-1832 - 4-24-1912)
BERNARD, Elizabeth Pelter (7-29-1847 - 3-6-1932) age 84yrs 7m & 7d
BERNARD, Weston O. (3-12-1882 - 3-9-1889) S/o S.H. & Elizabeth.
BERNARD, Elliot Preston (1-9-1905 - 2-15-1905) S/o E.O. & E.N.
BERNARD, Madeline Virginia (1914 - 1915)

BILLIPS, Eugene E. (2-26-1915 - 7-21-1997) {S/O Wm. & Louvenia}
BILLIPS, Ruth Rose (8-20-1932 -   ){W/O Eugene E.}
BILLIPS, Alonzo W. (1908 - 1969)
BILLIPS, Lucille T. (1918 -   ) Wife of Alonzo.
BILLIPS, William Floyd (10-17-1872 - 9-10-1940)
BILLIPS, Louvinia C. (3-7-1877 - 7-30-1964)
BILLIPS, Nettie Ethel- (d. 6-4-1992, age 86) {D/O W.F & Louvinia}

BLANKENSHIP, Addie Ellen (Adeline) 1867 - 1925) {D/O Nancy Corner}
BLANKENSHIP, George Washington (1864 - 1947)
BLANKENSHIP, William Vaden-(8-12-1891 - 6-19-1973) {S/O G.W. & Addie}
BLANKENSHIP, Annie Thomas (7-24-1896 - 11-20-1993) W/o Vaden
BLANKENSHIP, Harold "Bill" Sr. (8-18-1917 - 12-5-1985) {S/o Vaden}
BLANKENSHIP, Elizabeth "Billie" (10-9-1920 -   ) { W/o Bill. }
BLANKENSHIP, Robert Vance (6-22-1894 - 2-10-1980){S/O G.W. & Addie}
BLANKENSHIP, Lula Mitchell- (3-31-1901 -   ){D/O Esca Mitchell}
BLANKENSHIP, Marjorie (8-17-1898 - 8-29-1977){D/O G.W. & Addie}

MECHANICSBURG CEMETERY

BLANKENSHIP, Louise Beatty (8-11-1915 - 12-26-1989) {W/o Irvin E.}
BLANKENSHIP, Irvin E.- (9-18-1915 - 2-23-1997) {S/O Vaden & Ann}
BLANKENSHIP. Aleta Mae (Durham)-(6-24-1928 - 3-20-1997) {W/O Raymond}
BLANKENSHIP, Raymond, K.- (10-27-1919 -   )

BOGLE, David Garth (2-20-1946 - 6-17-1986) { S/o John L.& Parke C}
BOGLE, James Daniel (6-29-1917 - 5- 1977) { S/o John & Nannie }
BOGLE, Mary Franklin,- (12-2-1927 - 6-15-1993) {W/O James Daniel }
BOGLE, Jessee Clement (3-27-1923 - 8-2-1961) { S/o John & Nannie }
BOGLE, John Lockhart [Jr.]- (6-29-1917 - 7-30-1970) {S/O J.L. Sr.}
BOGLE, Parke Coleman- (3-26-1920 -   ) {W/o John Jr. & George W.}
BOGLE, John Lockhart Bogle, Sr. (8-11-1872 - 11-22-1940)
BOGLE, Nannie M. (10-25-1886 - 3-25-1974) D/o D.A. & M.E.N. Miller
BOGLE, Lillian Miller- (9-7-1913 - 10-21-1981){D/o John & Nannie}

BREEDLOVE, Amos R.- (1-18-1895 - 12-1-1977)
BREEDLOVE, Dolly D. (6-10-1906 -   )
BREEDLOVE, Kenneth R. (2-17-1940 - 6-27-1987)
BREEDLOVE, Harold James-(2-18-1922 - 12-23-1997){H/O Blanche Mustard}
BREEDLOVE, Blanche M.-(8-8-1925   ) {D/O W.T. & Narcie Mustard}

BROOKMAN, Robert (5-27-1873 - 7-3-1932)
BROOKMAN, Emma Patton (5-12-1873 - 5-19-1958)
BROOKMAN, Cleo (5-10-1910 - 2-12-1983)

BROWN, Otis C. (1900 - 1987) {H/O Segal Mustard}
BROWN, Segal Mustard (1901 - 1976) D/o Newton Shell Mustard.

BRUNK, Crystal (7-18-1982 - 7-20-1982)

BURTON, J. (John) (9-4-1844 - 11-27-1909)
BURTON, Victoria E. Hare, w\o J. Burton, (3-30-1848 - 12-24-1907)

CARNER, Grace Orey (3-22-1904 - 6-19-1980)

CARROLL, Alfred H. (1914 - 1960)
CARROLL, Mable P. (1916 -   ) wife of Alfred.
CARROLL, Harvey L. (6-4-1894 - 11-21-1963)
CARROLL, Larmie M. (9-6-1898 - 4-14-1964)
CARROLL, Lewis Lee- (10-20-1916 - 2-8-1995) {H/O Louise Walker}
CARROLL, Louise W.- (11-6-1925 -   ) D/O Bert & Floyd Walker}

CHAPMAN, Samuel B. Jr. (6-11-1928 - 3-8-1988) H/o Billy Sue Mustard

CLEMMONS, Millie Asbury (1906 - 1986)
CLEMMONS, Edd (1929 - 1991)

COFFEE, Raymond A. (1900 - 1970)
COFFEE, Josephine P. (1901 - 1975) [Wife of Raymond, nee Powers)

COMPTON, Kate Wohlford (2-18-1885 - 8-27-1956)

COMPTON, R. Frazier (6-9-1886 - 6-28-1944)

CONNER, George Stuart (3-24-1857 - 6-22-1934) { S/O Nancy Corner}
CONNER, Jennie (1859 - 1915) {D/O Harvey R. & Mariah W. Mustard }
CONNER, Maggie Mae, 3-4-1894 - 12-9-1896) child of G.S. and Jennie.
{ Archives notes Maggie Mae Conner as being only one day old, and as
   dying on December 1, 1896. The stone is badly eroded, so the dates
   I have entered here, may possibly be wrong. Weather and erosion do
   strange things to tombstones. Etchings that are not really there,
   seem to appear. Parke C.Bogle. }

CONOR, Harve (10-12-1857 - 3-16-1931)
CONOR, Nannie (10-27-1860 - No other dates)

CORNER, Maggie, (died June 1945) age 92
CORNER, Tip (age 81) No other dates on stone.

CRAWFORD, John M. (7-23-1896 - 3-27-1915)
CRAWFORD, William (1808 - 5-4-1875)
CRAWFORD, Margaret Webb (1816 - 12-10-1888) { W/O William}
   { According to information given to me by Mrs. Francis St Clair,
   William Crawford was the first person buried in the Mechanicsburg
   Cemetery. He and Margaret Webb Crawford were Mrs. St. Claire's
   great grand parents. {There are no stones to mark their graves.}

CRIDER, Benjamin- (1923 - 1993)
CRIDER, Connie (Repass)- 1923 -   )

DAVIS, Addison (1810 - 2-15-1900) [S\o Hiram & Betsy Burke Davis]
DAVIS, Juliet (1813 - 3-9-1901) [D\o Hiram & Betsy Burke Davis.
DAVIS, Theresa Loraine (2-29-1972 - 3-1-1972)
DAVIS, Emory Carl (1-20-1975 - 11-7-1987)

DILLOW, Samuel (9-4-1846 - no death date)

DURHAM, Celina L. (1879 - 1967)
DURHAM, Charles Franklin (1900 - 1959)
DURHAM, E.C. "Chap" (1903 - 1973)
DURHAM, J. Harve (5-5-1898 - 11-30-1988)
DURHAM, Roxie V. (9-9-1901 - 5-1-1981)

EATON, Georgia M. (12-3-1921 -   ) [Dau. of Arthur Melvin.]
EATON, Robert Lee (1-20-1919 - 1-1-1986) { H/O Georgia Melvin }

FANNING, Annie A. (2-12-1885 - 8-9-1890) Dau.of G.W. & M.H. Fanning
FANNING, Cecil M. (4-8-1902 - 6-16-1983) W/o W. Herbert Fanning.
FANNING, W. Herbert (10-27-1896 - 4-4-1976) [S/o James & Nannie.]
FANNING, George C. (1879 - 1918) [S/o George W. & Matilda Fanning]
FANNING, Grace M. [Mustard] (1875 - 1946) [W/o George C. Fanning]
FANNING, George W. (5-8-1835 - 12-4-1912) [S/o Joseph & Jane]
FANNING, Matilda D. (1845 - 1925) 2nd w/o George W.] Nee Davidson

FANNING, Robert E.- (2-23-1919 - 1-17-1998) {S/O Glenn & Grace}
FANNING, Ella Mae- (1-26-1919-   ) {Md Robert E. 9-29-1941}
FANNING, Glenn (10-16-1899 - 8-23-1977) [S/o James & Nannie Fanning]
FANNING, Grace H. [Havens] (9-21-1901 - 7-16-1970) W/o Glenn
FANNING, Willard L (5-23-1932 - 9-10-1954) S/o Glenn
FANNING, Gerald Benton III, (born & died 8-19-1964)
FANNING, John Wesley (1887 - 1959)
FANNING, Nellie Peery (1887 - 1961)

FERGUSON, Ruth A. Bernard- (9-30-1826 - 4-5-1888) {W/O Otey Ferguson}

FLETCHER, C. Snow (1874 - 1954)
FLETCHER, Larson   (1908 -1987) S/o Snow & Lula Fletcher.
FLETCHER, Lulu M. (1885 - 1960) W/o Snow, nee Ray.

FRANKLIN, Andrew W. (11-18-1886 - 12-9-1954)
FRANKLIN, Pearl Baker (10-27-1899 - 9-19-1989) W/o Andrew W.

FRENCH, William K. (1851 - 1923)
FRENCH, Virginia M. (1856 - 1930)
FRENCH, M. Bane (1916 - 1936)
FRENCH, G. Baber (1878 - 1937)

GILLIAN, Kyle C. (died 5-12-1962, age 52 yrs. 8 mos. & 9 da.)

GILLISPIE, Flora Bruce (9-4-1891 - 7-31-1967) W/o Arch
GILLISPIE, Robert Arch (5-12-1880 - 3-21-1949)

GORDON, Alice Mustard (8-22-1888 - 6-8-1942) W/o John R. Gordon.
GORDON, John R.   (3-1-1890 - 8-24-1951) S/o Francis M. & Ellen.
GORDON, Ellen Powers (8-30-1858 - 3-3-1941) 2nd W/o Francis M.
GORDON, Francis Marion (1-22-1838 - 3-9-1896)
GORDON, Fred T.   (10-12-1894 - 2-19-1961) S/o Francis & Ellen.
GORDON, Infant Daughter of Fred & Goldie , (born & died 5-21-1928)
GORDON, Grace Stuart (2-25-1890 - 6-27-1972) W/o Irvin Renn
GORDON, Irvin Renn (6-18-1892 - 8-13-1947) S/o Francis & Ellen
GORDON, Infant of I.R and Grace Gordon, (born & died 7-24-1922)
GORDON, John Irvin (2-2-1921 - 5-2-1976) S/o John R. & Alice.
GORDON, Rosa Stowers (7-3-1905 - 12-1-1988) W/o John Irvin.
GORDON, Nell F. [Nee Franklin] (8-19-1929 - 1-3-1991) W/o Donald
GORDON, Donald F. (10-2-1922 - 9-26-1993)

GRANBERG, Erik (12-19-1904 -   1992)H/O Mary Newberry
GRANBERG, Mary N. (12-16-1912 - 7-6-1997) D/O Jesse Newberry

GRAVES, Ella Sue, (3-29-1916 - 8-2-1916) D/o H.E. & Anna Graves.
GRAVES, Infant of H.E. & A.M. Graves (born & died 3-4-1918)
GRAVES, Robert Keith (11-25-1924 - 12-27-1924) S/o H.E. & Anna.
GRAVES, Anna Mustard (8-23-1890 - 9-7-1960)
GRAVES, H.E. (9-23-1892 - 4-6-1978)
GRAVES, Ralph M. (8-9-1919 - 3-6-1968) [S/o H.E. & Anna Graves]

HAMILTON, Emma B. (12-9-1895 - 7-22-1931) [W/o Wm. Hoge Hamilton]
HAMILTON, William Hoge (12-15-1883 - 1-29-1962)
HAMILTON, William Hoge, Jr. (9-16-1922 - 1-1-1929)
HAMILTON, Eugene (7-14-1931 - 7-19-1931) S/o William & Emma.
HAMILTON, Sanders M. (8-12-1844 - 1-20-1933)
HAMILTON, Sally A. (9-19-1858 - 10-28-1916) W/o Sanders, nee Mustard.
HAMILTON, Grover C. (1888 - 1972) S/o Sanders & Sally Hamilton.
HAMILTON, Sally S. (1890 - 1972) W/o Grover, nee Stinson.

HARDEN, Bertie H. (10-27-1921 - 5-11-1975) Nee Havens.
HARDEN, Linda Diane (9-17-1955 - 9-5-1966) Dau. of Bertie.
HARDEN, Paul C. (4-3-1932 - 1-15-1993) {US Army, Korea}
HARDEN, Stella McPeak- (5-27-1938 - 7-25-1998)

HARMAN, Ada Elizabeth (1896 - 1916) D\O Dr. James W. Harman
HARMAN, Dr. James W. (1824 - 1905)
HARMAN, Tommy Hoilman (1894 - 1915) S/O Dr. James W. Harman
HARMAN, Willie Dewey (1898 - 1899) S/O Dr. James W. Harman

HARNER, William Lawrence (10-17-1923 - 3-13-1988)H/O Sue Melvin
HARNER, Ellen Sue (11-3-1925 -) {W/O William L. Harner, D/O
                                    Arthur & Maggie Stanley Melvin.}

HAVENS, Alexander (Co. F. 8th Va. Cav. C.S.A. no dates)
HAVENS, Cannie (died May 5, 1929)
HAVENS, Earston Sheppherd (6-25-1873 - 4-4-1946)
HAVENS, Lillie Woods (6-25-1877 - 7-16-1959)
HAVENS, Hattie V. (1904 - 1979) [W/o Sidney]
HAVENS, Sidney E. (1908 -)
HAVENS, Huston C. (5-22-1882 - 3-18-1926)
HAVENS, Marvin C. (8-2-1897 - 6-21-1981)
HAVENS, Nannie T. (7-4-1884 - 10-18-1932)

HENSLEY, Pearl McPeak (1911 - 1985)

HETHERINGTON, J. Hoge (6-17-1876 - 10-27-1944)
HETHERINGTON, Cynthia Wohlford (9-27-1882 - 3-12-1965)
HETHERINGTON, Joseph B. (5-19-1914 - 4-15-1962)

HOGE, Edward Meek- (3-31-1908 - 4-27-1997) {S/O Wm. H. & Vicie Hoge}
HOGE, Georgia H.- (2-11-1910 - 3-15-1995) {D/O Grover Hamilton, w/o
                                    Edward Meek Hoge}

HOILMAN, Thomas Henry (1865 - 1927)
HOILMAN, Jenette Patton Harman (1870 - 1922) 2nd w\o Dr. J.W.Harman.
         Married 2nd to Thomas Henry Hoilman.

HOLLOWAY, Jessee E. Miller- (1898-1937){W/O William, D/o D.A. Miller}

JOHNSON, Dale (1921 - 1978 [Funeral Home marker.

JOHNSTON, Clarence Cecil (7-11-1901 - 7-20-1980) [Twin to Lawrence]
    "   Lawrence Lee (7-11-1901 - 5-6-1989) [Twin to Cecil]
    "   Chapman L. (6-29-1892 - 3-14-1964)
    "   Pearlie Syres (11-14-1889 - 8-8-1945) W/o Chapman.
    "   Harvey R. [Robert] (8-17-1894 - 12-17- 1963)
    "   Lucy Mustard (6-6-1862 - 12-29-1945) D/o J.H. & Marcia M-
    "   Stella [nee Munsey] (1899 -1995) {D/O R. Ezra & Gertrude}

JONES, Lee (11-4-1885 - 3-3-1908) { Shot accidently by Cary Allen }

KANODE, Carol Jean (9-16-1965 - 6-20-1967) D/o Junior & Mary.

KEISTER, Charles W. (1856 - 19??)
KEISTER, Rhoda Lou Cubine (1863 - 1894) 1st wife of Charles.
KEISTER, M. (Mag) R. (1861 - 1934) 2nd w/o Charles.
KEISTER, Birdie Mae Lou (1894 - 1894) Dau. of Charles & Rhoda.

KELLY, Gay M.- (10-13-1926 - 12-4-1996) {D/O Jo Ed & Flora McGuire}

KIDD, Harold E. {Everette} (11-28-1912 - 11-7-1989)
KIDD, Martha Ann (1894 - 1973)

KIRBY, Harve E. (1909 - 1996) { H/O Crystal Talbert}
KIRBY, Crystal T. (1907 - 1989) {W/O Harve}

MANN, William Kenneth (7-8-1925 - 4-13-1986) {H/O Gladys Rae}
MANN, Gladys Rae (Asbury)- (2-20-1939 - 1-2-1996) {D/O Tom & Lydia}

MARTIN, James Artes (3-14-1916 - 7-11-1917)
MARTIN, Sylvia Lorine (6-20-1920 - 12-3-1920)

MAY, Noah (8-23-1914 -   )
MAY, Daisey L. (4-18-1920 - 12-2-1984) W/o Noah.

MAYS, Charles Leo (12-11-1890? - 8-17-1906?) S/o M.B. Mays.

MCCURDY, Goldie Harman (4-17-1900 - 8-7-1984) (Dau.\O Dr. J.W.
        Harman and Jennette Patton Harman.)

MCGUIRE, Joseph E. (1897 - 1972) {H/O Flora Harman}
MCGUIRE, Flora H. (1905 -   ) (D/O James W. Harman}
MCGUIRE, Harry Thomas- (5-4-1940 - 1-31-1998) {US Airforce}
MCGUIRE, Catherine B. (Blankenship)- (9-13-1944 -){Md. 2-16-1962,
        D/O Harold & Creasie Dalton Blankenship}

MCNEIL, Daniel O. (1831 - 1915)
MCNEIL, Sarah E. (1844 - 1909) Nee Wohlford.

MCPEAK, David Clifford (2-28-1932 - 6-2-1932)
MCPEAK, Arnold Russell- (1-27-1917 - 12-2-1997)
MCPEAK, Lelia Patton- (9-25-1919 -   ) {W/O Arnold R.}

MECHANICSBURG CEMETERY

MELVIN, John C. (11-28-1866 - 8-26-1929) S/o Stantford Melvin.
MELVIN. Ella M. (5-13-1878 - 4-3-1970) Nee Mustard, w/o John C.
MELVIN, Martha Louella (born & died 5-27-1948)
MELVIN, Archie W. (2-3-1912 - 2-4-1940)
MELVIN, Arthur F. (4-24-1882 - 11-4-1956)
MELVIN, Maggie B. (3-11-1891 - 3-15-1980) W/o Arthur
MELVIN, Charles C. (12-27-1875 - 4-9-1946) {S/O Edmond "Doc" M.}
MELVIN, Carrie P. (8-10-1877 - 11-12-1957) W/o Charles, nee Price.
MELVIN, Boman (no dates)
MELVIN, Roy Preston- (4-30-1903 - 12-2-1995){S/O John & Ella M. }
MELVIN, Eve Love- (4-29-1908 -   ) { W/O Roy P.}
MELVIN, Frank Straley (4-15-1911 - 5-5-1970){S/O Arthur & Maggie}
MELVIN, John Elliot- (11-13-1915 - 9-13-1994) {S/O Arthur & Maggie}
MELVIN, William Edward- (1-13-1914 - 2-24-1993) {S/O Arthur & Maggie}

MILLER, Dr. Daniel Alexander (6-1-1853 - 7-15-1906)
MILLER, Mary Elizabeth, (Nee Newberry) 11-14-1861 - 12-19-1941)
MILLER, Maggie Pearl (6-12-1882 - 1-18-1886) Dau./ Daniel & Mary.
MILLER, John Robert (9-15-1884 - 8-24-1950) S/o Dr. Daniel.
MILLER, Cecil W. (4-6-1889 - 1-22-1971) W/o John Robert.
MILLER, Daniel Wohlford (4-6-1909 - 9-30-1962) S/o John & Cecil.
MILLER, George E. (4-15-1864 - 6-15-1933)
MILLER, Ella H. (6-10-1868 - 6-20-1928) W/o George E.
MILLER, Grady Hampton (12-1-1894 - 10-10-1970)
MILLER, Nellie Mustard (5-9-1897 - 1-18-1990) W/o Grady Hampton.
MILLER, Dewey M. (12- 1898 - 5-3-1978)
MILLER, Gladys M. (12-29-1900 - 3-21-
MILLER, Paul (4-9-1909 - 12-31-1962)
MILLER, Mossie G. (7-20-1916 - 9-7-1977) W/o Paul, nee Gibson
MILLER, John Earl (5-19-1912 - 2-25-1963)
MILLER, Harvey Vaden (7-11-1910 - 4-10-1988)
MILLER, Ina Kathryn L. (3-18-1911 -   ) W/o Vaden.

MITCHELL, Ardelia Wohlford (3-12-1844 - 11-9-1913) W/o Timothy.
MITCHELL, Timothy E. (12-17-1832 - 2-20-1916)
MITCHELL, Jessie M. (10-19-1832 - 1-25-1967)
MITCHELL, W. Homer (1892 - 1948)
MITCHELL, C. Alfred (1867 - 1960) S/o Timothy & Ardelia
MITCHELL, Minnie A. Dulaney (1867 - 1948) W/o C. Alfred
MITCHELL, Esca (2-10-1877 - 3-10-1954) S/o Timothy & Ardelia.
MITCHELL, Minnie Miller (9-1-1879 - 11-27-1942) W/o Esca.

MOORE, Etta Mae Hamilton (6-19-1879 - 12-31-1955) W/o A.Brown Moore
MOORE, Luther (4-4-1885 - 4-7-1896) S/o Jacob & Nannie Moore.
MOORE, Nannie N. (6-1851 - 7-12-1892) 1st w/o Jacob Moore.
MOORE, Nora (9-21-1882 ? - 1-2 ?- 1896) ??

MOREHEAD, Harry Maxwell, (1927 - 1993) {Md. Nell Stuart 7-15-1950}
MOREHEAD, Nell (Stuart)- (1930 -   ) {D/O Ed & Reba Stuart}

MORGAN, Virginia (4-10-1829 - 10-9-1890) W/o G.H. Morgan.

MUNSEY, Gertrude,   (1870 - 1961) D/o A.G.Updike, w/o R.Ezra Munsey.

MUSTARD, Newton Shell   (12-23-1856 - 7-5-1932) S/o Harvey R.
MUSTARD, Ella Crockett (3-7-1862 - 9-29-1928) W/o Newton Shell.
MUSTARD, Grat Harvey (12-8-1885 - 11-2-1954) S/o Newton Shell.
MUSTARD, Ora Stafford (11-20-1884 - 6-28-1961) W/o Grat.
MUSTARD, Robert Henry (11-25-1888 - 11-29-1958) S/o Newton Shell.
MUSTARD, Clanie Bird (6-2-1895 - 10-25-1948) W/o Robert Henry.
MUSTARD, King Hanson (11-21-1892 - 7-6-1958) S/o Newton Shell.
MUSTARD, Zozo Dixon (5-11-1891 - 3-16-1976) W/o King Hanson.
MUSTARD, Betty Jane (11-25-1927 - 3-10-1928) Dau. of King & Zozo.
MUSTARD, Walter E. (5-28-1897 - 11-12-1986) S/o Newton Shell.
MUSTARD, Irene Lynn (2-20-1903 - 9-19-1988) W/o Walter E.
MUSTARD, Estol Shell (7-20-1899 - 7-9-1967) S/o Newton Shell
MUSTARD, Georgia Byrnes (1902 - 1970) D/o Newton Shell & Ella C.
MUSTARD, Thomas Harvey (8-28-1870 - 7-2-1959) S/o Harvey R.
MUSTARD, Maggie Caroline (9-12-1876 - 3-14-1937) W/o Thomas H.
MUSTARD, Jezreal Robinett (6-25-1865 - 2-22-1918) S/o J.H.& Marcia
MUSTARD, Ina Wohlford   (11-8-1869 - 2-11-1928) W/o Jezreal.
MUSTARD, Fred Mason (6-5-1894 - 6-10-1951) S/o Jezreal & Ina.
MUSTARD, Ford Robinett (8-11-1895 - 3-30-1990) S/o Jezreal & Ina.
MUSTARD, Inez Snider (7-5-1909 - 1-12-1980) W/o Ford Robinett.
MUSTARD, William T. (11-29-1885 - 12-1-1980) S/o Jasper & Fannie.
MUSTARD, Narcie Miller (10-27-1890 - 7-29-1942) W/o William T.
MUSTARD, R.G. [Robert Gray] [Stone is missing] S/o Paulina Mustard
MUSTARD, Eva Moore [stone is missing] W/o Robert Gray Mustard.
MUSTARD, Oren S. (Jack) (4-20-1892 - 5-24-1954) S/o Robert G. & Eva
MUSTARD, Wayne Elwood (4-7-1911 - 11-17-1983) S/O Robert & Eva.
MUSTARD, Vera Irene- (11-19-1913 - 12-3-1994){W/O Elwood, nee Walker}
MUSTARD, George Ellis (3-19-1917 - 1-14-1923){S/o Robert G. & Eva}
MUSTARD, Jack Hunter (1945 - 1976) S/o Albert & Betty Rose.
MUSTARD, Larry Owen (1945 - 1967) S/o Albert & Betty Rose
MUSTARD, Jerry D. (1945 - 1967) S/o Wayne & Essie Nowlin Mustard.
MUSTARD, Essie Nowlin (1917 - 1950) 1st w/o Wayne Mustard.
MUSTARD, Frances- (d. 10-6-1995, age 75) {2nd w/o Wayne Mustard }
MUSTARD, Charlie L. (1866 - 1952) S/o Henry & Fronzinia C. Mustard.
MUSTARD, Henrietta (9-11-1858 3-6-1920) 1st w/o Charlie L. Mustard.
MUSTARD, Mary Jane P. (11-15-1876 - No death date) 2nd w/o Charlie.
MUSTARD, James Garland- (5-22-1914 - 4-15-1995) {S/O J.C. & Effie W.}

NEAL,   James Frank (1901 - 1978)

NEWBERRY, Robert L. (1-1-1834 - 1-1-1919) S/o Allen & Eliz. Bogle.
NEWBERRY, Margaret Hunter (11-14-1836 - 5-16-1925) W/o Robert L.
NEWBERRY, Samuel P. (12-9-1863 - 10-15-1922) S/o Robert L.
NEWBERRY, M. Rose (1-17-1869 - 4-30-1940) W/o Samuel P., nee Miller
NEWBERRY, Ellis H. (4-18-1900 - 10-19-1990) S/o Samuel P. & Rose
NEWBERRY, Kathleen Wohlford, (6-13-1905 - 6-25-1982) W/o Ellis H.
NEWBERRY, John A. (5-20-1887 - 10-13-1975) S/o Samuel P. & Rose.
NEWBERRY, Kate E. (2-17-1888 - 9-1-1971) W/o John A.
NEWBERRY, Curtis E. (5-3-1912 - 12-23-1958) S/o John & Kate.

NEWBERRY, John Price (1919 - 1990) S/o John & Kate.
NEWBERRY, Evelyn Hamilton, 1917 - 1962) 1st w/o John Price.
NEWBERRY, Ralph A. (10-31-1910 - 7-12-1960) S/o John & Kate.
NEWBERRY, Samuel Landis (1-24-1918 - 12-4-1976) S/o John & Kate.
NEWBERRY, Frank Roney (1-14-1892 - 12-29-1978) S/o Samuel & Rose.
NEWBERRY, Wreathe Harouff (9-21-1894 - 1-23-1958) W/o Frank Roney.
NEWBERRY, Leighton Price (3-18-1914 - 10-17-1988)
NEWBERRY, Mary "Brownie" (10-30-1924 - 11-29-1986) W/o Leighton.
NEWBERRY, Sylvia Harouff (1915 - 1938) D/o Frank & Wreathe.
NEWBERRY, Robert S. (4-26-1896 - 7-31-1951) S/o Samuel P. & Rose.
NEWBERRY, Zella E. (4-29-1896 - 4-6-1990) W/o Robert S., nee Burton
NEWBERRY, W. White (1866 - 1943) S/o Robert L. & Margaret H.
NEWBERRY, Jesse Hunter (8-29-1870 - 1-27-1954) S/o Robert Lemuel
NEWBERRY, Mellie Stafford (9-15-1874 - 8-11-1948) W/o Jesse Hunter
NEWBERRY, Robert L. (1905 - 1944) S/o Jesse H. & Mellie.
NEWBERRY, Harry M. (1907 - 1939) S/o Jesse H. & Mellie.
NEWBERRY, Paul Washington, (6-27-1963, age 52yr 11mo 12 da. S/o Jesse
NEWBERRY, Elizabeth Mustard, (2-28-1851 - 8-16-1916) [D/o John and
    Lovisa Mustard and wife of Wythe C. Newberry.]

NICEWANDER, Andrew J. (9-11-1897 - 12-8-1985)
NICEWANDER, Lelia T. (4-6-1905 - 5-5-1980) W/o Andrew, Sr.
NICEWANDER, Andrew J. Jr., (9-11-1942 - 4-1-1989) S/o Andrew J. Sr.
NICEWANDER, Clarence Edward (5-18-1888 - 3-21-1906) S/o Toby & Clydie
NICEWANDER, Edd Lee (11-18-1864 - 6-5-1944)
NICEWANDER, Bettie H. (2-3-1865 - 8-11-1938)
NICEWANDER, Harry Crockett (1900 - 1956)
NICEWANDER, Hilda Coledge (1902 - 1986) W/o Harry Crockett.
NICEWANDER, Ann E. (12-3-1842 - 4-21-1898)
NICEWANDER, Flora A. (12-9-1873 - 6-11-1953)
NICEWANDER, Robert R. (10-6-1894 - 2-3-1946) WWI Cpl. 323 Inf.
NICEWANDER, Susan (1840 - 1916)
NICEWANDER, William H. (8-26-1867 - 7-14-1947)

OREY, Flossie Patton (2-15-1908 - 6-29-1989)
OREY, John Schuler (12-27-1902 - 12-14-1977)

OWENS, Hampton Jordon- (2-21-1922 - 11-25-1981){2nd h/o Betty Rose
                                            Newberry Mustard.}
OWENS, Elizabeth Rose (1926-1989) {D/o Ellis & Kathleen Newberry}

PALMER, Georgia- (10-20-1922 - 1998) { Nee Thompson, W/o James E.}
PALMER, James E. (11-22-1910 - 5-24-1987) Md. 6-13-1942.

PARCELL, Anna Mustard (1-12-1899 - 1-12-1953) D/o Jezreal Mustard.
PARCELL, William H. (1904 - 1977)

PATTON, Arnold (1877 - 1963)
PATTON, Charles Okles (8-13-1893 - 4-26-1917)
PATTON, Robert Kelley (1-20-1908 - 10-10-1970)
PATTON, Ethel D. (1910 -   ) Nee Dillow. W/o Robert Kelley.

PATTON, Fayette G. (4-8-1902 - 11-3-1910)
PATTON, Floyd Wayne (7-1-1922 - 5-10-1942)
PATTON, George, age 26. (no other dates)
PATTON, Ida A. (1879 - 1960)
PATTON, John W. (1876 - 1952)
PATTON, Mary (12-12--1846 - 1-2-1921)
PATTON, Norice B. (?? 1913 - ?? illegible)
PATTON, Susie Davis (1889 -   )
PATTON, Charlie R. (1897 - 1977)
PATTON, Sadie Mae (1899 - 1951) W/o Charlie R.
PATTON, Robert (5-18-1842 - 1-21-1908)
PATTON, William Miller (8-11-1923 - 3-12-1979)
PATTON, Avela Hughs (8-30-1928 -   )
PATTON, Thomas Gerome (3-15-1886 - 12-25-1960)
PATTON, Lucy Hamilton (5-16-1887 - 6-10-1977
PATTON, Thuly (8-16-1869 - 4-7-1942)
PATTON, James H. (8-2-1886 - 12-24-1945)
PATTON, Son of James E. Patton (1-11-1920 - 4-16-1930)
PATTON, William M. (9-17-1878 - 5-23-1954)
PATTON, Poca D. (3-22-1879 - 2-24-1970)

PENDELTON, Ardelia (10-10-1858 - 3-11-1921) Badly eroded stone.
PENDELTON, Flora B. (1887 - 1960)
PENDELTON, James (Co. F. VA. Cav. CSA. (no dates)
PENDELTON, Nichodemus (18889 - 1949)
PENDELTON, William D. (5-30-1927 - 1-16-1976)
PENDELTON, William D. Jr., (10-15-1954 - 1-21-1955)

PENLEY, Lena E. Bernard, w/o W.S. Penley (5-4-1887 - 10-13-1919)

POWERS, Carrie- (5-4-1904 - 2-6-1995){D\O Harvey Crow & Rose Powers}
POWERS, Harvey C. [Crow] (1864 - 1947)
POWERS, Rose (1860 - 1939) W/O Harvey C.--Nee Nicewander.
POWERS, Ocie O. (1890 - 1967) Dau\ O Crow and Rose.
POWERS, Hubert (1884 - 1901) S/O J.J. and Jennie Powers.
POWERS, Jasper J. (1852 - 1926)
POWERS, Jennie B. [Baker] (1863 - 1920)
POWERS, John (8-28-1814 - 2-22-1898)
POWERS, John A. (1891 - 1970)
POWERS, Marie B. - (1897 - 1979) W/o John A. Nee Baker.
POWERS, Julia Ann (3-23-1826 - 5-5-1906)
POWERS, Thomas M. (8-8-1861 - 12-5-1922)

PRUITT, Walter H. (9-7-1910 - 4-30-1972)
PRUITT, Flora H. (6-4-1913   )
PRUITT, Avery H. (1-15-1909 -   )
PRUITT, Lula A. "Elizabeth" (5-4-1912 - 6-20-1988)

RAMSEY, William Jackson (6-24-1908 - 5-26-1985)
RAMSEY, Nora Billips (5-18-1902 - 10-6-1991) W/o William Jackson.

RAY, Samuel D. (1866 - 1929)
RAY, Sarah F. (1857 - 1934)

REED, Joseph (8-28-1828 - 11-30-1909) 2nd hus. of Ellen Powers Gordon

REPASS, L. Donald (1927 - 1962)
REPASS, Maxine F. (1925 -   ) { Nee Fanning, w/o L. Donald }

RICHARDSON, Wayne W. (6-29-1923 -   ) Hus. of Genevive
RICHARDSON, Genevive T. (8-3-1925 -   ) D/o Joe Thomas.

RIDER, Thomas A. (8-9-1845 - 12-10-1908)
RIDER, Jane Ann (8-23-1855 - 7-5-1913) Wife of Thomas A. Rider.

SANDS, Idell Patton (2-21-1909 - 1-31-1941) W/o Dewitt Sands.

SARVER, Laura French (6-30-1882 - 2-5-1969)
SARVER, William M. (3-22-1923 - 2-5-1969) US Navy.

SEXTON, Ruby Ball- (d. 1-17-1995, age 81) {Niece of Billy B. Mustard}

SHEPPARD, W.? (1835 - 1919)

SHEPPHERD, Cosby Wohlford (d. 6-23-1880, age 31yrs. 6 mos.){1st wife
        of James M. Sheppherd, & d/o Samuel Wohlford.}
SHEPPHERD, James M. (1848 - 1927)
SHEPPHERD, M.J. [Mary Jane] (6-30-1838 - 3-18-1919) 2nd w/o James

SIMMONS, John Randolph (1941 - 1950) S/o Ruby Gordon Simmons.

SINK, Beulah B. (1927 - 1987) Nee Brunk.
SINK, George L. (1910 -   )
SINK, Virginia P. (1912 - 1992)
SINK, William D. (1908 - 1966)

SMITH, Mae Ruth (9-24-1935 - 6-10-1964)

SONGER, Andrew J. (9-8-1832 - 1-10-1907)
SONGER, Ward (8-18-1863 - 7-1-1944)
SONGER, Carrie Fizer (1-6-1870 - 5-6-1864) W/o Ward Songer.
SONGER, John Ward (3-17-1890 - 5-4-1956) S/o Ward & Carrie.
SONGER, Macie Waddell (10-25-1898 - 8-15-1974) W/o John Ward.
SONGER, Jerry Wayne Songer (9-25-1955 - 3-29-1996) S/O Jack & Margie
SONGER, Lucinda C.- (3-9-1960 -   ) {Md Jerry, 8-24-1879}

SPARKS, Rachel M., (7-20-1932 - 2-22-1993)

STAFFORD, Montgomery S. (1889 - 1971) S/o Ralph Montgomery.
STAFFORD, Mable N. (1900 - 1961) W/o Montgomery S.
STAFFORD, Thelma N. (1922 - 1934) Dau. of Mont and Mable Stafford.
STAFFORD, Mary E. (1853 - 1923) Nee Crawford, W/o Ralph M. Stafford

STAFFORD, Ralph M.   (1834 - 1929) S/o Ralph & Margaret Orr Stafford
STAFFORD, William Henry (11-20-1882 - 1-9-1944) S/o Ralph M.
STAFFORD, Emma Wright (4-5-1881 - 1-6-1923) 1st w/o William Henry.
STAFFORD, Emma Davis (10-2-1879 - 6-16-1957) 2nd w/o Wm. Henry.
STAFFORD, William Henry, Jr. (b & d 1-4-1923) S/o Wm. & Emma Wright
STAFFORD, John C. (8-30-1914 - 4-4-1964) S/o Wm. & Emma Wright.
STAFFORD, J.W. (8-11-1861 - 7-25-1925)
STAFFORD, Flora Wohlford (5-28-1868 - 6-16-1928) W/o J.W. Stafford.
STAFFORD, Albert M. (11-25-1919 - 1-18-1966) S/o William Henry.
STAFFORD, Jane A.   (2-21-1918 - 2-4-1972) W/o Albert M. Stafford.
STAFFORD, Vicy M. (6-3-1847 - 2-6-1885) W/o James E. Stafford.
    { Vicy was a daughter of Edmond and Catherine Melvin, who came
        here from North Carolina in the mid 1840's. James E. Stafford
        was a son of Ralph Montgomery Stafford. }
STAFFORD, Oscar Brown   (12-6-1866 - 3-21-1955) Unmarried.

ST.CLAIR, Gordon P.   (8-9-1924 - 5-29-1980) H/o Frances Stafford.

STRADER, Charlotte Mae (1-14-1940 - 1-15-1940) D/o Everette & Flossie
STRADER, John David (2-10-1862 - 8-6-1928)
STRADER, Mary Evelyn (2-24-1863 - 9-28-1938)

STROCK, John F. (5-18-1838 - 3-10-1921)
STROCK, Zachariah Whitten   (7-16-1880 - 7-11-1966)
STROCK, Hassie Mitchell (10-29-1896 - 5-21-1969) W/o Zachariah.
STROCK, Lacy Allen (10-31-1934 - 3-20-1938) S/o Zach. & Hassie.
STROCK, Lorena V. (12-25-1923 - 9-19-1925) D/o Zach. & Hassie.
STROCK, Zachariah Whitten, Jr. (12-14-1921 - d. at sea, 1-26-1944)
        { Son of Zachariah Whitten and Hassie Mitchell Strock }
STROCK, Larry Earl (3-22-1940 - 12-28-1943)
STROCK, Sidney Charles- (7-12-1918 - 10-5-1993) {S/O Whitt & Hassie}

STUART, Ed (1897-1980) S/o Sally Mustard & William B. Stuart.
STUART, Reba M. (1905-1986) W/o Ed Stuart, nee Melvin.
STUART, Myrtle (1902 - 1977) D/o Sallie Mustard & Wm. B. Stuart.
STUART, William B. (1856 - 1920) Husband of Sally Mustard
STUART, Sally M. (1863-1951) D/o Harvey R. & Mariah W. Mustard
STUART, William (9-4-1818 - 11-17-1881) Father of William B.
STUART, Mary Edmona-(d. 11-29-1992, age 97) {D/O W.B. & Sally M. }

TAYLOR, Cynthia Wohlford (12-28-1850 - 9-18-1909) { Cynthia was
        the first wife of James T. Taylor. }
TAYLOR, Walter Howe (1894 - 1980)
TAYLOR, Reanie F. (1915 - 1991) Wife of Walter Howe Taylor.
TAYLOR, Lydia Bell,- (8-9-1917 - 11-11-1993){Wife of George Taylor }
TAYLOR, George (   ) Son of Walter Howe Taylor

THOMAS, Annie W. (1895 - 1973) W/o Joseph Thomas.
THOMAS, Joseph Arthur (8-13-1887 - 8-28-1958) S/o R.G. & Susan.
THOMAS, Warren S. (10-30-1920 - 12-26-1990) S/o Joe & Annie.
THOMAS, Muriel P. (4-13-1925 -   ) W/o Warren, born in England.

THOMAS, Charlie S. (1893 - 1974) Husband of Elizabeth Flick. WWI
THOMAS, Elizabeth F(lick) (1-11-1894 - 3-22-1981) W/O Charlie Thomas
THOMAS, L. Clarence (1910 - 1976) WWII.
THOMAS, Pauline S. (12-30-1917 -   )
THOMAS, R.G. (8-3-1851 - 2-9-1922)
THOMAS, Susan V. (9-25-1857 - 2-23-1909)

THOMPSON, Byrnes Patton (3-19-1902 - 11-22-1981)
THOMPSON, Samuel C. (4-7-1897 - 9-23-1963)
THOMPSON, Helen Virginia (11-9-1927 - 6-20-1943)
THOMPSON, Oran Price- (4-29-1924 - 12-3-1997)
THOMPSON, Evelyn Ann- (2-28-1930 -   ) {W/O Oran Price}

TOLBERT, Thelma Woods (3-22-1922 - 10-14-1990)
TOLBERT, C. Otho (12-10-1917 - 4-8-1993) {H/O Thelma Woods}

TOWNLEY, Leona Mustard (11-4-1892 - 4-3-1927) D/o Jezreal Mustard.
TOWNLEY, Victor Mason (11-6-1912 - 7-13-1913) S/o Leona.

TUGGLE, William D. (1885 - 1973)
TUGGLE, Wanda Wohlford (1905 - 1965) W/o William D.

VAN DEN DUNGEN, Johannes C. [Cornelious] (10-28-1937 - 8-6-1978)
        { He was born in Amsterdam, Holland, reared in the Phillipines
        and now sleeps beneath our beautiful Virginia sod. He was
        the husband of Janeth C. Bogle. }

VINYARD, Martin V. (1-3-1970 - 12-1-1989) US Marine.

WADDLE, Linda Mustard- (10-5-1945 - 3-29-1995) {D/O Garland Mustard}

WAGNER, Claude H. (9-1-1890 - 12-28-1969)
WAGNER, Pearl Mustard (12-13-1886 - 4-1-1971) W/o Claude, d/o
        Newton Shell and Ella Crockett Mustard .
WAGNER, Frank R. (1905 1984)
WAGNER, Lorine U. (2-6-1910 - 5-16-1996) W/o Frank R. Wagner, D/o
        Frank and Bertha Mustard Updyke.
WAGNER, Frank R. Wagner, Jr. (7-24-1938 - 11-19-1976) S/O Frank &
        Lorine Updyke Wagner.

WALKER, Arminta A. (1854 - 1921)
WALKER, Howard C. (6-10-1885 - 10-4-1972)
WALKER, Callie H. (7-1-1892 - 6-28-1986) W/o Howard C.
WALKER, Lloyd B. (11-29-1922 - 10-13-1955) S/o Howard & Callie.
WALKER, Rex G. (10-9-1926 - 10-12-1983)
WALKER, Blanche S. (3-3-1927 -   ) W/o Rex G.
WALKER, Claude Wagner (5-8-1939 - 10-25-1939)
WALKER, Diana Pearl (3-31-1941 - 4-23-1941)
WALKER, Floyd A. (10-12-1880 - 3-26-1943)
WALKER, Mary Elizabeth Brown (1-21-1892 - 1-18-1924) W/o Floyd A.
WALKER, Bertie S(arver) (3-20-1903 - 10-27-1991) 2nd w/o Floyd A.

WALKER, Margaret Mae (Nee Taylor) (1919 -1978) W/o Jim Walker.

WALKER, Willis Craig - (8-19-1924 - 10-19-1992) { S/O H.C & Callie }
WARDEN, Dorothy I. (11-7-1932 - 12-14-1987)

WEBB, Maude Bogle (3-12-1915 - 12-7-1940) D/o of John & Nannie Bogle.
     { Wife of Price Webb, who died and is buried in Pulaski, Co. }

WHALEN, Allen J. (CSA stone, no dates)
WHALEN, Hiram (CSA stone, no dates.
WHALEN, Lizzie P. (6-11-1856 - 8-24-1939)
WHALEN, Mary A. (11-10-1840 - 12-22-1888)
WHALEN, Lula N. (1833-1901)

WHITE, Mark A. (1966-1986)

WILSON, Frank (12-3-1896 - 12-10-1983)
WILSON, Bessie Durham (10-11-1908 - 6-3-1954) 1st w/o Frank Wilson
WILSON, Linda Carol (11-24-1944 - 3-26-1945)
WILSON, Louise Joy (11-14-1932 - 11-15-1938)
WILSON, Lucy Cook (4-6-1920 -   ) 2nd w/o Frank Wilson.

WOHLFORD, Caroline Sheppard, (1882 - 1954) W/o L. Phillip Wohlford.
WOHLFORD, Lewis Phillip (1872-1929)
WOHLFORD, Charles B. (8-26-1874 - 7-25-1944) S/o Gordon Wohlford.
WOHLFORD, Maude K. (10-13-1879 - 4-3-1959) W/o Charles B.
WOHLFORD, Gordon (1-26-1846 - 2-14-1910) S/o Samuel, Sr.
WOHLFORD, Matilda Byrnes (1-18-1846 - 1-29-1927) W/o Gordon.
WOHLFORD, John Samuel (1866 - 1934) S/o George & Jane.
WOHLFORD, George (1837 - 1882) S/o Samuel Sr.
WOHLFORD, Jane (1839-1912) W/o George, d/o John & Louvisa Mustard'
WOHLFORD, Robert Vernon (1869 - 1932)
WOHLFORD, Charles R. (CSA stone, no dates.)

WOODS, Hattie Pearl Havens (6-24-1886 - 7-2-1958)
WOODS, John Winfield (3-5-1867 - 4-20-1970) (Census, b date 1875)
WOODS, L.M. [Leatha Mustard] (1906-1976) W/o T.W. "Tomp" Woods.
WOODS, T.W. "Tomp" (1902 - 1965) S/o John & Hattie.

WOODYARD, Lelia (10-21-1880 - 1-28-1902) D/o H.W. & Hettie.
WOODYARD, Sally E. (1863 - 1890) D/o Paulina Mustard, w/o James W.

WRIGHT, Cecilia Susan (6-22-1856 - 4-7-1933) W/o C.M. Wright.
          { C.M. Wright is buried in the old Bogle cemetery on Walker's
          Creek. Cecilia was a daughter of Elizabeth Bralley and
          Thompson A. Bussey. }

--------, Infant son, with no surname (11-27-1896 - 11-27-1896)

YATES, Ruby, (died in 1991){D/O Wm. & Louvenia Billips}
 { Cemetery was updated in October of 1998 by Jo Ann Tickle Scott}

GOSHEN CEMETERY
[West of Goshen Church in the Little Creek section of Bland County }
{ Copied in October of 1998 by Jo Ann Tickle Scott }

BANES, Colleen Davis- (4-4-1928 - 5-30-1969) {Mother}
    "   Wayne Kenneth- (9-20-1925 - 12-18-1968) {Father}
    "   Jessie L. Bond- (10-1-1900 - 10-16-1983) {W/O Edgar A. Bond}
    "   Edgar A.- (6-4-1897 - 1-6-1976)
    "   William D.- (3-18-1893 - 4-1-1956)
    "   On 3 hand made stones, are the names, Charley, Mary and
           Chester BANES. (No dates)
    "   Margaret A.- (1855 - 1924) {Age 69}
    "   James Ellis- (8-8-1987 - 8-11-1987)
    "   Joseph Nelson- (B. & D. 10-29-1988)

BRUNK, Opal Belle- (6-6-1940 - 4-15-1941) (D/O Huston & Genoa }
    "   Huston N.- (1896 - 1979) {Father}
    "   Genoa D.- (1901 - 1987) {Mother} [Nee Davis]
    "   Infant son of Robert Bruce- (4-27-1960 - 4-27-1960)
    "   Robert Huston- (2-4-1958 - 2-6-1958)
    "   Nancy Mae- (6-9-1954 - 11-7-1996) D/o Robert & Catherine)
    "   William S.- (10-3-1848 - 8-21-1950)
    "   Nancy C.- (6-21-1858 - 6-24-1909)
    "   Elizabeth "Lizzie"- (1-11-1877 - 4-21-1950)
    "   Walter Hubert- (3-29-1886 - 2-27-1962)
    "   Nannie Cathern- (6-22-1886 - 9-29-1951)
    "   George Clayton- (1-26-1930 - 11-17-1935)
    "   Clarence Herbert- (3-15-1908 - 10-14-1935)
    "   Ethel May- (11-15-1913 - 10-14-1918)

BURTON, Emmer- (7-28-1922) {Birth or death date? } [Homemade stone]
    "   Mitchell M.- (1863 - 1942)
    "   Willie Bane- (1876 - 1934)
    "   Charles Eulus- (4-?9-1926 - 12-14-1978) {US Army WW II}
    "   Bertha Brunk- (4-7-1900 - 9-11-1930)
    "   Charles Calvin- (10-25-1900 - 6-3-1949)
    "   May J.- (9-30-1965 -   ) {W/O Walter M. Crockett }
    "   John Henry- (4-10-1898 - 3-13-1973)
    "   Clayton A.- (4-5-1924 - 12-20-1973) {US Army WW II }
    "   Clarence Draper- (9-17-1930 - 9-18-1991) { US Army WW II}
    "   Joseph Eugene- (6-8-1966 - 10-18-1997)
    "   Charles William- (7-2-1927 - 8-6-1994) { US Army WW II }

CARPENTER, Lorine M.- (1927-1927) {Infant D/O Edagr & Allie }
    "   Edgar A.- (6-27-1897 - 10-28-1958)
    "   Allie B.- (2-24-1897 - 4-6-1968)

CORDER, Lula Ann Brunk- (7-6-1897 - 4-25-1926) {W/O Edward Corder }
    "   Martha Brunk- (10-21-1949 - 10-21-1998) {Age 49}
    "   Ruth D.- (1-4-1919 - 2-11-1996)
    "   James L.- (8-7-1911 - 4-15-1998)
    "   Calvin Larkin- (3-31-1936 - 7-8-1936) {S/O James & Ruth}

GOSHEN CEMETERY
[West of Goshen Church in the Little Creek section of Bland County }
{ Copied in October of 1998 by Jo Ann Tickle Scott }

CRISCO, Calvin Orrin- (2-27-1930 - 6-28-1996)

DAVIS, Annie Kate- (11-29-1895 - 4-29-1947) {W/O Albert T. Davis}
    "   Albert T.- (5-18-1885 - 6-16-1959)
    "   Stewart P.- (12-8-1881 - 10-9-1944)
    "   Ethel D. Shelton- (1-23-1886 - 3-25-1981)
    "   Gladys C.- (2-1-1910 - 7-26-1952) { W/O Claude S. Davis }
    "   Claude S.- (5-14-1905 - 12-25-1975)
    "   Elizabeth C. Farmer- (5-13-1866 - 12-30-1945) W/O Hiram N. D-
    "   Hiram Newton- (1-27-1863 - 9-30-1931)
    "   Infant son- (B.& D. 4-30-1940) { S/O Gilbert & Ola Bell M.}
    "   Gilbert F.- (1919 - 1951)
    "   Ola Bell M.- (1920 - 1984)
    "   Herman Milton- (1912 - 1975) {FHM}
    "   Emmett M.- (4-4-1885 - 12-13-1955)
    "   Willie J.- (3-13-1888 - 12-14-1953)
    "   Lester N.- (4-7-1929 - 11-6-1936)
    "   Robert Newton- (6-30-1887 - 3-10-1934)
    "   Julia King- (12-6-1892 - 12-28-1967)
    "   Elmer Lawrence- (4-2-1910 - 1-6-1955)
    "   Mary Lou- (4-1-1911 - 6-5-1985)
    "   Louis Baxter- (1-21-1924 - 11-14-1986) { US Army WW II }
    "   Willie F.- (9-17-1877 - 4-18-1942) { W/O C.C. Davis }
    "   C.C. - (6-27-1875 - 6-15-1932)
    "   Wilma- (12-23-1905 - 3-12-1919) { D/O Willie & C.C. }
    "   Infant Son- { of C.C. & Willie F. Davis}
    "   Infant Son- { of C.C. & Willie F. Davis)
    "   James E.- (5-1-1864 - 10-24-1934)
    "   Ollie E.- (4-2-1866 - 10-27-1934) W/O James E. Davis }
    "   Robert Lee- (6-14-1867 - 12-15-1956)
    "   Josie E.- (1870 - 1942)
    "   Henry- (5-5-1844 - 2-15-1906)
    "   Margaret- (3-7-1841 - 5-2-1905)
    "   Fred P.- (4-5-1903 - 10-27-1982)
    "   Martha F.- (1-16-1907 -   )
    "   Lockie L.- (1-10-1927 - 12-26-1942)
    "   Peggy Jane- (9-15-1939 - 10-26-1939)
    "   Ruby V.- (4-18-1920 - 11-26-1920)
    "   Susanna- (5-25-1880 - 11-4-1921)
    "   Flavius- (12-13-1868 - 12-17-1957) { Spanish American War }
    "   Lee Earl- (9-17-1906 - 5-4-1966)
    "   Ida A.- (9-14-1891 - 7-26-1957)
    "   Joseph Donald- (10-28-1930 - 1-2-1991)
    "   Vance Calvin- (12-3-1911 - 12-30-1960)
    "   Ethel Kitts- (12-5-1901 - 10-2-1978)
    "   Infant daughter of Vance & Ethel Davis- (8-7-1949)
    "   Nannie E.- (11-29-1876 - 12-7-1912) { Age 36 Yrs, 8 das. }
          { First wife of Comie Albert Davis)
    "   Comie Albert- (2-4-1872 - 3-17-1945) {S/O Henry & Margaret F.}

GOSHEN CEMETERY
[West of Goshen Church in the Little Creek section of Bland County }
{ Copied in October of 1998 by Jo Ann Tickle Scott }

DAVIS, Edna K.- (9-15-1891 - 10-12-1973) {2nd W/O Comie Albert Davis}
  "   Lucy C.- (1894-1938)
  "   Charles C.- (1887 - 1929)
  "   Viola King- (12-9-1914 - 12-2-1985) { Mother }
  "   Phillip A.- (12-3-1912 - 8-23-1968) { Father }
  "   Ruby M.- (1918-   )
  "   Norman H.- (1916 - 1961)

FARMER- Sarah Hudson- (2-15-1923 - 2-25-1994) { US Navy WW II }

GREENE- Dorothy Meadows- (3-12-1909 - 2-2-1994)

HAMBLIN- Hugh D.- (3-18-1892 - 12-22-1920)
  "   John S.- (5-21-1855 - 2-2-1947)
  "   Sarah G.- (9-23-1953 -
  "   Ruby- (11-12-1921 -   )
  "   Infant Daughter (11-1-1910 - 10-10-1927) ??
  "   Frank- (8-5-1839 - 1-3-1911) { S/O S.G. & Emma }
  "   Stewart C.- (4-13-1882 - 3-18-1946)
  "   Estel Crockett- (12-11-1893 - 3-23-1970)
  "   Lena Davis- (5-4-1902 - 10-29-1952)
  "   Clinton Davis- (8-9-1943 - 8-16-1943)
  "   Raymond Alton- (2-4-1917 - 7-12-1990) { Pfc. US Army }
  "   Grace Brunk- (9-30-1923 -   )
  "   Ethel- (1889-1976)
  "   Hoge- (1877-1965)

HANCOCK, Sidney E.- (11-17-1887 - 2-6-1944) { US Army WW I }
  "   Walter Tarter- (6-18-1898 - 6-26-1918)
  "   J. R.- (2-18-1905 - 2-22-1936)

HARDY- Violet- (9-1-1924 - 9-3-1924) {D/O H.E. & L.J. Hardy }

HARPER, Frank B.- (8-13-1940 - 6-14-1973)

HODGES, Eva Corder- (6-2-1905 - 8-25-1974)

KING, Joseph S.- (8-18-1957 - 3-6-1929)
  "   Emily Pegram- (7-13-1870 - 4-1-1959)
  "   John D.- (2-19-1891 - 6-19-1959) { PFC. US Army WW I }

KITTS, Alford Robert- (10-8-1908 - 8-13-1936)
  "   Robert Hutzell- (9-10-1874 - 12-5-1961) {Father}
  "   Bertha Davis- (12-22-1879 - 5-24-1938) {Mother}
  "   Fay Rena- (12-22-1919 - 12-27-1924)
  "   Viola E. Lee- (2-1-1916 - 3-25-1916)
  "   Jacob F.- (No dates) { Co. F. VA Inf. CSA }
  "   Cynthia Wyrick- (about 1850 - 8-9-1905) {D/O Asa Wyrick &
                       2nd w/o Jacob Kitts}

GOSHEN CEMETERY
[West of Goshen Church in the Little Creek section of Bland County }
{ Copied in October of 1998 by Jo Ann Tickle Scott }

LINKOUS, Leonard L.- (9-2-1921 - 8-3-1983) {Md. 3-2-1942 }
    "   Kathleen C.- (4-23-1924 - 5-14-1979) {W/O Leonard}
    "   Raymond Eugene- (9-15-1926 - 2-16-1987)

MEADOWS, Mary Alberta- (1-5-1897 - 10-1-1924)
    "   John Jess- (5-28-1890 - 5-2-1978)
    "   Albert Terry- (6-19-1895 - 8-23-1972)
    "   Laura Millirons- (4-3-1898 - 5-23-1973)
    "   James Victor- (9-2-1919 - 9-4-1919) {S/O J.J. & M.A. }
    "   Ida Bell- (10-1-1861 - 3-13-1945) {W/O J.W. Meadows }
    "   J.W. - (3-1-1863 - 11-19-1917)
    "   Betty Naomi- (3-17-1899 - 6-12-1900){ D/O J.W. & Ida B.}
    "   Dager- (7-1-1888 - 8-3-1926)
    "   Wylie V.- (9-13-1884 - 12-3-1960)
    "   James- (B. & D. 6-5-1941) {S/o Mr. & Mrs. Trenton Meadows}
    "   James Russell- (6-24-1913 - 6-28-1913)

PARSELL, Charles Lee- (12-10-1856 - 3-1-1917)
    "   Martha J.- (2-23-1859 - 6-11-1929)

PEGRAM, J.H.- (4-22-1832 - 3-21-1902)
    "   Frances L.- (8-31-1832 - 5-23-1911)

RATCLIFFE, Charlie Robert- (12-29-1925 - 11-23-1997)

RITTER, David S.- (6-8-1842 - 4-7-1911) {Pvt. Co F. 54 VA.Reg. CSA}
    "   Georgia- (1-1-1902 - 9-27-1902) Infant of F.D. Ritter }
    "   Margaret- (3-6-1905 - 3-18-1905) { "   " " "   "   }
    "   Nannie- (7-28-1909 - 8-26-1910) { "   " " "   "   }
    "   David A.- (3-4-1874 - 12-5-1962)
    "   Della H.- (11-16-1880 - 1-1-1968)
    "   Leonard A. - (1-22-1903 - 9-12-1928)
    "   Elbert R.- (6-29-1909 - 3-31-1917)

ROOPE, John C.- (12-17-1883 - 4-2-1971)
    "   Bertie C.- (4-13-1896 - 11-8-1994)
    "   J. Darnell- (1-8-1936 - 6-30-1963)
    "   Edith D.- (12-28-1935 -   )

WILLIAMS, Ellet W.- (2-25-1894 - 12-15-1960) { Pvt. US Army, WW I.}
    "   Ella D.- (5-26-1891 - 4-28-1960 }

WOLFE, Hoge Harvey- (10-4-1935 - 4-28-1983) {US Army, Korea-Vietnam}
    "   Charles O.- (4-26-1960 - 7-19-1996) {Father}

[There are several illegible stones, field stones and stakes here.
Also several homemade stones with no names or dates. Jo Scott]

UPDYKE CEMETERY
[Copied by Jo Ann Tickle Scott in October of 1998]
{ Cemetery is behind the house of the late Gilmer Updyke, just off
State Route 42. According to Timothy Harman, Gilmer told him that
there used to be a little store near the house and a mule lot. This
area is called "The Slide". Thanks to Timothy Harman for his help and
good memory. } Jo Ann Tickle Scott.

UPDYKE, J.M. { Junius Marcellus }- (5-20-1859 - 8-1-1935) {Father }
        {S/O Albert Galatin and Mary Smith Updyke.}
    "   Ada Lee- (1-6-1883 - 3-14-1972) {Nee Davis }
    "   Infant- (7-11-1912) {Child of J.M. and Ada Lee Updyke}
    "   Albert Gilmer- (7-28-1913 - 7-5-1997) { Cattleman }

BLANKENSHIP CEMETERY
[Cemetery is located to the north of Route 601, called "Ruby's Road".
It is about 2 miles from Interstate 77.]
{ Copied in October of 1998 by Jo Ann Tickle Scott.}

BLANKENSHIP, Dixie B.- (3-31-1929 - 12-23-1987) {Nee Breedlove}
            "An Angel hovered in the room, patiently waiting there,
            To take her home to Jesus and leave her in His care.
            A halo was in his hand to place on her silvery hair,
            A reward for a life of toil and the grief she had to bear.
            One night the Angel took her, God had called her home,
            He needed another Angel to stand before His throne."
BLANKENSHIP, Michael Jackson- (2-20-1951 - 8-30-1987)
    "   Kyle Nye- (7-16-1953 - 8-30-1987)
{Both Michael & Kyle were killed in a car wreck on this same road}

BRUCE CEMETERY
[Located on the Michael Pauley farm. 5 miles above a two story grey
brick house on left of Route 98. Bruce's once owned this land.]
{Copied by Jo Ann Tickle Scott}

BRUCE, Joshua H.- (5-5-1825 - 2-2-1904)
    "   Margaret- (d.-2-5-1870, age 44 yrs, 6 mo. & 18 das.)
                {W/O Joshua Henderson Bruce}
    "   Josiah- (8-17-1834 - 12-11-1890)
    "   James- (d. 4-2-1876, age 46 yrs, 6mos. & 19days)
    "   Newton A.- (3-25-1862 - 7-30-1916)
    "   Lily Caroline- (2-8-1862- 8-2-1886){1st W/O Newton A. Bruce}
    "   Bertha Maud- (8-17-1879 - 12-2- 1894} {2ndW/o Newton A Bruce }
    "   Elizabeth - (d. 8-1867, age 61 yrs, 1 mo.)
    "   Erastus M.- (11-1-1867) Only date legible.

LOCKE, Melissa J.- (d. 10-13-1855, age 28 yrs 8 mo. & 15 days)

THOMPSON, A.N.- (7-15-1840 - 4-15-1919) { Our Father }
THOMPSON, Julia Harriet- (2-20-1845 - 1-18-1902) {W/O A.N)
{ 3 fieldstones & 4 markers destroyed except for their bases}

HANCOCK CEMETERY
[Located south of Route 601 and east of Shrader's Chapel Church]
{ Copied in October of 1998 by Jo Ann Tickle Scott }

ABRAMSON, Vergie Hancock- (1910-1961)

COLLINS, George William- (9-16-1897 - 1-29-1970)
    "   Bessie Hancock- (11-27-1894 - 7-1-1975)
    "   Samuel William- (1924-1948)

CORDER, Mary E.- (12-18-1890 - 2-24-1967)
    "   Jas. L.- (7-25-1855 - 4-1-1923)

HANCOCK, Marcus Lee- (10-22-1856 - 1-29-1938)
    "   Margaret V. Wyrick-(5-27-1856 - 3-15-1928) {W/O Marcus Lee}.
    "   Jesse James, Jr.- (4-4-1932 - 3-4-1962) { Pvt. US Army }
    "   Letha V.- (8-8-1915 -   )
    "   Richard Lee, Sr.- (3-4-1935 - 5-6-1991)
    "   Elma- (1-30-1911 - 7-17-1913)
    "   Jordan I.- (5-10-1901 - 12-9-1918)
    "   Stella E.- (3-10-1897 - 11-8-1979)
    "   Riley H.- (6-25-1889 - 3-3-1966)
    "   Ribble J.- (11-27-1923 - 11-7-1992) {US Army WW II.}
    "   Virginia H.- (10-22-1917 - 3-15-1994)
    "   Lucy E.- (12-2-1893 - 1-15-1986)
    "   Mary J.- (6-15-1822 - 3-5-1899)
    "   George W.- (1858-1937)
    "   Isabella S.- (1868-1956)
    "   R.E.- (7-22-1921 -   )
    "   W.H.- (4-9-1866 - 1897)

SHRADER, Leona B.- (5-30-1932 - 7-13-1962)
    "   Sherrie Lane, infant- (12-13-1963)

MILLER CEMETERY
[Located on Vaden Miller, Jr. home place on Route 612 at top of hill.
Is not accessible by car. Hard to get to as brush, briars and weeds
have taken over. Impossible to restore.]
        { Copied in October of 1998 by Jo Ann Tickle Scott }

MILLER, Dr. L.J.- (1828-1896) { S/O Charles & Ann Mcniel Miller }
    "   Martha L. (Lois)- (1829-1904) { Nee Bird, b. Floyd Co. VA}
    "   John H. (Harvey)- (6-1-1870 - 4-25-1946) {S/O Dr. L.J.}
    "   Minnie C.- (12-5-1872 - 2-15-1951) {Nee Wright & w/o Harvey}

MOREHEAD, Mary Belle-(1856-1884) { 1st wife of Gordon Morehead and
            a daughter of Dr. Lorenza John Miller }

HELVEY CEMETERY

[Cemetery is located on teh south side of Kimberling Road (Rt. 612)
on a hill to the west ot the old L.J. Helvey home. Land is now
owned by Dr. Jessup Skewes. Can only get there by walking and you
have to cross the creek.]
{ Copied in October of 1998 by Jo Ann Tickle Scott }

HELVEY, Naomi S. - (1871- 1960) { Nee Shufflebarger, W/O Archie H-}
"   Minnie Sue- (5-13-1887 - 9-26-1940)
"   Samuel H. (Houston)- (12-25-1860 - 7-6-1939)
"   Nickiti K.- (6-7-1865 - 12-12-1944) { W/o Houston, D/o Dr.
                 L.J and Martha Bird Miller}.
"   L. James- (7-4-1897 - 3-6-1975) {S/O Samuel Houston and
                 Nickiti Miller Helvey.}
"   Clara M.- (9-29-1900 - 4-23-1962) { Nee Morehead } { W/O L.
                 James Helvey }

BURTON FAMILY CEMETERY

[Cemetery is located on route 603 off state route on George T.
Burtons farm. Can be accessed by 4x4 or must walk.}
{ Copied in October of 1998 by Jo Ann Tickle Scott. }

BURTON, Cora E. Corder- (6-23-1825 - 7-11-1907) {W/O Jas. A.Corder}
"   Ethel- (2-12-1907 - 9-11-1907)
"   George W.- (1875-1927) {Father}
"   Elizabeth C.- (1865-1954) {Mother}

CORDER, John R.- (5-28-1935 - 5-30-1935)
"   Elizabeth M.- (4-9-1936 - 4-10-1936)
{ The above stones are enclosed by a chain link fence. The following
stones were at one time within this enclosure. The posts are still
there but the fence is gone. }

EPPERSON, Telia E.W.- (8-10-1871 - 12-30-1883) { D/O E.E. &
 Danielle F } [Stone is flat on the ground and cattle roam over it]
{ Note by Jo Ann Scott: Mary E. Epperson, b. 1851, md. W.L. Hancock
in 1882 in Bland County. Edward E. Epperson b. 1863, md. Mary A.
Hancock in 1881. }

PAULEY, Thomas G.- (No dates) {Jacksons VA Artillary, CSA }

HIDDEN VALLEY CEMETERY # I
[Cemetery is located north of State Route # 601 on Little Creek. It is well kept and easy accessible by automobile.]
{ Compiled by Jo Ann Tickle Scott in 1998 }

CORDER, Amy Ruth- (5-30-1917 - 9-6-1917)
   "   Edna Bell- (9-3-1904 - 2-8-1911)
   "   Frances Davis- (11-19-1879 - 2-25-1956)
   "   Benjamin Larken- (3-6-1877 - 3-19-1952)

DAVIS, Infant Daughter of Claude S. & Gladys C. Davis- (No dates)
   "   Samuel David- (11-5-1881 - 11-22-1940){ Age 59 yrs. 17 das.}
   "   Della Rose King- (11-20-1885 - 4-10-1957)
                              { Age 71 yrs, 4 mos. & 20 days }
   "   Nancy J.- (7-14-1859 - 6-23-1899) { Mother }
   "   James Whitten- (10-30-1852 - 7-19-1928) { Father }
   "   Ressie Kitts- (12-23-1877 - 3-28-1958) { W/O Meek H. Davis }
   "   Meek Hoge, Sr.- (2-13-1878 - 7-10-1941 }

FRENCH, Frank E.- (5-1-1918 - 12-13-1937)

GRAY, James William- (12-14-1881 - 7-21-1936)
   "   Emily- (6-25-1885 - 1-8-1953)
   "   Yates Kelby- (5-18-1909 - 12-20-1949) { In Memory of Dad }
   "   Hubert M.- (1907-1961)

MATZ- Bertha- (6-4-1899 - 8-6-1961) {Mother}
   "   Louie- (1-5-1886 - 2-4-1931) {Father}

MUNCEY, Harry Thornton- (1-4-1941 - 7-6-1941) { S/O Earl & Beulah }

TERRY, Sandra Ann- (1-8-1957 -   )
   "   William A.- (2-3-1953
   "   Garnett S.- (6-25-1904 - 1-3-1960)

1 stone, no name or dates.
4 indentations, occupants unknown.

HIDDEN VALLEY CEMETERY # 2
[Same location as Cemetery # 1]
{ Compiled by Jo Ann Tickle Scott in 1998 }

BRUNK, Charles Neal- (7-1-1906 - 6-5-1971)
   "   Nellie Davis- (4-4-1904 - 9-21-1976)
   "   Robert K.- (7-21-1887 - 5-4-1971)
   "   Effie D.- (7-14-1892 - 8-15-1954)

CROCKETT, ------ (8-28-1915 - 11-17-1993) { Pvt. US Army, WW II }

CORDER, Archie C.- (11-4-1908 - 2-11-1990)
   "   Samuel R.- (10-16-1906 - 9-9-1979) { US Army, WW II }

HIDDEN VALLEY CEMETERY # 2
[Same location as Cemetery # 1]
{ Compiled by Jo Ann Tickle Scott in 1998 }

DAVIS, Amy Jane- (1-28-1889 - 8-21-1971)
    "   Richard Floyd- (1-14-1886 - 9-25-1971)
    "   Vernie Eliza Brunk- (1-11-1889 - 11-2-1957)
    "   James William- (3-15-1924 - 9-16-1978) { US Army, Korea }
    "   Trinkle W. Sr.- (10-13-1916 - ?-26-1994)
    "   Vivian C.- (3-27-1925 -   ) { Md. 7-6-1946 }
    "   John Thomas- (9-2-1906 - 4-20-1970)
    "   Mable Kitts- (3-1-1910 -   )
    "   Rev. Floyd Clayton- (10-12-1919 - 11-18-1974){Minister }
    "   Gilford Lafayette- (11-25-1905 - 7-5-1966)
    "   Beatrice Kitts- (8-25-1911 - 3-19-1983)
    "   Charles Newton- (12-8-1923 - 6-11-1988) { US Army WW II }
    "   Margaret Powers- (6-10-1927 -   )
    "   Wade H.- (2-5-1911 - 1-10- 1980)
    "   Hazel Faw- (7-21-1914 - 4-2-1993)
    "   Hubert Raymond- (11-26-1919 - 3-19-1982)

FREEMAN, Annie M.- (9-29-1946 - 5-14-1986)
    "   Rodney L. "Stubby"- (3-25-1952 - 10-30-1998)
    "   Hobert F.- (1921-1994) { A loving Father }

HAMBLIN, Martha A.- (11-15-1903 - 12-13-1990)
    "   Goven T.- (8-22-1913 - 8-27-1993)

LAMBERT, Irvin Kelly- (8-4-1908 - 9-27-1971)
    "   Florence Gray- (2-25-1912 - 10-10-1994)
    "   Arthur A.- (9-3-1921 - 5-4-1987)
    "   Lula V.- (2-13-1915 - 11-5-1989)

LAWRENCE, Frank A.- (1896-1911) {Uncle Frank }
    "   Mary D.- (1903-1989) { Aunt Mary }

MILLIRONS, George Louis- (1-7-1902 - 8-4-1995)
    "   Genoa B.- (4-12-1919-   ) { Beloved wife }
    "   Ruby Matthews- (3-7-1914 - 4-5-1996)

TERRY, James Hampton- (9-11-1894 - 6-19-1963) { US Army WW II }
    "   Lula Williams- (11-1-1898 - 11-21-1984)
    "   Raymond A. Sr.- (5-4-1929 -   )
TERRY, Irene R.- (11-29-1933 - 8-11-1997) { Md. 7-1-1949 }

TURNER, The Family of William D. Turner, Sr.

TOWNLEY, Ruth Ann Turner- (11-14-1958 - 10-7-1986)

WALKER, Ruth Collins- (10-8-1913 - 12-4-1995)

KEGLEY FAMILY CEMETERY
{ Located on the farm formerly owned by Dr. G.B. Kegley }
[Copied in October of 1998 by Jo Ann Tickle Scott]

CLINGENPEEL, W.M.- (2-2-1868 - abt 1904)
CLINGENPEEL, Jennie G.- (1874 - abt 1904) {W/O W.M. Clingenpeel}

KEGLEY, Isaac- (4-10-1810 - 3-18-1886)
KEGLEY, Prudence- (4-14-1815 - 1-31-1894) {W/O Isaac, dau. of James
            Devor and Margaret Dunn.}
KEGLEY, Mitchell- (3-30-1835 - 3-12-1894) { S/O Isaac & Prudence }
KEGLEY, Matilda Jane- (8-2-1840 - 2-9-1909) {W/O Mitchell Kegley }
KEGLEY, Judge Fulton- (7-12-1865 - 3-20-1927) {S/O Mitchell Kegley}
KEGLEY, Mary J. Hayes- (9-19-1872 - 2-15-1958) {W/O Fulton Kegley}
KEGLEY, Samuel Fulton- (6-22-1903 - 9-20-1908) {S/O Fulton & Mary J.}
KEGLEY, Judge Pierce Clinton- (11-10-1906 - 4-1-1970) {S/O Fulton and
            Mary J. Kegley. Murdered in his office.}
KEGLEY, Ruth Brown- (6-13-1907 - 1-8-1997) {W/O Judge Pierce and dau.
            of James & Ethel Miller Brown}
KEGLEY, Fulton Brown- (5-13-1931 - 11-6-1980) {S/O Pierce & Ruth}
KEGLEY, Betty Meyers- (7-4-1933 -   ) {W/O Fulton Brown Kegley}
KEGLEY, George Barnard II and Mary Ellis- (2-14-1942) {Stillborn
            twins of Dr. George B. & Virginia Lewter Kegley }
KEGLEY, George Barnard- (1913-1981) {S/O Fulton & Mary Hayes Kegley
            and a most beloved physician of the county.
            Capt. US Army WW II, M.D.}
KEGLEY, Virginia Lewter- (4-14-1912 - 9-7-1987) {W/O Dr. G.B. Kegley}

{Five generations of the Kegley family are buried here. The farm is
 owned by George B. Kegley, Jr. son of Dr. George & Virginia Kegley}

OLD NEAL BURYING GROUND
{ On farm now owned by J.P. Munsey. The old house was long ago torn
 down and only field stones remain in a hay field. Located on north
side of Route 42. It is not known by this compiler just who is buried
here. If you have any information as to who is buried here, please
notify, Jo Ann Tickle Scott and we will enter it into our records. }

HORBARGER CEMETERY
{ Cemetery is located on Route 636 to the north of Route 615 about
one half mile from Bastain Union Church. }
[Copied in October of 1998 by Jo Ann Tickle Scott.]

BRITT, Clifton H.- (1854-1936)
BRITT, Mary E.- (1860-1924)

BRUCE, William Johnston- (11-16-1862 - 5-9-1947)
BRUCE, Amanda Starks- (5-3-1865 - 7-4-1954) {W/O William J. Bruce}
BRUCE, Ruth Catherine- (11-28-???? - 5-16-1910)
BRUCE, Robert James- (11-16-1892 - 11-29-1892)
BRUCE, Gladys Verona- (2-19-1908 - 6-5-1910)
BRUCE, Jessie Demaris- (11-16-1896 - 7-28-1942?)

COBURN, *Henry* ‾   (8-24-1887 - 9-1-1966)
COBURN, Annie- (1896-1921) { W/O H.C.}
COBURN, Thomas C.- (no dates) Co. C 45th VA INF CSA
COBURN, J.W.D.- (1874-1950)

HARMAN, John W.- (5-14-1919 - 3-13-1920)
HARMAN, E. Swanson- (5-14-1905 - 2-2-1918)
HARMAN, G. Kenneth- (3-6-1907 - 1-24-1918)

HORNBARGER, William P.- (no dates) Co C 54 VA Inf CSA
HORNBARGER, Francis E.- (1-16-1866 - 5-23-1909)
HORNBARGER, James H.E.- (1-23-1875 - 10-25-1899) {S/O W.P. & Mary }
HORNBARGER, Beatrice A.- (6-25-1837 - 4-15-1884)
HORNBARGER, Nancy K.- (9-1-1873 - 7-11-1934)

JAMES, Paul- (1881 - 11-2-1912) age 31 yrs. Born in England.

STARKS, Martha A.- (4-14-1883 - 6-16-1883)
STARKS, J.M.- (no dates) Co C Echols Brig. CSA

THOMAS, Helen Marie- (12-21-1912 - 2-22-????) D/O C.E & Virginia.
THOMAS, Junious C.- (1-20-1910 - 2-11-1910) S/O C.E. & Virginia.

22 field stones at various places in Cemetery.

OLD MILLER CEMETERY

[On land now owned by Mrs. Trubie Chewning. Formerly owned by Alexander and Jane Hamilton Miller and passed down to his son Ronie John Miller. The farm was sold at auction the early 1950's and was purchased by W.A. Chewning. The land lays under the north side of Big Walker's Mountain. The graveyard is past restoration. Cattle have roamed over it until it is hard to even tell where the graves are. My young nephew, Philip Bogle went up the steep hill and copied the names and dates from the remaining stones in 1987. Parke C. Bogle]

HAMILTON, Margaret- (1811 - 1896) wife of Timothy Hamilton and daughter of Enos Moore and his wife Mary "Polly" Bogle Moore. Polly Bogle, daughter of the pioneer James Bogle.

HAMILTON, Timothy- (1816 - 1882) No one seems to know who his parents were. Family records say he was born in Botetourt County.

MILLER, Nancy Jane- (1842 - 1930) Daughter of Timothy & Margaret Hamilton and wife of Alexander F. Miller.

MILLER, Alec- (1841 - 1928) Son of Charles and Ann McNiel Miller. Husband of Nancy Jane Hamilton Miller.

MILLER, John Albert- (1907 - 1908) Son of Ronie & Mary Miller.

MILLER, Rosie Jane- (1894 - 1895) Daughter of Ronie & Mary Miller.

MILLER, Ronie John- (1871 - 1959) Son of Alexander and Jane Miller. {Ronie was the last person buried in this old graveyard}

MILLER, Mary Estelle- (1867 - 1935) Wife of Ronie J. Miller. She was a "Williams" before marriage. No stone could be found for her grave. When I was a young girl I remember going to her grave and putting bunches of butterfly bush blooms on it. She made this request of me when she was leaving our yard and the bush was in full bloom. It was the last time I ever saw her alive. I am no longer able to walk up the steep hill but each time I drive up the road toward Mechanicsburg, I glance up the hill toward the Old Miller graveyard, where a huge tree has grown up in the middle of it. For a few fleeting moments I relive the pleasant days spent with "Cousin" Mary Miller. Her home was a haven to young people. One never left her house without first eating or drinking of some sort of refreshments. Her table was always set with fine china and crystal. Her graciousness knew no bounds. I remember how lovingly "Cousin" Mary would talk about her two dead babies. Two heavily framed pictures of them hung above her mantle. (No stone here now for Ronie John or Mary E. Miller)

MILLER, Hugh Fleming- (1890 - 1941) Only child to live to adulthood of Mary & Ronie J. Miller. He fell from a cherry tree and died from complications. He was diabetic. After the death of his first wife he married Virginia Munsey from Giles County. She survived him and is buried at Pearisburg, VA. (No stone)

MILLER, Margaret Newberry- (9-5-1886 - 2-22-1927) 1st wife of Hugh Miller and daughter of Henry Newberry and his 2nd wife, Laura Porter Newberry. [Hugh & Margaret had two sons, Paul and Earl. They are both dead and buried at Mechanicsburg.] (No stone for Margaret now}

WILLIAMS, Sallie G.- (1836 - 1906) Mother of Mary Estelle Miller.

WILLIAMS, Robert W.- (1877 - 1906) Brother of Mary E. Miller

NUNN CEMETERY

{ Cemetery located Southwest of where Kimberling Road (612) enters
State Route 606, upon a hill. The fence can be seen from the road
and one can take a 4x4 truck and drive to it. Thanks to Donald
Helvey for his help.}

[Copied by Jo Ann Tickle Scott in 1998]

HOLLINS, Effie M.- (10-22-1892 - 11-27-1960)

MILLER, Jasper W.- (4-20-1850 - 5-4-1928)
MILLER, Rhoda- (5-15-1857 - 6-15-1949) {Nee Helvey}

NUNN, Herbert Wayne- (5-30-1910 - 8-1998)
NUNN, Maudie Ella Elkins- (4-4-1908 - 8-27-1991)
NUNN, Jimmy- (born & died 2-7-1936) {S/O Herbert & Maudie}
NUNN, Argle P.- (8-17-1942 - 3-3-1979)
NUNN, Henry P.- (5-31-1910 - no death date)
NUNN, Mae Norris- (3-13-1915 - 9-26-1977)
NUNN, Louella- (4-15-1875 - 6-20-1910){ W/O W.T.Nunn, D/O Jasper W.
               Miller and Rhoda Helvey Miller}
NUNN, Roxie- (died 4-19-1923) { D/O W.T. & Luella Miller Nunn} On a
          field stone and her last name was not visible. According
          to the Bland County 1910 Census she was born about 1893}
NUNN, Thomas- on a field stone, dates illegible. {Believe this to be
               W.T. Nunn, H/O Luella Miller Nunn. Census gives his
               birth date as about 1868. He was 42 in 1910 }
NUNN, Ethel- (1905 - 4-14-1923) {D/O W.T & Louella Miller Nunn}
NUNN, Herschel- (died 7-2-1923) {S/O W.T. & Louella Miller Nunn, born
               about 1898, was 12 in 1910}
NUNN, Gilbert- (1906-   )
NUNN, Francis M.- (1905 - 1989)
NUNN, Dwayne Lewis- (1965 - 1982)

One field stone with no inscription.

HARMAN BURYING GROUND AT HOLLYBROOK

[The old Harman house stood where a trailer now sits on property now
owned by Clovis Cox. The grave site is owned by Gary & Wanda Carroll.
Wanda told me that the log house had been torn down, the pieces
numbered and moved to Tazewell County. Also stolen was a marker with
a plaque stating that "Old Skyduska" was buried here. Nothing now
remains except a flat stone with Henry Harman's name on it. According
to Mr. Carroll, there are over 100 graves here.]

Compiled by Jo Ann Tickle Scott.

HARMAN, Henry, Sr. (Old Skyduska) (1726-1822)
         { Pvt. Capt Osborn's Regiment Revolutionary War }

RAMSEY, Anvah K.- (3-18-1916 - 3-13-1918)
RAMSEY, Charles B.- (8-22-1848 - 11-19-1901)
RAMSEY, Willie Angeline Harman- (7-16-1854 - 6-17-1932) {W/O Charles}
RAMSEY, Winnie- (7-1-1874 - 2-1-1893)

MOREHEAD CEMETERY
[On farm formerly owned by Kyle and Emmarilla Miller Morehead]
{ Route 612, Bland County Virginia }

CROY, Wm. M.- (9-14-1896 - 3-26-1967) Md. 10-31-1920.
CROY, Lillie M.- (9-1-1892 - 12-13-1976) Wife of Wm., dau of L. K.
    and Emarilla Miller Morehead.

MILLER, James M.- (1866 - 1884)
MILLER, Rachael Herron- (9-10-1827 - 5-25-1865) 1st wife of A.W.
MILLER, A.W. (Abraham Woodson)- 4-20-1824 - 4-15-1897)
MILLER, Elsie- 3-17-1828 - 1-10-1911) 2nd wife of A.W. Miller. { She
    was first married to James Waggoner. She was a daughter of
    Jacob and Mary Fanning Munsey. }
MILLER, Johnny W.- (1-31-1880 - 10-30-1880)
MILLER, Charles W.- (11-18-1853 - 9-23-1930)
MILLER, Mary Lou (Ramsey)- (3-17-1858-7-22-1947) Wife o Charles.
MILLER, Lou Emma- (9-19-1881 - 9-29-1896)

MOREHEAD, Henry Vance- (8-31-1911-9-26-1986) Son of Kyle & Emmarilla.
MOREHEAD, Wanda L. Morehaed- (6-16-1925 -   ) Wife of Henry.
MOREHEAD, Lee K. (Kyle)- (10-23-1867 - 5-2-1900)
MOREHEAD, Emmarilla C.- (3-18-1873 - 8-12-1958) Wife of Kyle and
    daughter of Abraham Woodson and Elsie Munsey Wagner Miller.
MOREHEAD, Nelson- (8-8-1900 - 3-6-1901) Son of Lee K. & Emmarilla.
MOREHEAD, Oren Price- (1909-1972) Youngest son of Lee K. & Emmarilla.
MOREHEAD, Edna C.- (1916-1954) Oren's 2nd wife.

PRUETT, John Milton, Jr- (2-12-1921 - 9-18-1963) Son of Effie and
    John Milton Pruett, Sr.
PRUETT, John Milton- (3-12-1893 - 11-17-1986)
PRUETT, Effie E.- (1896 - 1953) Wife of John Milton and daughter of
    Lee K. and Emmarilla Miller Morehead.
PRUETT, Edwin Kyle- (died 1-19-1971, age 40 yrs., 10 mos., 17 days.
    Son of Effie and John Milton Pruett.

WAGNER, David Waugh- (2-15-1859 - 8-19-1942) Son of James Waggoner
and Elsie Munsey Waggoner and a brother of Dr. J.A. Wagner. A half
brother of Emmarilla Miller, wife of Lee K. Morehead. There is no
marked stone at his grave. Perhaps his grave is marked with one of
the several plain cinderblocks, which bear no inscriptions.

Five cinder blocks with no markings.

(Information on the cemetery was sent to me by Mary Margaret Beach.)
  Parke C. Bogle

MOREHEAD FAMILY CEMETERY # 2

[Cemetery is located on the old Morehead farm on Route 607 to the right of Route 608 from Crandon. Cemetery is in excellent condition and one can easily walk to it from the road.]
{ Copied by Jo Ann Tickle Scott in October of 1998 }

MERRIX, Adeline M.- (1929-1979) {D/o Peter & Zelda Morehead }
    { In loving memory of Mother, Mary, Sandi and Mike.}

MOREHEAD, Charles- (5-11-1894 - 8-17-1895)
   "   J.A.- (11-1-1886 - 5-6-1907)
   "   G.A. {Gordon A.}- (4-17-1849 - 11-30-1922)
   "   Tacy A. {Adeline}- (10-10-1868 - 1-26-1920) {2nd W/O G.A }
   "   Alma- (5-15-1926 -   ) {D/O Luther & Margaret }
   "   Margaret L.- (1893-1969) {Mother} { W/O Luther Morehead }
   "   Luther- (6-8-1896 - 11-22-1944){Father} [PVT US Army]
            { S/O Gordon & Tacy Pruett Morehead.}
   "   Peter H.{Harrison}- (1-20-1900 - 1-24-1973){ Father} { S/O
                Gordon & Tacy Pruett Morehead }
   "   Mary Z.(Zelda)- (5-24-1905 - 3-4-1994) {Mother}
       { D/O Miller & Poca Pauley Patton, md. to Peter H. Morehead
       on 10-27-1923.}

HELVEY FAMILY CEMETERY # 2
{ Copied in October of 1998 by Jo Ann Tickle Scott.}

[Located on north side of Kimberling Road (Rt. 612) on the old Henry Helvey farm, now owned by Warren Faulkner. It is on a high hill about 1 1/2 miles from the main road. Can be reached in a 4x4 vehicle. Cattle are grazing the cemetery. Thanks to Donald Helvey in helping find this cemetery.}

HELVEY, Henry Franklin- (1884-1962)
HELVEY, Woodie Morehead- (1882-1949
HELVEY, John K.(Kennerly) (1816-1898) { S/O Baltzer & Rhoda Helvey.
                He was 1st married to Nancy Hutzell in 1842
                and 2nd to Sally Dorn Munsey in 1850. Some
                family historians say the other 2 wives are
                also buried here.}
HELVEY, Louvenia- (- d. 1901) { 1900 Bland Census gives her birth
                date as February 1852. Nee Pruett. She was the 3rd
                w/o John K. Helvey. She was a d/o Henry M. &
                Isabel Pruett. She md. John K. Helvey, 1-25-1882 }

STOWERS CEMETERY
[Above Bland, down a lane off Route 42]
{ Copied in 1991 by Parke C. Bogle and Alma Newberry Waddell }
[Cemetery checked again in 1998 by Jo Ann Tickle Scott]

BILLINGS, Weire- (a young child- no dates.)

BURGE, Paul- (1910 -   ) { Married 4-7-1939 }
BURGE, Elsie B.- (1922 - 1987) { Married 4-7-1939 }

CREGER, John- (2-11-1789 - 12-13-1868)
CREGER, Mary Ann- (11-2-1798 - 4-19-1893) Wife of John.
CREGER, Rosanah- (5-22-1823 - 2-5-1834) Dau. of John & Mary.
CREGER, Susie- (no stone) Dau. of John & Mary.

DEVOR, Sarah E.- (3-24-1850-9-23-1902) D/o Jas.& Dicy Creger Stowers.
DEVOR, John- (7-7-1839 - 1-25-1917) S/o Wm. & Julia Ingram Devor.

----------, triplet children, names not known.
----------, 5 graves with no stones.

DILLOW, James, (no dates)
DILLOW, Willie Gray- (no dates) FHM -faded away.
DILLOW, Jessee G., (12-8-1892 - 1-13-1918)
DILLOW, Laura- (home-made stone- no dates.)
DILLOW, Elmer- (no stone)
DILLOW, Luther G.- (5-11-1900 - 10-21-1970)

EAGLE, Samuel M.- (no dates, CSA marker.)
EAGLE, Martha J.- (1837 - 1923) Nee Neese

HEDRICK, Mary- (5-20-1880 - 2-12-1936)

JENNELL, B.R. "Rusty"- 8-27-1907 - 8-1-1954)

KIDD, John M.- (1-22-1864 - 1-3-1927)
KIDD, Elizabeth Stowers- (9-20-1867 - 2-24-1928) Wife of John Kidd.
KIDD, Infant dau. of C.C. & B.B. Kidd. (Born & died 10-20-1942)
KIDD, Infant dau of C.C. & B.B. Kidd. (born & died 6-28-1933)

KIRBY, G. Alice Stowers, (12-21-1864 - 9-1-1926) {W/O Monroe Stowers}
KIRBY, M. (Monroe) S.- 11-5-1855 - 6-1-1926)

LAMBERT, Jackie Carson- (1960 - 1960)
LAMBERT, James Edward- (12-2-1870 - 8-23-1954)
LAMBERT, Cynthia Stowers- (7-22-1872 - 4-4-1956) W/o James Edward.
LAMBERT , Peery E.- (11-18-1909 - 1-19-1960)
LAMBERT, Elmira Leon- (8-6-1897 - 1-6-1898)
LAMBERT, Rutha Ola- (1-27-1896 - 7-31-1896)

NEWBERRY, Henry T. (Tartar)- (1-29-1893 - 2-17-1939) S/o Wythe N-
NEWBERRY, Wanda G.- (3-2-1895 - 8-20-1930) { Nee Kirby }

STOWERS CEMETERY
[Above Bland, down a lane off Route 42]

SCOTT, Lillie Mae- (4-8-1880 - 11-17-1965)
SCOTT, Mary A.- (9-25-1854 - 10-27-1919)
SCOTT, Eldred M.- (9-23-1854 - 4-4-1894)
SCOTT, Louisa E.- (7-16-1883 - 12-31-1887)
SCOTT, John Bill, (1910 - 1943)
SCOTT, Carrie Randolph- (1-10-1919 - 6-25-1919)
SCOTT, Henry James- (10-3-1903 - 6-10-1922)
SCOTT, Bertha Elizabeth- (5-21-1883 - 1-29-1928) {Mom}
SCOTT, Luther Brown- (10-20-1877 - 4-5-1959) {Dad}

SEXTON, Bessie Mae Lambert- (7-13-1918 - 2-1-1918)

STOWERS, John- (12-1922 - death date illegible) {Jo says 1912-1922)
STOWERS, Name and dates illegible.
STOWERS, Emily, (2-11-1857 - 8-13-1868)
STOWERS, James M.- (3-29-1829 - 6-11-1900)
STOWERS, Dicy- (9-1-1820 - 4-29-1885){ Jo says, d. 1887}
STOWERS, William- (11-27-1812 - 1-25-1902)
STOWERS, Christina- (7-29-1816 - 8-13-1861) 1st wife of William.
STOWERS, Ellen- (3-23-1832 - 1-26-1870) 2nd wife of William.
STOWERS, Anna- (9-28-1822 - 11-16-1891) 3rd wife of William.
STOWERS, Mary B.- (4-22-1898 - 7-29-1989) { Nee Barger}
STOWERS, Clarence E.- (8-11-1896 - 2-19-1960)
STOWERS, Frank S.- (12-23-1869 - 11-20-1946)
STOWERS, Fannie B. Wilson- (11-9-1869 - 1-27-1929) Wife of Frank S.
STOWERS, Grover W.- (1907 - 1962)
STOWERS, Nellie A.- (1905 - 1994)
STOWERS, Shirley C.(Turner) - (8-3-1937 - 4-22-1990) { W/o Vernon }
STOWERS, Elizabeth Creger- (5-23-1835 - 11-10-1923) W/o J.M. Stowers
STOWERS, Nannie J.- (12-2-1867 - 11-4-1914)
STOWERS, John P.- (3-5-1866 - 2-1-1924)
STOWERS, Wylie Mason- (12-18-1897 - 10-11-1954)
STOWERS, Paul Cecil- (12-1-1902 - 6-28-1971) {USAF- WW II}

TICKLE, John N. (Nye)- (10-6-1919 - 12-10-1992) {US Army WW II PH)
TICKLE, Helen C.- (2-6-1923 -   ) {Nee Carroll}

WADDELL, Michael Jackson- (3-22-1948 - 1-21-1950){S/O Leonard & L.C}
WADDELL, Louise C.- (1-28-1865 - 1-21-1950)
WADDELL, Leonard- (3-27-1862 - 8-31-1940)
WADDELL, Earl E.- (5-11-1910 - 10-5-1992)
WADDELL, Virginia H.- (5-10-1926 -   )
WADDELL, Wythe G.- (10-10-1860 - 12-15-1920)
WADDELL, Rebecca A.- (11-29-1859 - 10-9-1925)
WADDELL, R. Everette- (1-15-1902 - 5-1-1981)
WADDELL, Alma N.- (2-10-1908 -   ) {W/O Everette, nee Newberry}
WADDELL, Lenore- (8-14-1928 - 12-24-1958)
WADDELL, Michael- (9-8-1821 - 4-15-1905)
WADDELL, Margaret- (5-9-1822 - 2-11-1909)
WADDELL, Ada Gray- (2-16-1886 - 3-12-1890)

STOWERS CEMETERY
[Above Bland, down a lane off Route 42]

WADDELL, Louisa C.- (7-22-1860 - 2-8-1943)
WADDELL, Robinett J.- (12-5-1850 - 6-6-1930)

WIMMER, Richard Lee- (4-12-1944 - 9-15-1960) Son of Clyde & Ruth.
WIMMER, Clyde Arnold- (8-20-1922 - 11-30-1975)

{ Many graves are without markers and many are illegible bcause of
time and the elements. Mrs. Alma Newberry Waddell went with me to
this cemetery and filled in the information for the graves where the
stones were illegible and for those which had no stones. Copied,
April 14, 1991 by Parke C. Bogle and Mrs. Alma Waddell.

[Cemetery was copied again in October of 1998 by Jo Ann Tickle Scott]
The cemetery is easily accessable by car.

CEMETERY AT ESCA MITCHELL FARM
{ Located on the former Esca Mitchell farm which is now owned by Mrs.
Lula Mitchell Blankenship and her nephew, Joe Carr. }
[Copied in 1998 by Jo Ann Tickle Scott]

BROWN, Cynthia P.- (4-2-1805 - 6-23-1817)

CORNER, James M.- (No dates) {Co. C. 36th VA Inf. CSA}

MCTEER, Drayton- (no dates)

WILSON, Samuel W.- (10-1844 - 7-1918) {Co. C. 10th KY Reg. CSA}

{ There are six or more field stones with no markings }

{ The original brick house on this farm was built by Col. John
Compton in 1852. The brick was burned on the upper end of the meadow
near Kimberling Creek. William Hoge and Timothy Mitchell bought the
farm in 1890. C. Alfred Mitchell bought Hoge's part in 1910. The home
was called "Gap View" at the time it was owned by George and Barbara
Lopp Harman. Their daughter Betsy Harman who married Ephraim Dunbar,
lived there until Dunbar's death. Betsy then married Lewis Neel.
   During the Civil War the owners hid their guns and other valuables
in the huge fireplaces. The house which has been remodeled is now
owned by Mrs. Lula Mitchell Blankenship and her nephew Joe Carr.}
 (From Bland History, pages 122-123) Parke Bogle }

OLD MUSTARD CEMETERY ON WALKERS CREEK
[On land now owned by Carl Newberry]

BYRNES, Dr. J.W.- (7-6-1825 - 4-9-1861). { Some family members say
        that Dr. Byrnes is buried in Wise County and that this stone
        is only a memorial to him. }
BYRNES, Sarah, wife of Dr. Byrnes- (1-6-1826 - 2-4-1905)
BYRNES, Joseph N.- (born 7-6-1855 in Wise Co., died 4-9-1894, age 38
        yrs., 9 mos & 3 days. Son of J.W. & Sallie Byrnes.

MUSTARD, William- (10-27-1793 - 4-15-1878) age 84 yrs, 5 mos. & 18
        days. { Our Father }
MUSTARD, Annah- (10-16-1801 - 12-20-1865) Consort of William
        Mustard. Married, 1-29, 1822. Dau of Wm. & Agnes Patton P-
MUSTARD, Edward Brown- (born in 1868 died in 1925. There is no stone
        for him here and probably never was.
MUSTARD, J. (James) Thomas- (1-15-1832 - 3-16-1896)
MUSTARD, J. (John) Jasper- (9-29-1842 - 5-21-1920) " He was a
        friend to the poor and needy."
MUSTARD, Fanny M, (2-26-1844 - 21-1920) { Wife of John Jasper, Dau.
         of William and Margaret Myers Stuart.}
MUSTARD, Estel Campbell- (6-30-1844 - 6-20-1864) Wounded at New
        Market by a bursting shell, died at Staunton. The only
        casualty of the seven sons of William & Annah P. Mustard,
        who fought in the Civil War.
MUSTARD, H. (Harvey) R.- (11-25-1827 - 3-10-1905)
MUSTARD, Mariah- (8-2-1835 - 6-2-1918) Wife of Harvey R. Mustard.
         (Daughter of Samuel and Elizabeth Nicewander Wohlford]
MUSTARD, Barbara India- (3-20-1881 - 11-6-1886) Daughter of Samuel
        Patterson Mustard and Matilda Peery Moore.
MUSTARD, Vicki C.- (8-27-1861 - 1-27-1880) Dau. of Harvey R. and
         Mariah Wohlford Mustard.
MUSTARD, Myrtle Blanche- (1-30-1871 - 2-1888) Dau of John Jasper
MUSTARD, Anna M.- (1879 - 1890) Archives, State Library. Dau of
        John Jasper.
MUSTARD, Mary C.- (1872 - 9-15-1891) Archives, State Library.
        Daughter of John Jasper. { The stones for the preceeding two
        graves are no longer there. The dates of death were taken
        from the Vital Statistics of Bland County from the Archives
        of the Virginia State Library. }

UPDIKE, Mary Gladys- (10-16-1899 - 6-26-1907){D/O A.F & Berrtha
                        Mustard Updike.}
    There are several sunken spots, denoting a burial spot, but no
stones to tell who is buried there. Some of the stones are made of
alabaster marble and have withstood the ravages of time, animals and
the elements. It was sad indeed to see this old resting place in such
a pitiful condition. It is beyond restoration. These were the
legible stones in 1982. There have been no other burials here since
then.   Parke C. Bogle
                            1117 High Street
                            Pulaski, VA 24301
                        Email-<parkebog@swva.net>

OLD BETHEL CEMETERY
[Cemetery is located north of Route 42, about 5 miles from where
Route 52 and Route 42 divide. It is east of Leon Lambert's home, up
on a hill. It can be reached by automobile.]
(Copied in October of 1998 by Jo Ann Tickle Scott)

CRIDER, Kelly Lee- (8-3-1987 - 2-17-1988)

FORTNER, Ellen and her baby. (Between Harlow & Rhoda Lambert)

HOUNSHELL, Lena L.- (8-22-1927 - 5-8-1997) {Mother}

INGRAM, Sallie D.- (1874 - 1962)
INGRAM, Harmon- (1855 - 1938){ He has 2 stones, 1 home made one
INGRAM, gives dates -(1885, age 83, 1938 }
INGRAM, Allie H.- (5-8-1914 -   )
INGRAM, Leroy- (1-30-1902 - 12-28-1970)
INGRAM, Randolph Johnson- (1870 - 1935)
INGRAM, Samuel V.- (4-30-1859 - 5-24-1943)

LAMBERT, Charles Henry- (7-23-1898 - 7-24-1967)
LAMBERT, A. Dewey- (7-20-1899 - 6-7-1976)
LAMBERT, L. Pearl- (4-23-1902 - 7-13-1967)
LAMBERT, Corale- (11-8-1878 -   )
LAMBERT, Glen- (11-29-1880 - 12-1-1966)
LAMBERT, James Clair- (4-4-1917 -   )
LAMBERT, Dorothy Lee- (10-27-1920 - 6-29-1900)
LAMBERT, Arlin G.- (10-4-1910 - 7-1-1983)
LAMBERT, Ethel A.- (9-22-1924 -   )
LAMBERT, Lawrence- (9-13-1908 - 10-5-1969)
LAMBERT, Alice H.- (1884 - 1969)
LAMBERT, Thomas W.- (1873 - 1957)
LAMBERT, Julian P.- (2-19-1942 - 4-7-1967)
LAMBERT, Edith Chloas- (9-9-1947 -   )
LAMBERT, Sheila June- (8-20-1963 - 12-23-1963)
LAMBERT, Harlow- (Cement hand written, no dates)
LAMBERT, Rhoda- ("   "   "   "   ")
LAMBERT, Wesley- (No dates) { Co. G. 36 VA Inf. CSA }
LAMBERT, Harrison Morton- (11-9-1888 - 11-11-1941)
LAMBERT, Myra A.- (9-15-1888 - 12-23-1972)
LAMBERT, Everett H.- (1913 - 1966)

LAMPERT, Gideon- (No dates) { Co. G. 36 VA Inf. CSA }
LAMPERT, 6 field stones & 2 wooden posts on Lampert plot.

MELVIN, Michael A.- (9-10-1992? - 12-2-1992)
MELVIN, Michael Vance- (6-20-1966 - 3-19-1995)

PAULEY, Vivian S.- 6-7-1920 - 8-25-1965)
PAULEY, Hubert W.- (4-15-1920 - 11-13-1993)
PAULEY, Roach- (4-10-1916 - 9-17-1964)
PAULEY, Marie- (6-23-1919 - 5-11-1977)

OLD BETHEL CEMETERY
[Cemetery is located north of Route 42, about 5 miles from where
Route 52 and Route 42 divide. It is east of Leon Lambert'shome, up on
a hill. It can be reached by automobile.]
(Copied in October of 1998 by Jo Ann Tickle Scott)

PERKEY, Tommy S.- (5-22-1953 - 2-9-1992)
PERKEY, Trubie Bane- (1900 - 1979)
PERKEY, Carrie Cregar- (1908 - 1989)

SHEWEY, Hallie Lambert- (1-13-1914 - 12-4-1992)
SHEWEY, Frank O.- (3-28-1909 - 4-13-1965)
SHEWEY, Henry L.- (1-19-1931 - 12-7-1997)
SHEWEY, Rosa Burton- (5-4-1934 -   )

STOWERS, Cannie M.- (1890 - 1937)
STOWERS, Thomas M.- (1885 - 1963)
STOWERS, Elbert Smith- (5-3-1847 - 8-21-1922)
STOWERS, Loudeema Thompson- (10-28-1847 - 5-31-1929){W/O Elbert S.}
STOWERS, Infant son of Carl & Wayne Stowers, (b.& d. 2-2-1958)

THOMPSON, James David- (11-10-1926 - 1-27-1998) FHM
THOMPSON, Brady M.- (4-5-1902 - 12-5-1979)
THOMPSON, Edith L.- (2-20-1908 - 12-26-1983)
THOMPSON, 2 stones, 1 cement on Thompson plot, no names or dates
THOMPSON, Estel- (1930 - 1936)
THOMPSON, Kent- (1935 - 1939)
THOMPSON, Ella- (1942 - 1959)
THOMPSON, Dean- (1954 - 1963)
THOMPSON, Lois- (1940 - 1964)
THOMPSON, Charlie M.- (5-10-1882 - 12-15-1935)
THOMPSON, Mary R.- (5-26-1894 - 12-11-1977)
THOMPSON, Hazel Kate- (10-21-1924 - 9-25-1946) D/O C.M. & M.T. T--.
THOMPSON, James F.- (1869 - 1900)
THOMPSON, Ibbie F.- (1869 - 1940)
THOMPSON, Therry- (1892 - 1964)
THOMPSON, Vance- (1930 - 1931)
THOMPSON, Elmer- (1927 - 1964)
THOMPSON, V. Frances- (10-31-1924 - 3-29-1994)
THOMPSON, Josie A.- (1-8-1879 - 4-29-1945)
THOMPSON, John H.- (1-1-1875 - 10-19-1941)
THOMPSON, Margaret K.- (3-11-1841 - 1-13-1915)
THOMPSON, James W.- (No dates) { Co. G. 36, VA inf. CSA }

TIBBS, Ronald Perry- (b&d 9-13-1949) S/O Mr. & Mrs. W.D. Tibbs.

UMBARGER, A. Dewey- (1936 - 1979)
UMBARGER, N. Jean- (1931 -   )

SECOND PART OF OLD BETHEL CEMETERY
[Located in Southeast corner of Old Bethel, next to Route 42.]
{ Copied in October of 1998 by Jo Ann Tickle Scott }

HAVENS, Margaret Ann- (1836 - 1921)

KITTS, Glen- (1885 - 1935)

LAMPERT, John T. (No dates) { Co. G. 36 VA Inf. CSA }

LINDAMOOD, Ollie Perkey- (1880 - 1906)
LINDAMOOD, Joseph Stephen- (11-15-1974 - 2-3-1991)
LINDAMOOD, Billie H.- (8-6-1901 - 3-180-1910)
LINDAMOOD, Martha Jane- (2-19-1832 - 12-25-1874
LINDAMOOD, John Henry- (3-31-1831 - 8-23-1906)
LINDAMOOD, Charles Harlo- (9-15-1866 - 7-23-1940)
LINDAMOOD, Lillie T. Purkey- (5-12-1875 - 8-23-1906) {W/O C.H. L--.

PERKEY,   Martha Sophira- (1880 - 1906)

PURKEY,   William A.- (11-7-1841 - 8-17-1879)
PURKEY,   Virginia May- (9-3-1877 - 1-14-1880)

THOMPSON, Sophia Cline- (1835 - 1925)

TUELL, Harry A.- (10-10-1927 - 12-27-1982)
TUELL, Donna Jo- (5-16-1935 - 3-18-1981) { D/O Beaulah Newberry and
       Chloe Lindamood and wife of Harry Tuell.}

STEEL, Henry W.- (No dates) { Co. G. 36 VA Inf. CSA }

{ In a little offset at east end of cemetery are these stones }
STOWERS, Mary U. (1829 - 1893) { D/O Joseph & Elizabeth Lambert
       Thompson and W/o James M. Stowers,Jr., who is buried at
       Bethany. Her parents are also buried here. Other names near
       this plot but with no dates are:
       KATY OTEY
       G.H.S.
       No Name stone.
       J.L.
       E.T.L.
       Polly Ann NEAL.

OLD MUSTARD CEMETERY ON STATE ROUTE # 42, NEAR MECHANICSBURG, VA.
[Cemetery is on land owned by the Randall Price family]
{ Compiled by Parke C. Bogle and Jo Ann Tickle Scott}

EASLEY, Emily- (1826-1855) {1st W/O Dr. John W. Easley, nee Thompson,
        born, Pittsylvania County, mother of Judge George W. Easley}
BRUCE, Susan- (died 1-31-1853, consort of Harvey C. Bruce.{born
                        3-17-1820, d/o Daniel Hoge & Ann Stafford}
DAVIS, Isaac- departed this life Jan. 24, 1842 ?
FANNING, Mary- (11-15-1834 - 12-30-1871) W/o George Fanning and a
        twin to ALLEN MUSTARD. She died in childbirth, as did her
        child. George Fanning later married Matilda Davidson.
HOGE, Ann- (died 1-12-1853, age 72) {W/O Daniel Hoge}
HOGE, Ann- (age 15 years, died May 25, 1832) D/o Daniel & Ann
        Stafford Hoge. She was born Feb. 2, 1817.{Born 2-2-1817}
HOGE, Julia- (died June 16, 1836, consort of James Hoge.) { She was
        a "KERR" before marriage. James was s/o Daniel & Ann Stafford
        Hoge. Ann was born in Ireland. James Hoge was s/o Gen. James
        Hoge & his wife Eleanor Howe Hoge. Julia was 1st w/o James.
MITCHELL, Shirley K.- (12-11-1865 - 8-31-1867) {D/O T.E & Ardelia}
MITCHELL, child of T.E & Ardelia Mitchell. (Name and dates missing.)
MITCHELL, Burmontie-(June 4, 1870 - June 8, 1872){S/O T.E. &Ardelia}
MITCHELL, Birda- (Sept. 29, 1874 - Oct. 10, 1875){D/O T.E. & Ardelia}
MUSTARD, James- (May 18, 1770 - Feb. 1, 1847) Age 76 yrs 8 mos & 12
        days. "This tribute of respect is erected to his memory by
        Sarah Mustard consort of J.M."
MUSTARD, Sarah (Nee Munsey) No doubt she is buried here. She died
        after 1850, when she appeared on the 1850 Giles County
        Census as being 80 years old. Dinah Harman, a black woman,
        age 60 lived in the household. They lived in the house next
        door to Sarah's son William Mustard. Sarah married James
        Mustard in Montgomery County, VA, in 1791.
MUSTARD, John- (Oct. 27, 1795 - May 23, 1875) Second son of James &
        Sarah Munsey Mustard. H/o Lovisa Patterson.
MUSTARD, Luvicie- (Mar. 7, 1803 - Mar. 1, 1867) d/o William &
        Agnes Patton Patterson. Agnes was a daughter of the noted
        Capt. Henry Patton of Revolutionary fame. W/o John Mustard.
                " Our mother is still beneath this sod
                The dearest friend we ever had
                Oh, her sweet voice so full of love
                Is gone to sing in realms above."
MUSTARD, Allen- (Nov. 15, 1834 - June 5, 1892) [a twin to Mary
        Fanning] Married Sarah Matilda Shumate. They had no issue.
MUSTARD, John T. [Thomas]- (Sept. 1844 - Dec. 6-1871) S/o John and
        Lovisa Patterson Mustard. He was unmarried.
RIDER, Semphronia- (July 22, 1820 - Dec. 11, 1857) Age 37 yrs, 5 mos
        & 21 days. Nee WILMORE. Married Hiram Rider, April 2, 1839.
WOHLFORD, Samuel- (April 1, 1804 - Mar. 23, 1855) H/o Elizabeth
        Nicewander. Father of Mariah Wohlford Mustard.
WOHLFORD, Elizabeth Nicewander- (Nov. 2, 1809 - Dec. 8, 1874)
        [No stone. Dates taken from the family Bible.
{ There are spaces for many more graves here. Time and neglect has
almost destroyed the resting places of these old ancestors of mine]

NEWBERRY CEMETERY ON A.T. NEWBERRY FARM
[Copied in 1989 by Parke Bogle and checked again by Jo Ann Tickle
Scott in 1998. Cemetery located on land owned by the A.T. Newberry
family. There are steps leading from the road up into the cemetery.]

KING, Van Crockett- (7-20-1902 - 4-19-1921) {S/o Painter & Fannie}
KING, David Painter- (10-14-1864 - 2-28-1929)
KING, Frank Crockett- (4-16-1895 - 6-6-1930)

MUSTARD, Bascom Newton- (11-27-1876 - 6-12-1943) {S/O Wesley Newton
                    and Elizabeth Caroline Newberry Mustard}
MUSTARD, Mattie Crabtree- (4-23-1882 - 4-24-1918) W/o Bascom N.
MUSTARD, C. Bascom- (5-3-1913 - 6-9-1955) S/o Bascom & Mattie. WW II
MUSTARD, Infant (no dates) {daughter of W.N. & E.C. Mustard.}
MUSTARD, Callie May- (4-30-1874 - 7-20-1875) D/o W.N & E.C.
MUSTARD, William Newberry- (3-8-1860 - 5-4-1888) S/o W.N. & E.C.
MUSTARD, Daisey Pearl- (11-22-1879 - 1934) D/o W.N. & E.C. Mustard
MUSTARD, Elizabeth Caroline Newberry- (2-29-1838 - 12-30-1898) " To
    the memory of our mother, w/o W.N. Mustard." { D/o Allen
    Taylor Newberry and his first wife, Elizabeth Bogle.}
MUSTARD, W.N. (Wesley Newton)- (1836 - 1910) Son of William and Ann
                    Patterson Mustard. { A Civil War Veteran }
MUSTARD, John G. (Gratton)- (1857 - 1931){ S/o W.N. & E.C.} { He was
                    a deaf mute who was very self sufficient}.
NEWBERRY, Rev. Samuel- (12-25-1773 - 2-12-1857){ S/o Immigrant
    Samuel Newberry and his 2nd wife Bethia Brannon (Begley).}
NEWBERRY, Eunice Powers- (1771 - 2-13-1882) W/o Rev. Samuel.
NEWBERRY, Nancy E. Gross- (1857 - 1930) 3rd w/o Allen Taylor Newberry
NEWBERRY, Allen Taylor- (1803 - 1887) {S/o Rev. Samuel & Eunice.}
NEWBERRY, Caroline Painter- (1827-1882) { 2nd w/o Allen T. Newberry.}
    { Allen Taylor Newberry is buried between his 2nd and 3rd
        wives. His 1st wife, Elizabeth Bogle died in 1846 and is
        buried at Oaklawn Farm, now owned be Lucy Bowen Litton.
        Elizabeth Bogle was born in 1804 & died in 1846. She had
        10 children by Allen Taylor Newberry. }
NEWBERRY, (Mary Lois- (9-21-1915 - 2-11-1916){D/o A.T. Jr & Maude}
NEWBERRY, Allen T.(Jr.)- (4-29-1885 - 11-16-1970) { S/o A.T. Sr. &
    his third wife, Nancy E. Gross Newberry.}
NEWBERRY, Maude S.-(1-29-1887 - 4-26-1966) {W/o A.T. Jr.& D/o William
    and Sally Mustard Stuart.}
NEWBERRY, Jasper Livingston- (11-14-1910 -8-24-1987) { S/o Maude
    Stuart A.T. Newberry, Jr.}
NEWBERRY, Rosemary (Dillow) -(2-8-1913 - 11-24-1987) { Wife of Jasper
    L. Newberry.}
NEWBERRY, Lois Gayle-(1-27-1932 - 12-2-1940) D/o Jasper & Rosemary
NEWBERRY, Allen Taylor, III- (5-8-1921 - 6-26-1992)(H/O Beulah Tibbs}
NEWBERRY, Beulah T.- (7-24-1921 -   ) W/O A.T. Jr. Nee Tibbs}
NEWBERRY, Virginia Eunice- (3-24-1894 - 8-11-1981) { D/o Dunn Bogle
    Newberry and Arbana Hancock Newberry.}
NEWBERRY, James Sherrill- (6-15-1892 - 1-16-1968) { S/o Dunn Bogle
    Newberry & Arbana Hancock Newberry.}
NEWBERRY, Dunn Bogle- (1-1-1842 - 4-13-1918) S/o Allen Taylor & his
    1st wife, Elizabeth Bogle Newberry.

NEWBERRY CEMETERY ON A.T. NEWBERRY FARM

[Copied in 1989 by Parke Bogle and checked again by Jo Ann Tickle
Scott in 1998. Cemetery located on land owned by the A.T. Newberry
family. There are steps leading from the road up into the cemetery.]

NEWBERRY, Arbana C. (2-29-1868 - 10-6-1929){D/o Pleasant Hancock
          and Theresa Wyrick Hancock. W/o Dunn Bogle Newberry.}
NEWBERRY, Samuel Dunn Newberry- (6-13-1905 - 4-4-1925) S/o Dunn &
          Arbanna C. Hancock Newberry.
NEWBERRY, William H. Newberry- (died 6-10-1938){ S/o Dunn Bogle
                    Newberry & h/O Bertha Thompson. }
NEWBERRY, Samuel H. (Henderson)- (6-19-1830 - 4-18-1917) {S/o Allen
          Taylor & Elizabeth Bogle Newberry. Was a State Senator,
          poet and Captain in the Civil War.}
NEWBERRY, Mary A. (Nee Repass)- (7-15-1849 - 4-18-1905) W/o Samuel H.
NEWBERRY, Clara Beaumont- (7-6-1872 - 8-12-1872) D/o Samuel & Mary A
NEWBERRY, Edmond Livingston-(4-16-1870 - 5-11-1908) { S/o Samuel &
          Mary Adeline Repass Newberry.}
NEWBERRY, Allen Taylor, Jr. (III)- (5-8-1921 - 6-26-1992) { S/O A.T.
          and Maude Stuart Newberry, h/O Beulah Tibbs }
NEWBERRY, Wythe C.- (1852 - 1930) { S/O Henry & Elizabeth Robinett
          Newberry & h/o Elizabeth Mustard, a daughter of John and
          Louvisa Patterson Mustard. She is buried at Mechanicsburg }

PATTERSON, William Edward- (3-13-1864 - 1-31-1938)
PATTERSON, Frances Jane- (7-12-1871 - 11-13-1940)
PATTERSON, Frank- (3-2-1898 - 1-18-1985)
PATTERSON, Ballard H. "Pete"- (1907 - 1968)

PAULEY, Snydor Franklin- (11-24-1926 - 2-22-1996) { US Army WW II }
PAULEY, Floyd F.- (1894-1959)
PAULEY, Zollie- (1901-1964)
PAULEY, Paul G. "Speed"- (1-12-1924 - 2-5-1996)

RICHARDSON, Infant of S.S. & Artie (B & D 7-1-1922)

{ Jo Ann counted 10 fieldstones with no names or dates and one badly
eroded stone, illegible. There were several indentations, but the
occupants are unknown }

OLD WRIGHT CEMETERY
[Commonly called "The Mountain Field Cemetery]

BLANKENSHIP, Archie Walter- (4-6-1922 - 2-11-1991)
BLANKENSHIP, Pearlie M.- (10-29-1927)   {Md. 40 yrs}
BLANKENSHIP, Edison Lee- (9-9-1919 - 5-30-1991)
BLANKENSHIP, Richard Bowman- (9-19-1925 - 5-15-1945)
BLANKENSHIP, Fred Daniel- (1883 - 1961)
BLANKENSHIP, Oda Bell- (1889 - 1977)
BLANKENSHIP, J. C.- (9-5-1929 - 9-17-1931)
BLANKENSHIP, William E.- (7-15-1881 - 2-14-1946)
BLANKENSHIP, Annie Ethel- (8-7-1892 - 4-10-1964)
BLANKENSHIP, Clinton- (1927 - 1947)
BLANKENSHIP, Stella G.- (11-20-1916 - 10-2-1992)

CARROLL, Quinton- (11-18-1918 -   )
CARROLL, Lila Blankenship- (4-11-1925 - 1-11-1980)

COMBS, Ula Blankenship- (1914 - 1936)

FARLOW, Louise- (1867 - 1952) [Nee Wolfe]
FARLOW, Mildred Geneva- (2-19-1937 - 2-28-1937)

GUSLER, Infant of W.B. & Audrey Gusler- (b. & d. 1945)

RAMSEY, George Clarence- (7-4-1905 - 12-6-1969)
RAMSEY, Thurman Riley- (3-25-1918 - 4-6-1973)
RAMSEY, Alvis D.- (1877 - 1940)
RAMSEY, Allie- (1887 - 1951)
RAMSEY, Grover- (1903 - 1904) Son of A.D. Ramsey
RAMSEY, Polly A.- (11-10-1850 - 11-29-1927)
RAMSEY, W. H. - (10-7-1840 - 1-4-1909)
RAMSEY, Infant (no name or dates
RAMSEY, Sidney Orland- (3-27-1920 - 12-30-1992)
RAMSEY, W. W.- (5-1-1872 - 2-19-1955)

SPANGLER, Mary Steele- (d. 6-18-1964, age 42?) Badly eroded
SPANGLER, Larry V.-(5-27-1941 - 8-26-1972){S/O Mary Steele Spangler}
SPANGLER, Latha, (11-6-1944 - 7-18-1964) S/O Mary Steele Spangler}
SPANGLER, Ernest Lee- (11-21-1915 - 2-12-1977)
SPANGLER, James DeWayne- (1980 - 1980) Son of Jimmy & Darlene.
SPANGLER, Herbert Paul- (12-30-1918 - 4-10-1985)
SPANGLER, James Earnest- (1946 - 1998)
SPANGLER, Anna Darlene- (1952 -   )
SPANGLER, Stella K.- (12-28-1921 - 6-18-1961)

WALL, Coy- (4-13-1922 - 5-28-1990)

WILLIAMS, Hurley R.- (1946 -   )
WILLIAMS, Mark Elmo- (1950 - 1989)
WILLIAMS, Marvin Ellis- (5-7-1925 - 3-28-1985) {US Army WW II }
WILLIAMS, Mark E.- (1950 - 1989)

OLD WRIGHT CEMETERY
[Commonly called " Mountain Field Cemetery]

WRIGHT, Talmadge Lee- (1957 - 1988)
WRIGHT, Wesley Allen- (1965 - 1988)
WRIGHT, Tony R.- (1936 - 1984) { H/O Minnie Burton }
WRIGHT, Minnie B.- (1941 -   ) { D/O Mason & Gladys M. Burton}
WRIGHT, Francis D.- (8-27-1947 - 5-4-1968)
WRIGHT, Ollie Mae- (2-11-1911 - 2-4-1986)
WRIGHT, William Olney- (11-10-1894 - 6-16-1979)
WRIGHT, Otis- (11-9-1927 - 3-31-1987) {US Army WW II }
WRIGHT, Otis, Jr.- (1-9-1956 - 1-9-1956) [Two hours old]
WRIGHT, Alvis Dewey- (11-24-1931 - 10-22-1984)
WRIGHT, Allie- (1887 - 1951)
WRIGHT. Lessie R.-(1941 - 1964)
WRIGHT, Lee J.- (5-12-1863 - 5-9-1939)
WRIGHT, Matilda E.- (8-4-1865 - 2-12-1930)
WRIGHT. Dorothy L.- (12-3-1932 - 3-11-1933)
WRIGHT, Margaret L.- (9-12-1931 - 10-4-1932)
WRIGHT, A.A.- (12-29- 1857 - 10-15-1926) [Carved on fieldstone]
WRIGHT, Della Ruth- (1912 - 1918)[Daughter of J.B. & L.J. Wright]
WRIGHT, D. W. M.- "Father" (11-15-1854 - 2-13-1944) [His full name
        was "Doctor" William McComas Wright. He was not a medical
        doctor. He married Sarah A. Bruce, Nov. 17, 1874.
WRIGHT, Sarah A.- "Mother" (6-3-1852 - 12-8-1925) Wife of D.W.M.
        Wright. [She was a daughter of John G. Bruce and his first
                wife, Elizabeth Jane Robinson of Wythe County.)
WRIGHT, Nellie F.- (1900 - 1923)
WRIGHT, Edna Myrtle- (10-14-1922 - 9-5-1953)
WRIGHT, Robert L.- (4-26-1901 - 12-23-1942)
WRIGHT, Daisy E.- (6-15-1909 - 4-16-1994)
WRIGHT, Nina F.- (10-12-1914   ) { Md 60 yrs }
WRIGHT, Homer Neal- (1932 - 1998)

{ There are 14 field stones near the back fence, with no
inscriptions or dates. Also several grave sites with no stones or
other markers. Some of the Funeral Home Markers are still in place
but weather and time have rendered them unreadable. If you know of
any one who is buried here, please let your Bland Historical Society
know their names and dates of birth and death.
 We thank Mrs. Audrey Gusler, for her kindness in helping us find
this old cemetery. She went with us and was very helpful in
identifying some of the hard to read stones.
 We apologize for any mistakes that we have made in copying this
cemetery. Mistakes are easily made, at the time of copying and again
when the names are typed. We ask your indulgence.
                        Mrs. Garman Lester
                        Mrs. Parke C. Bogle
{ Cemetery was checked again in 1998 by Jo Ann Tickle Scott and
several new dates were added.}

RED OAK CHURCH CEMETERY
[On Route 623 off State Route # 42, west of Bland Courthouse]

AKERS, Lorenza D.- (2-13-1933 - 10-6-1990)

ALDERMAN, James Wesley- (2-20-1937 - 12-26-1985)
ALDERMAN, Josephine T.- (3-23-1937 -   )

BALES, Sarah J.- (12-7-1846 - 10-25-1879) { Was murdered }
BALES, Mary M.- (6-24-1825 - 12-19-1906)
BALES, James R.- (6-26-1822 - 6-4-1908)
BALES, V. H.- (4-10-1854 - 1-14-1875)

BANE, Ida- (1907 - 1980)
BANE, Virginia Kimberling- (10-27-1867 - 4-30-1929) W/o Henry Bane.
BANE, William Henry- (5-10-1877 - 5-22-1963)

BARGER, John W.- (2-18-1891 - 3-3-1976)
BARGER, Lois W.- (11-30-1907   )
BARGER, Charles R.- (4-20-1893 - 11-22-1974) Married 11-18-1917.
BARGER, Martha L.- (2-13-1899 - 2-25-1969) Married 11-18-1917.
BARGER, Geo. W.- (2-12-1861 - 4-17-1934)
BARGER, Annie Belle Walker- (5-17-1863 - 3-19-1950)

BARTON, Joseph M.- (10-13-1870 - 5-8-1961)

BAUGH, Pansy- (8-21-1894 - 6-27-1985)
BAUGH, Phillip C.- (3-20-1886 - 8-26-1964)
BAUGH, Hallie U.- (7-2-1902 - 2-29-1976)
BAUGH, Edgar Neel- (4-10-1932 -   )
BAUGH, Charlotte Byerley- (4-2-1934 - 3-20-1990)
BAUGH, John T.- (11-20-1883 - 7-27-1964)
BAUGH, Bettie K.- (12-22-1880 - 10-11-1966)
BAUGH, Idella- (11-20-1898 - 7-8-1915)

BEAM, Claude Barton- (10-16-1905 - 10-5-1980) US Navy
BEAM, Hattie N.- (7-13-1913 - 10-29-1981)

BEVIL, Joey Martin- (1959 - 1975)

BOWLES, Robert Bailey- (2-6-1923 - 2-25-1959)
BOWLES, Charles Kemper- (9-25-1892 - 6-26-1976)
BOWLES, Leona Harner- (6-12-1897 - 12-31-1957)
BOWLES, Charles Richard- (8-11-1918 - 4-26-1936)

BROWN, James E.- (1888 - 1957)
BROWN, Ada M.- (1891 - 1984)
BROWN, Nelson- (5-19-1914 - 1-27-1963)
BROWN, Marsha Sue- (8-17-1954 - 6-30-1955)
BROWN, Ralph- (1919 - 1991)
BROWN, Mary Epperson- (11-25-1826 - 7-4-1893?) W/o John Brown

BURCHAM, Irvin E.- (5-24-18896 - 4-23-1960)

RED OAK CHURCH CEMETERY
[On Route 623 off State Route # 42, west of Bland Courthouse]

BURCHAM, Dorothy A.- (5-22-1897 - 7-6-1959)

BURGE, Paul- (1910 -   ) Married 4-7-1939.
BURGE, Elsie B.- (1922 - 1987) Married 4-7-1939

BURKE, James C.- (1891 - 1945) Father
BURKE, Alice D.- (1897 - 1965) Mother

CLEMONS, Samuel G.- (5-5-1889 - 4-5-1964)
CLEMONS, Samuel Anes, Sr.- (8-14-1928 - 3-16-1991)

COX, Cleta T.- (10-16-1908 - 10-4-1978)

CROW, Mary C.- (4-19-1864 - 3-5-1918)

CROWE, Christiana- (12-12-1831? - 5-6-1888?)
CROWE, Jonas M.- (2-17-1850 - 3-25-1917)
CROWE, Lena M.- (11-23-1898 - 11-20-1956)
CROWE, Daniel A.- (5-2-1853 - 2-11-1922)

CRUFF, Ballard S.- (1901 - 1970)
CRUFF, Eva G.- (1910 -   )

DAVIS, Samuel M.- (1-19-1922 - 4-5-1978)
DAVIS, Margie L.- (6-13-1930 - 10-26-1977)
DAVIS, Samuel A.- (8-22-1898 - 4-10-1975)
DAVIS, Hattie C.- (1-18-1904 - 7-31-1930)
DAVIS, Emma Bailey- (10-20-1902 - 8-4-1986)
DAVIS, Samuel S.- (5-5-1849 - 3-10-1927) ‾Father
DAVIS, Sarah Ann- (9-12-1859 - 1-3-1941)   Mother.
DAVIS, Oscar Cadell- (USN WW I- 6-27-1920)
DAVIS, Joseph H.- (12-31-1901 - 1-1-1969)
DAVIS, Hiram G.- (1827 - 1900)
DAVIS, Cosby J.- (1830 - 1903)
DAVIS, Henry B.- (1868 - 1957)

DEACON, Moretimer- (12-6-1900 - 7-26-1974)

DILLMAN, Pearl K.- (1921 - 1925)
DILLMAN, Ethel L.- (1916 - 1925)
DILLMAN, Willie K.- (1891 - 1944)
DILLMAN, Eliza M.- (1894 - 1932)
DILLMAN, Paul- (1-20-1911 - 11-16-1990)
DILLMAN, Daisy H.- (12-7-1912 - 6-27-1986)
DILLMAN, Lucinda Jane- (2-12-1857 - 6-29-1935)
DILLMAN, George- (No dates) CSA Marker
DILLMAN, Arby W.- (2-10-1893 - 1-27-1956) WW I

DUNCAN, Tommy Wayne- (11-21-1932 - 4-5-1953)
DUNCAN- Frank B.- (7-24-1894 - 2-13-1963)

DUNCAN, Estelle H.- (11-22-1893 - 5-18-1969)
DUNCAN, Lawrence- (6-20-1918 - 8-17-1989)
DUNCAN, Dorothy- (2-14-1925 -   )

DURHAM, Buford W.- (1-7-1913 - 8-26-1987)
DURHAM, Trula B.- (6-29-1916 -   )

EDWARDS, Alice K.- (1895? - 1952)

FOGLESONG, Martin E.- (3-23-1892 - 5-17-1941)
FOGLESONG, Infant son of Martin E. & E.J. Foglesong. b & d 3-29-1922.

HANCOCK, Kenneth W.- (11-4-1967 - 2-8-1971) S/o Mary & Edgar.
HANCOCK, Dunn N.- (10-13-1908 - 1-10-1974)
HANCOCK, Pearl H.- (5-22-1914 -   )

HARDEN, Gilbert R.- (3-26-1914 - 8-26-1986)
HARDEN, Irene W.- (1-14-1924 -   )
HARDEN, Charles Corbett- (2-6-1894 - 9-1-1968)
HARDEN, Lena Turley- (5-25-1891 - 11-19-1976)
HARDEN, Calvin W.- (3-22-1924 - 9-1-1925)
HARDEN, Fred Byron- (4-28-1917 - 4-6-1980)
HARDEN, Mayme Lambert- (11-21-1914 -   )
HARDEN, Samuel H.- (4-1-1851 - 4-14-1922)
HARDEN, Frances V.- (3-11-1857 - 3-2-1923)
HARDEN, John S.- (5-12-1891 - 7-2-1921)
HARDEN, Margaret M.- (10-31-1876 - 9-26-1888)
HARDEN, David M.- (6-16-1874 - 5-19-1927)
HARDEN, Mary Hollins- (6-19-1884 - 4-14-1946) W/o David M. Harden.
HARDEN, Infant son of D.M. & M. Neel Harden (B & D 4-14-1914)
HARDEN, Henly H.- (9-26-1873 - 2-19-1950)
HARDEN, Mary Ann- (11-22-1876 - 4-15-1952)
HARDEN, Burbridge B.- (1899 - 1973)
HARDEN, Samuel R.- (1886 - 1942)
HARDEN, Nora C.- (1887 - 1930)
HARDEN, Henry W.- (1907 1930)

??????, 2 infant graves near Harden plot. (B & D 4-21-1896)

HARNER, M.M.- (4-4-1822 - 11-22-1883?)
HARNER, Lawrence L.- (3-22-1891 - 6-25-1963)
HARNER, Lute B.- (12-27-1895 - 9-11-1977)
HARNER, William T.- (8-30-1861 - 6-5-1947)
HARNER, Elvira R.- (11-2-1871 - 6-11-1911)
HARNER, Aubrey Arthur- (12-15-1889 - 9-16-1942)
HARNER, Mae Neal- (6-14-1887 - 8-7-1932)
HARNER, J.J.- (dates illegible- partly underground)
HARNER, Hubert N.- (4-14-1902 - 10-25-1936)

HAYTON, Ballard P- (11-1-1904 - 10-30-1973)

RED OAK CHURCH CEMETERY
[On Route 623 off State Route # 42, west of Bland Courthouse]

HAYTON, Kathleen S.- (3-31-1917 -   )
HAYTON, Charles Benton- (7-19-1971 - 2-26-1942)
HAYTON, Lena Rose- (7-18-1884 - 5-31-1955)
HAYTON, T. Otto- (12-23-1888 - 7-13-1969)
HAYTON, Nannie B.- (2-21-1895 - 7-12-1980)
HAYTON, Howard P.- (10-3-1914 - 9-5-1916)
HAYTON, Robert B.- (8-27-1913 - 6-27-1947)

HOUNSHELL, Estle B., Sr.-(6-16-1889 - 6-11-1980) Married 9-12-1923.
HOUNSHELL, Mary Harden- (10-30-1904 - 9-10-1973) Married 9-12-1923
HOUNSHELL, Elmo- (born & died 3-17-1934)
HOUNSHELL, Estle B., Jr.- (Died 5-14-1994, age 58) { Obit.}

HUBBLE, Charles H.- (3-4-1906 - 7-24-1972)
HUBBLE, Myrtle C.- (6-29-1897 - 5-7-1972)

KIDD, Bertie B.- (2-29-1904 - 2-29-1964)
KIDD, Carl C.- (5-28-1898 - 11-28-1963)
KIDD, Infant dau of J.C. & Helen Kidd- (4-23-1967)
KIDD, Infant son of J.C. & Helen Kidd- (12-30-1970)

KIMBERLIN, Harry Lynn- (8-27-1923 -   )
KIMBERLIN, Martha Neel- (1-30-1924 - 9-22-1978)
KIMBERLIN, Nellie Gray- (1884 - 1885)
KIMBERLIN, Flora E.- (1887 - 1889)
KIMBERLIN, Louisa Catherine- (1857 - 1916)
KIMBERLIN, Elijah Hawkins- (1858 - 1935)
KIMBERLIN, William D.- (1865 - 1929)
KIMBERLIN, Blanch M.- (1876 - 1944)

KIMBERLING, Eliza- (12-3-1837 - 1-25-1917)
KIMBERLING, Stephen- (12-26-1830 - 6-1-1898)
KIMBERLING, James- (12-13-1857 - 7-16-1925)

KINDER, Charles L.- (1879 - 1944)
KINDER, Julia A.- (1882 - 1959)
KINDER, Bennie L.- (1936 - 1986) FHM

KITTS, Ira Otis- (7-26-1897 - 7-7-1948)
KITTS, Flora H.- (7-11-1906 -   )
KITTS, Victoria Neel- (7-10-1856 - 5-26-1934)
KITTS, James Martin- (3-6-1889 - 12-8-1932)
KITTS, 4 stones near Kitts plot with no markings.

LAMBERT, Elmer L- (2-10-1918 - 7-31-1987)
LAMBERT, Trula N.- (7-23-1925 -   )
LAMBERT, G. Wesley- (1888 - 1970)
LAMBERT, Stella P.- (1902 - 1971)
LAMBERT, Mamie E.- (1924 - 1967)
LAMBERT, Bertha- (1-12-1921 - 11-29-1989)

RED OAK CHURCH CEMETERY
[On Route 623 off State Route # 42, west of Bland Courthouse]

LAMBERT, Stephen G.,Jr.- (1920 - 1979)
LAMBERT, Stephen G.- (1890 - 1970)
LAMBERT, Dorsie Dell- (1897 - 1961)
LAMBERT, James Wm.- (11-9-1868 - 3-19-1941) Father.

LANE, Henry Garland- (born & died 6-25-1936)

LINDAMOOD, James L.- (1882 - 1962)
LINDAMOOD, Thursa A.- (1891 - 1973)
LINDAMOOD, Emily C. Felty-(5-15-1846 - 6-29-1923) W/o J.H. Lindamood.
LINDAMOOD, Willis G.- (3-17-1871 - 1-10-1936)
LINDAMOOD, Martha B.- (11-8-1871 - 8-14-1938)
LINDAMOOD, Rush M.- (12-22-1898 - 6-4-1977)
LINDAMOOD, Ina Grey- (10-15-1911 - 6-8-1978)
LINDAMOOD, Everette B.- (11-27-1911 - 12-20-1979)
LINDAMOOD, Mildred N.- (7-25-1912 - 9-19-1981)
LINDAMOOD, E. Hayes- (11-14-1886 - 10-16-1964)
LINDAMOOD, Dora Thorn- (5-5-1891 - 5-2-1943)

MCCLELLAN, Florence W.- (4-24-1893 - 8-21-1920) W/o C.C. McClellan.

MUNSEY, William B.- (12-11-1886 - 12-16-1964)
MUNSEY, Nannie H.- (5-31-1908 - 10-19-1973)

NEAL, George L.- (6-15-1861 - 11-15-1943)
NEAL, Lucinda C.- (5-7-1859 - 8-10-1941)
NEAL, Frank- (10-25-1881 - 10-7-1936) { H/O Annie Bogle }
NEAL, Annie- (8-16-1882 - 8-27-1947) { D/O F.C. & Martha Bogle)

NEEL, Trubie- (1816 - 1972)
NEEL, Hottle Crockett- (11-17-1920 - 7-24-1967)
NEEL, Conley- (5-26-1897 - 5-3-1980)
NEEL, Eula B.- (6-2-1898 - 11-22-1990)
NEEL, Son of Mr. & Mrs. Conley Neel- (1925)
NEEL, Julia K.- (11-9-1887 - 7-31-1971)
NEEL, Alex J.- (3-26-1885 - 3-25-1978)
NEEL, Mary B.- (7-5-1890 - 9-21-1960)
NEEL, Hallie T.- (1-30-1904 -   )
NEEL, Robert S.- (6-13-1894 - 8-16-1974)
NEEL, Ollie Crowe- (1896 - 1934)
NEEL, Margie C.- (1931 - 1932)
NEEL, Maxie L.- (4-28-1928 - 6-4-1966)
NEEL, Marvin H.- (6-25-1908 - 8-7-1978)
NEEL, Mayme L.- (7-4-1906 -   )
NEEL, Henry Curtis- (10-4-1915 - 1-27-1976)
NEEL, William T.- (1890 - 1962)
NEEL, Edith J.- (1890 - 1965)
NEEL, Ted James- (1913 - 1979) WW I
NEEL, Iva Grey A.- (8-22-1915 -   )
NEEL, Richard W. "Dick"- (8-22-1915 -   )

NEEL, Bernice "Bee" Duncan- (9-21-1912 -   )
NEEL, Charles H.- (6-27-1886 - 1-18-1945)
NEEL, Annie E.- (7-18-1887 - 5-3-1972)
NEEL, Tammy Lynn- (Stillborn 1-5-1951)
NEEL, Joe Blaine- (8-5-1935 - 10-18-1936)
NEEL, Emory Wayne- (10-3-1922 - 7-27-1966)
NEEL, Ruby Pauline- (5-6-1926 -   )
NEEL, Elmer- (1916 - 1957)
NEEL, Anne- (1913 - 1979)
NEEL, W. Carrington- (7-13-1920 - 10-23-1959)
NEEL, Jacqueline- (5-7-1925 -   )
NEEL, R. Lee- (2-9-1865 - 10-28-1938 -)
NEEL, Sarah E.- (3-23-1863 - 4-12-1932)
NEEL, Myrtle R.- (3-26-1901 - 9-24-1915)
NEEL, Kent C.- (2-27-1887 - 6-30-1905)
NEEL, Arthur G.- (4-15-1892 - 6-4-1903)
NEEL, Carra C.- (11-1-1899 - 1-18-1960 ?)
NEEL, Jossie M.- (1-27-1889 - 4-12-1902)
NEEL, Stephen Craig- (5-15-1955 - 1-6-1985)
NEEL, Milton- (7-25-1912 - 9-22-1992) {H/O Mary E. Neqwberry }
NEEL, Mary Evans- (1-6-1910 - 8-25-1988) {D/O Walter Newberry }
NEEL, Donald Shaunn- (6-13-1968 - 4-7-1988)
NEEL, Lawrence L.- (1918 - 1920)
NEEL, Effie G.- (1884 - 1972)
NEEL, James D.- (1888 - 1945)
NEEL, Walter H.- (10-5-1877 - 2-23-1933)
NEEL, Ninnie B.- (9-2-1876 - 11-25-1967) {D/O F.C. & Martha Bogle}
NEEL, A. Fred- (9-13-1908 - 4-9-1925)
NEEL, Allen J.- (4-22-1873 - 2-18-1937)
NEEL, Nancy E.- (2-14-1872 - 3-15-1951)
NEEL, Mary M.- (11-2-1840 - 10-4-1920)
NEEL, Alexander- (1-1-1842 - 4-14-1910)
NEEL, 4 unmarked graves near Neel plot

NEESE, Clarence- (died age 3 months, son of Roxie & W. Grant Neese.)

PECK, Blaine- (8-29-1926 - 1-6-1989 - age 62) {Grubb Funeral Home }
PECK, T.J. Randolph- (1-5-1922 - 8-7-1925) Son of M.R. & M.J. Peck.
PECK, Garner D.- (10-24-1932 - 2-22-1935)
PECK, Marion R.- (7-16-1892 - 9-8-1959)
PECK, Mary D.- (7-12-1898 - 12-4-1986)
PECK, Peery G.- (3-13-1924 - 6-22-1976)
PECK, Thomas J.- (3-25-1861 - 5-5-1936)
PECK, Laura V. Bridges- (5-30-1873 - 1-16-1950) W/o Thomas J. Peck.

RAMSEY, Edward G.- (1912 - 1970)
RAMSEY, Lena P.- (1912 -   )

REPASS, Walter A.- (11-30-1925 - 1-5-1984)
REPASS, Shirley N.- (6-18-1933 -   )

RED OAK CHURCH CEMETERY
[On Route 623 off State Route # 42, west of Bland Courthouse]

REPASS, Infant dau of Walter & Shirley Repass (b.& d. 4-9-1951)
REPASS, A. Davis- (1900 - 1966)
REPASS, Mayme T.- (1900 - 1968)
REPASS, Samuel L.- (6-27-1864 - 7-1-1914)
REPASS, Lucinda U.- (2-26-1867 - 12-28-1904)
REPASS, Infant son of J.W. & S.E. Repass (no dates)

SADLER, Edgar H.- (1896 - 1953)
SADLER, Mable U.- (1902 -   )

SHAEFFER, John W.- (7-3-1892 - 6-25-1950) Married 7-1-1931.
SHAEFFER, Cleo Neel- (8-26-1904 - 11-17-1955)

SHEWEY, L.J.S.- (died 1895) Wife of Howard Shewey.

THOMPSON, Gray Cecil- (2-19-1899 - 8-1-1985)
THOMPSON, Lelia U.- (8-27-1905 - 6-29-1983)
THOMPSON, Hubert Walton- (8-4-1888 - 1-29-1979)
THOMPSON, A. Paris- (3-29-1885 - 11-14-1934)
THOMPSON, Alice V.- (8-6-1863 - 10-26-1927)

TURLEY, Bascom Allen- (12-19-1907 - 12-15-1984)

TURNER, James Michael- (2-2-1969 - 1-10-1977)

UMBARGER, Keith- (7-23-1941 - 5-24-1945)
UMBARGER, Elizabeth- (8-2-1828 - 6-21-1881)
UMBARGER, Jonas Jackson- (6-19-1917 - 4-25-1989) [Mausoleum]
UMBARGER, Stanley M.- (11-13-1942 -   ) [Mausoleum]
UMBARGER, Brooksie- (4-27-1918 -   ) [Mausoleum]
UMBARGER, Sandra Burge- (3-27-1947 -   ) [Mausoleum]
UMBARGER, Henry H.- (11-27-1886 - 10-9-1970)
UMBARGER, Evelyn L.- (6-3-1896 - 1-12-1956)
UMBARGER, Clarence M.- (5-9-1904 - 12-12-1981)
UMBARGER, Della Neel- (9-22-1910 -   )
UMBARGER, C.M., Jr.- (8-5-1931 - 8-6-1931) Son of C.M. & Della.
UMBARGER, David W.- (1885 - 1962)
UMBARGER, Josie F.- (1887 - 1968)
UMBARGER, Andrew E.- (4-3-1895 - 2-24-1947)
UMBARGER, Eliza Jane- (9-23-1866 - 3-9-1935)
UMBARGER, Howard- (1-6-1922 - 10-5-1984)
UMBARGER, Arnold A.- (3-10-1890 - 10-13-1923)
UMBARGER, Ruth B.- (6-11-1892 - 8-15-1966)
UMBARGER, William P.- (11-9-1864 - 1-11-1916)
UMBARGER, Jemima- (4-20-1827 - 7-31-1885) Wife of Peter Umbarger.
UMBARGER, Peter- (1-??-???? - 2-2-1890)
UMBARGER, David B.- (4-7-1854 - 3-26-1918)
UMBARGER, Christine E.- (3-21-1856 - 11-3-1933)
UMBARGER, William- (CSA marker- no dates)
UMBARGER, Christina- (9-11-1831 - 10-7-1906)

UMBARGER, Walter Peery- (11-20-1894 - 12-28-1917)
UMBARGER, Henry- (10-4-1832 - 6-11-1911) Confederate Vet.
UMBARGER, Mary Jane Henderson- (1-29-1853 - 3-15-1932) Wife of Henry.
UMBARGER, David- (1850 - 1928)
UMBARGER, Amanda- (1851 - 1942)

UMBERGER, William Jennings- (5-1913 -   )
UMBERGER, Mary Frances S.- (8-1911 -   )
UMBERGER, William T.- (1885 - 1971)
UMBERGER, Minnie Pearl- (1894 - 1952)
UMBERGER, Jonas- (3-9-1859 - 2-3-1941)
UMBERGER, Barbara E. Neel- (2-27-1869 - 1-1-1937) Wife of Jonas.
UMBERGER, Rufus M.- (3-9-1855 - 3-22-1925)
UMBERGER, Samuel L.- (12-6-1886 - 11-16-1956)
UMBERGER, Vinnie M.- (3-26-1889 - 7-9-1952)
UMBERGER, Leida G.- (2-29-1912 - 12-8-1913) D/o S.L. & V.M. Umberger.

WADDELL, Wanda Baugh- (1935 - 1958)

WINESETT, Arthur B.- (3-14-1902 - 1-1-1969)
WINESETT, Lottie U.- (2-20-1892 - 5-25-1964)
WINESETT, Alberta Chloe- (9-29-1907 - 5-28-1970)
WINESETT, Lemuel G.- (8-18-1907 - 11-6-1957)
WINESETT, Jimmie- (1-18-1937 - 10-4-1976)
WINESETT, H. Cleve- (11-25-1888 -   )
WINESETT, Maye S.- (3-19-1888 - 12-25-1975)
WINESETT, Nathan E.- (5-1-1860 - 5-11-1948)   Father.
WINESETT, Susan B.- (8-19-1866 - 2-10-1919)   Mother.
WINESETT, Infant d/o Nathan E. & Susan B. Winesett- (b.&d.12-12-1902)
WINESETT, Darthulia- (4-2-1825 - 1-19-1900) Wife of Noah Winesett.
WINESETT, Infant son of N.E. & S.B. Winesett- (b. & d. 2-8-1899)
WINESETT, J.C.- (5-21-1890 - 11-20-1964)
WINESETT, Henry M.- (8-15-1867 - 2-3-1925)
WINESETT, Rhoda E.- (7-21-1869 - 2-13-1948)
WINESETT, Minnie Grey- (7-16-1887 - 3-29-1980)

[There are several field stones without markings, as well as stones
which time and the elements have rendered unreadable. Some have been
mended and reset so deeply in the soil that the lettering is not
visible.
    This is a well kept cemetery and most of the stones are in a
reasonable state of repair. The person or persons who attend to this
cemetery are to be commended for a beautiful job well done.
    The names and dates from the stones in this cemetery, were copied
on June 8, 1991, by Mrs. Garman Lester and Mrs. Parke C. Bogle. Some
dates have been added from obituaries gleaned from newspaper obits.
    We beg your indulgence, if we have erred. First, we may have copied
the dates incorrectly, or erred again when typing. We will appreciate
any corrections that any one may care to make. P. Bogle]

AGEE, Dickie- 6-21-1938 - 12-25-1938) Son of Annie & Oran Agee.
AGEE, ORAN- (8-30-1914 - 6-15-1966)
AGEE, Rosa Lee- (8-9-1881 - 5-13-1933).
AGEE, James L.- (9-24-1879 -   ).
AGEE, Otis Eugene- (10-13-1955 - 7-27-1975)
AGEE, Ray O.- (1927 -   )
AGEE, Margaret V.- (1930 - 1985)
AGEE, James Cleveland- (4-5-1955 - 2-8-1956)
AGEE, Dorothy B.- (1927 -   )
AGEE, Paul E.- (1923 - 1968)

BIRD, Mary (nee Sands)- (5-1-1892 - 11-17-1918)
BIRD, Geneva J.- (5-12-1862 - 11-18-1896) D/o G.W. & S.A. Miller
       and wife of A.L. Bird.
BIRD, Austian Letcher- (6-13-1861 - 3-16-1926)

BLANKENSHIP, Creasie M. (11-24-1927 - 9-5-1983)

CHARLES, Cyrril Ambrose- (2-25-1887 - 9-26-1956) Pvt. US Army, WW I

CROMER, Dolly Faulkner- (1-31-1931 - 8-27-1989)

DALTON, Truman- (3-11-1878 - 7-13-1966)
DALTON, Vinia- (3-2-1884 - 5-23-1974)
DALTON, Everett Warren- (Born & died 2-25-1921)
DALTON, R.H.- (Born & died 12-20-1941)
DALTON, James J.- (1915 - 1981)
DALTON, Ruby Lee- (1917 -   )
DALTON, Troy Jefferson- (1902 - 1984)

DAVIS, Walter Pierman- (11-24-1902-12-23-1902) S/o J.A. & Nannie K.

FAULKNER, Infant- (no dates)
FAULKNER, Chester A.- (1-30-1890 - 5-23-1974)
FAULKNER, Nola P.- (8- 1898 -   ) Nee Pruett
FAULKNER, Elbert- 10-1932 - 1-1934)

HELVEY, Elizabeth Bruce- (3-1855 - 3-1929)
HELVEY, Infant son of H.C. & W.B., born & died 6-23-1919

MILLER, Byrd F. (Finley)- (4-14-1891 - 9-5-1958) { S/o Lorenza Meek
       and Rebecca Finley Miller.}
MILLER, Robert M. (Montague "Mont")- (11-2-1889 - 3-19-1960) { S/o
       Lorenza Meek and Rebecca Finley Miller.}
MILLER, Mary E.- (5-22-1894 - 5-27-1969 { W/o R. Mont and daughter of
       Ballard W. and Roxie Pruett Miller. }
MILLER, Ballard W.- (3-13-1869 - 1-8-1923) F/o Mary E.
MILLER, James W.- (3-18-1903 - 1-24-1920)
MILLER, Roxie B.- (3-9-1872 - 5-20-1912) {W/o Ballard, Nee Pruett.}
MILLER, Mellie Bird, (7-26-1884 - 9-4-1948)
MILLER, James L.- (6-11-1884 - 6-30-1975)
MILLER, George Hudson- (4-29-1889 - 2-29-1904)

SALEM CHURCH CEMETERY, - KIMBERLING, BLAND COUNTY VIRGINIA

MILLER, James Earnest- (5-21-1899 - 3-2-1901)
MILLER, Ada Mae- (6-7-1905 - 9-28-1905)
MILLER, Charles E.- (4-29-1865 - 1-26-1936)
MILLER, Sarah E.- (5-21-1861 - 12-31-1943)
MILLER, G.W.- (4-23-1845 - no death date) Enlisted, 1863
MILLER, S.A.- (2-2-1838 - 11-100-1920) Married, Sarah A. 4-12-1864
MILLER, Earl Jorden- (12-23-1907 - 5-16-12975)
MILLER, Evelyn Agee- (5-13-1912 - 6-28-1984) W/o Earl Jorden
MILLER, Emory Earl- (1932 - 1991) Son of Earl J. & Evelyn.

MOREHEAD, Leonard E.- (7-14-1847 - 11-7-1932)
MOREHEAD, Emma Louise- (4-2-1856 - 10-7-1926) Wife of Leonard

PRUETT, Hugh- (4-17-1879 - 10-24-1913)
PRUETT, Pearlie N.- (1-16-1883 - 3-21-1972)
PRUETT, James M.- 1870 - 1932)
PRUETT, Cora H.- (1874 - 1900)
PRUETT, Cpl. James Milton- (Co. F. 45th Va. Infantry, CSA. No dates
PRUETT, Elizabeth Arminta- (4-3-1845 - 12-2-1915) {Nee Fanning}
PRUETT, Emma- (8-29-1874- 4-30-1890)
PRUETT, Nellie- (12-10-1884 - 4-24-1890)
PRUETT, Arrena Ann- (5-15-1868 - 10-13-1889)
PRUETT, Rosa Ashworth- (died 1921) No age stated.
PRUETT, Margaret- (died 1921) No age stated.
PRUETT, Otto- (4-24-1877 - 10-22-1924)

ROI, Ulid A. "Blackie" - (12-9-1886 - 7-26-1952) Cpl. WW I

YATES, Charlie H.- (1906 -   )
YATES, Pearl D.- (1909 - 1955)

{ There are several sunken spots with no stones. I copied the stones
in this cemetery in 1993 and I am sure there have been other burials
here since then. I will appreciate any one telling me of any one else
who is buried here.   Parke C. Bogle
                          1117 High Street
                          Pulaski, VA 24301
                    Email- <parkebog@swva.net>

OAKLAWN FARM CEMETERY
[Newberry Cemetery on land now owned by Lucy Bowen Litten]

BOGLE, Nancy- (12-24-1844 - 5-20-1861) { D/o Elizabeth and Allen
        Taylor Newberry and w/o Creed Fulton Bogle. Creed Bogle was a
        son of George Bogle and Jane Ray Bogle. He died in the Civil
        War. Nancy's mother was a niece of Creed Fulton's father. }

BOWEN, Virginia Jamerson Newberry- (4-20-1909 - 4-25-1980) W/o Meek
        Hoge Bowen. D/o William A.T and Lucy Kidd Newberry.

GREGORY, Mildred Stone, (Feb. 21, 1917 - 8-14-1947) W/o R.F. Gregory.

KIDD, Sallie A.- (1-26-1840) - 4-15-1922)

LITTON, Robert Warren- (4-9-1928 - 12-15-1972){ H/O Lucy Bowen.}

MCDONALD, Richard Taylor- (7-1-1963 - 7-4-1963)
MCDONALD, William- (born 1798 - died 2-4-1862)

MULVEY, Mike- (died 1-1888) { Irish farm hand. }

NEWBERRY, Harman- (9-13-1826 - 8-10-1915) Oldest son of Allen
        Taylor and Elizabeth Bogle Newberry
NEWBERRY, Mary A.- (5-22-1831 - 10-17-1907) Nee McDonald, wife of
        Harman Newberry.
NEWBERRY, Lucie Kidd- (7-18-1878 - 3-1-1935) W/o W.A. Newberry
NEWBERRY, William A. (T)- (2-26-1868 - 6-23-1950) S/o Harman & Mary
NEWBERRY, Ida Kate- (2-4-1876 - 6-16-1897) Nee Kegley, 1st w/o Wm. A.
NEWBERRY, Ida Kate- (6-8-1897 - 7-11-1897) D/o William A. & Ida Kate
NEWBERRY, Robert Harman- (born & died May 8, 1900)
NEWBERRY, Mamie Louise- (12-27-1913 - 10-4-1923) D/O Lawrence & Kemp.
NEWBERRY, Harman Jackson- (12-22-1907 - 6-10-1909) S/o Lawrence Mc.
        and Kemp Grayson Newberry
NEWBERRY, Charlie H.- (8-23-1882 - 4-17-1885) S/o LaFayette &
        Louise Bird Newberry.
NEWBERRY, Layfayette M.- (2-6-1856 - 3-28-1925) S/o Harman & Mary A.
NEWBERRY, Mary Louise Bird- (3-23-1859 - 5-10-1944) W/o Lafayette.
NEWBERRY, Elizabeth-(1-1804 - 1-26-1846) W/o Allen Taylor Newberry.
        { D/o Robert Bogle and Rachael Dunn Bogle. }

STONE, Robert, Jr.- (1921 - 1942)

{ Cemetery copied in 1993. It is well kept and appeared to have been
mowed often. I had a nice conversation with Meek Hoge Bowen while
there. Lucy Litton is doing a beautiful job of refurbishing the
lovely house called "Oaklawn". Parke C. Bogle }

CEMETERY ON OLD MEEK MILLER FARM
{ Land is now owned by Charles and Shirley Cox }
[Copied in October of 1998 by Jo Ann Tickle Scott]

HELVEY, L.D. (Lorenza Dow}- (10-8-1853 - 2-15-1933) {Md. Sarah Ann
                              Elizabeth Miller, 2-12-1874}
HELVEY, Sarah M.-(8-14-1853 - 2-16-1925) {D/O Dr. L.J. Miller, W/O
                              L.D. Helvey}
HELVEY, Dora Bell- (4-21-1878 - 5-30-1901) {D/O Dow & Sarah, Sis. of
                              Bessie May Helvey who married James Ward Morehead}
HELVEY, Lorenza LaFayette- (3-14-1883 - 6-15-1895){ S/O Dow & Sarah}
HELVEY, Viola M.- (7-9-1877 - 7-26-1900)

RAMSEY, Elizabeth- (9-16-1829 - 6-1-1901) { Mother of Mary Ramsey who
                              married Charles Miller.}

[There are 26 graves in the cemetery, 7 have stones and 19 are field
stones. The cemetery is located to the south of Kimberling Road (612)
on land now owned by Charles and Shirley Cox. It is in the trees
slightly to the west of their home. My thanks to Donald Helvey for
his help. --Jo Ann Tickle Scott.

I. F. STOWERS CEMETERY
{Located west of Rocky Gap, to the north of State Route 61 and 16
miles east of Tazewell, north of route 61}
[Copied by Jo Ann Tickle Scott]

ROBINETT, Hiram- (4-4-1825 - 2-17-1865)
ROBINETT, Dicie- (9-14-1820 - 11-8-1892)
ROBINETT, Emily- (7-16-1856 - 12-29-1892) {W/O James H. Richardson}
ROBINETT, William M.- (Civil War stone- no dates)
ROBINETT, R.B.- (3-26-1854 - 10-2-1930}
ROBINETT, L. J. - (7-7-1864 - 1-3-1942) {W/O R. B.Robinett}
ROBINETT, Charles- No dates
ROBINETT, Mary- No dates
ROBINETT, Wes, son of Charles- No dates.

STOWERS, Virginia Robinett- (4-30-1837 - 3-7-1917)
STOWERS, Isaac F.- (2-15-1839 - 10-15-1919){H/O Virginia Robinett}
STOWERS, Mordica- (d. 7-21-1860) age 76 years.
STOWERS, Polly- (d. 3-29-1868, age 78 years) {W/O Mordica}
STOWERS, Rachel- (5-20-1832 - 7-22-1930) {W/O John W. Stowers}
STOWERS, JOhn W.- (d. 7-12-1862, age 31 years)
STOWERS, P.R.- (9-25-1836 - 12-31-1893} Age 57 yrs, 3 mos & 6 days.
STOWERS, Arminta- (10-14-1830 - 12-25-1892) {62 yrs. 2 mos. & 11da.}
STOWERS, B. P.- (3-17-1867 - 11-13-1927) {W/O P. R. Stowers}
STOWERS, Missouri May- (3-7-1869 - 7-11-1957) {W/O B.P. Stowers}
STOWERS, Claude- (3-16-1907 - 2-11-1979) {US Army WW II}

KITTS-TICKLE CEMETERY
{ Cemetery is located on route 604 in Cracker's Neck section of the county on the J.D. Tickle farm. One needs 4x4 or walk up the hill}
[Compiled by Jo Ann Tickle Scott]

KITTS, Nannie Edith- (12-5-1853 - 1-29-1935) Mother. {W/O W.R. Kitts
               and D/O James H. & Jane Detimore Burton}
KITTS, W. Ray- (6-21-1853 - 9-5-1923) Father {S/O Breckenridge Harvey
        & Emily Caroline Bowles Kitts. H/O Nannie E. Burton.}
KITTS, W. L.- (5-5-1887 - 11-11-1911) {H/O Myrtle N. Hancock}
KITTS, Elizabeth V. (Virginia)- (2-8-1828 - 10-21-1888) { W/O Harvey
       G. Kitts & D/O George & Jane Ray Ross Bogle}
KITTS, Harvey G.- (6-18-1830 - 12-24-1894) {H/O Elizabeth V.}
KITTS, Elizabeth J.V.- (5-10-1861 - 8-24-1883) {1st W/O Ballard G.}
KITTS, Jacob Creed Bogle- (1862 - 1945) {H/O Edna Nye Tickle & S/O
               Harvey G. & Eliz. Va. Bogle Kitts}
KITTS, Edney Nye Tickle- (3-19-1869 - 4-2-1961) {D/O Daniel L. & Mary
            "Polly" Bogle Tickle }[From family records.]

MYERS, William Harvey- (3-4-1883 - 8-4-1914) {H/O Mary Belle Myers,
          S/O James Fletcher & Painter Kitts Myers}
          { Was run over by engine 995 of B.of R.T & .O.O.}

TICKLE, Barnitz L. (Lemuel)- (5-1869 -1931) {S/O Hezekiah & Caroline
              Matilda Farmer Tickle}
TICKLE, Rosa Mariam-(10-1872 - 2-5-1948) {W/O Barnitz D/O Wm. Ray and
           Nannie Burton Kitts } [From family records]
TICKLE, Lona Bell- (1892 - 1908) {D/O Barnitz & Rosa Tickle}
TICKLE, Frank D.- (1898 - 1899) {S/O Barnitz & Rosa Tickle}
TICKLE, Stella May- (1895 - 1897){D/O Barnitz & Rosa Tickle }

[4 indentations and 5 field stones with no information on them.]

HOBBS CEMETERY
[Compiled by Jo Ann Tickle Scott.]
{ This cemetery is located on Hollybrook about 300 yards straight up a hill from the Appalachian Trail. Accordind to local history, th African-American Hobbs family owned this land at one time. The land was logged by another owner and the machinery destroyed what markers that were there. There is part of an old plow which may have been used to help dig the graves. There are 4 adult graves and 1 child's grave. The indentations are very deep and cannot be mistaken for anything except graves. The site can only be reached by foot.}
{Mrs. Scott gives thanks to Joey Brandon Cole and Joe Cole for their help.}

TICKLE-BOGLE CEMETERY
{ Located about 3 miles from the junction of state Route 42 and route
604, on the R.H. Tickle farm, now owned by Eddie Morehead. The site
is behind the old Bogle home now occupied by Joyce Tickle.}
[Compiled by Jo Ann Tickle Scott}

BOGLE, George William- (10-1-1800 - 9-1-1882) {S/O Ralph Bogle, Sr.}
BOGLE, Margaret Jane Ray Scott- (@1794 - 2-4-1879) {W/O George W.}

TICKLE, Daniel- (@1801 - aft. 1880) {B. in N.C.}
TICKLE, Sarah Elizabeth "Betsy) Lineberry- (1805 - 1-15-1880)
                    {W/O D Daniel Lineberry Tickle}
TICKLE, Mary "Polly" Bogle- (9-5-1838 - 1-3-1914) {D/O George Bogle
                    and W/O Daniel L. Tickle}
TICKLE, Daniel Lineberry- (10-13-1833 - 6-5-1916) {S/O Daniel & Eliz.
                    Lineberry Tickle. H/O Polly Bogle}
TICKLE, Mary Elizabeth Florence- (4-4-1867 - 2-24-1917) {1st W/O Ira
                    Lozier Tickle.}
TICKLE, Robert Mason- (1-11-1899 - 5-19-1912) {S/O Ira & Flora}
             { Hit by a rock and killed on way to a funeral}
TICKLE, Ella Gladys- (6-11-1906 - 4-20-1909) {D/O Meek & Ella P. }
                    (Died from Meningitis}

HAVENS CEMETERY
{ Located about 2 miles east of Bland to the left of Route 42 at the
                    Gordon C. Havens farm.
             [Copied in 1998 by Jo Ann Tickle Scott]

HAVENS, John- (11-14-1816 - 4-15-1891)
HAVENS, W.C.-(12-1-1903 - 6-2-1981){S/O Thompson & Emmer P. Havens}
HAVENS, Bernard Mason- (9-30-1901 - 12-8-1961) {S/o T.C & Emmer }
HAVENS, Thompson Crockett- (6-28-1859 - 10-29-1930)
HAVENS, Emmer Penley- (9-23-1870 - 3-12-1955) {W/O T.C Havens and d/o
                    Braxton Penley}

SIFFORD, Virginia H.- (3-13-1909 - 5-26-1935) {D/O T.C. & Emmer}

ROSE HILL CEMETERY
[Located on a hill North of State Route 52/21 about two miles North
of Bastian Union Church in Bastian, Virginia.]
{ Compiled by Jo Ann Tickle Scott }

AKERS, Nelsene Marie- (1-21-1930 - 9-17-1989)
AKERS, Wylie W.- (9-23-1925 -
AKERS,   (3-27-1954 - 8-5-1970)
AKERS, Edna C.- (1-6-1925 - 11-18-1985) {Mother}

BAILEY, Jack T.- (4-7-1931 - 5-4-1991)
BAILEY, Virginia B.- (4-5-1868 - 11-28-1941)
BAILEY, John W.- (8-29-1887 - 10-23-1936)
BAILEY, Alma Kidd- (7-6-1910 - 12-9-1998)
BAILEY, William Burke- (3-21-1904 - 7-28-1952) {H/O Alma K.}

BAKER, John Catron- (11-8-1902 - 3-12-1966)
BAKER, Martha Conn- (11-15-1893 - 10-17-1973)
BAKER, Emmett- (2-13-1871 - 5-23-1941)
BAKER, (Nellie K.- (6-8-1869 - 12-25-1943)
BAKER, Marie- (10-7-1927) {Infant}

BARNETTE, Clinton H.- (8-16-1919 - 5-18-1991) {Sgt. US Army WW II
BARNETTE, David T.- (9-11-1957 - 5-13-1993)

BIVENS, Richard Lee- (3-4-1947 - 8-3-1997)
BIVENS, Harold C.- (5-13-1928 -   ) {Husband}
BIVENS, Doris J.- (1-9-1930 - 9-5-1996) {Wife}
BIVENS, Larry Curtis- (3-25-1953 -   )
BIVENS, Ernest J. Jr.- (5-14-1955 -   )
BIVENS, Donald Ray- (11-21-1950 - 6-26-1952)
BIVENS, Ethel W.- (6-26-1924 -   )
BIVENS, Ernest J. Sr.- (7-17-1923 -   )

BLANKENSHIP, Estel McKinney- (7-30-1944 - 7-11-1997) Age 52
BLANKENSHIP, Helen Elizabeth- (9-5-1898 - 11-14-1936)
BLANKENSHIP, Zora- (9-14-1915 -   )
BLANKENSHIP, William B.- (12-31-1920 - 1-21-1990)
BLANKENSHIP, Estel M.- (9-5-1895 - 8-5-1939) {Father}
BLANKENSHIP, Lucy V. - (8-7-1899 - 2-7-1965)
BLANKENSHIP, Mary Ann- (4-15-1948 - 9-17-1948) {Our darling}
BLANKENSHIP, Randolph M.- (12-4-1922 - 1-27-1995)
BLANKENSHIP, Geneva A.- (11-15-1926 - 9-22-1997)

BLESSING, William Paul, Sr.- (1-26-1902 - 12-2-1971)
BLESSING, Calla Shristian- (10-25-1904 - 2-29-1988)
BLESSING, Herschel Mark- (1-29-1905 - 4-20-1991)
BLESSING, Audrey Heilman- (11-20-1910 - 9-9-1991)
BLESSING, Herschel H.- (11-23-1932 -   )
BLESSING, Danise K.- (12-4-1926 - 10-31-1991)

BOOTH, Gracie L.- (7-24-1906 - 11-4-1967)
BOOTH, Roy H.- (11-9-1907 - 4-24-1976)

ROSE HILL CEMETERY
{ Compiled by Jo Ann Tickle Scott }

BOWLES, Larry A.- (1980 - 1984) {FHM}
BOWLES, Darrell- (1-11-1969 - 1-30-1977)
BOWLES, Ruthie Pennington- (2-28-1924 - 11-19-1990)
BOWLES, Robert Guy- (1-7-1895 - 12-15-1962) {US Army WW I}
BOWLES, Annie Bane- (12-18-1898 - 2-22-1976)
BOWLES, William Guy- (1921 - 1977) {FHM}

BRUCE, Ruth Elizabeth- (8-11-1921 - 10-27-1988) {D/O Arthur & Ella }
BRUCE, Arthur C.- (1891 - 1971) {US Army WW I {H/O Ella Harman}
BRUCE, Ella Harman- (1903 - 1983) {W/O Arthur Carlton Bruce}
BRUCE, R. Donald- (3-19-1926 - 7-12-1988) {S/O Arthur & Ella}
BRUCE, Irene Rasnake- (9-2-1922 -   ) {W/O R. Donald}
BRUCE, John Lee- (8-28-1890 - 10-22-1974) {H/O Bell Thompson}
BRUCE, Bell Thompson- (2-17-1888 - 10-17-1984) { W/O John Lee Bruce}
BRUCE, John L. Jr.- (1917 - 1983) {US Army WW II}
BRUCE, Forrest Wayne- (5-31-1932 - 8-16-1959) {US Air Force}
BRUCE, Paul Edgar- (5-15-1894 - 4-27-1972) {US Army WW I }
BRUCE, Beulah- (1-16-1901 - 12-27-1990) { W/O Paul Edgar Bruce}

BUCKINGHAM, Flora Harman- (8-28-1917 - 8-11-1972){D/O J.H. & M.K.H.}

BURRESS, Gadia Pauline- (12-22-1926 - 9-13-1998) {FHM} {W/O G.B.}

BURTON, Clifford Paul- (4-16-1919 - 5-18-1996)
BURTON, Betty Lane- (2-16-1931 - 1-3-1993)
BURTON, Betty T.- (1950 - 1991)

CAHILL, Nora Bailey- (1-29-1900 - 12-20-1990)

CALVERT, Charles Eric- (8-14-1964 - 10-25-1976)

CARVER, Ethel Mae- (1911 - 1857) {Mother}
CARVER, John Tyler- (1906 - 1974) {Father}

CASSELL, Mary E.- (1841 - 1949)
CASSELL, John S.- (1869 - 1931)
CASSELL, Lillie A.- (1888 - 1947)

CHILDRESS, J. Bryan- (12-19-1907)
CHILDRESS, Mamie S.- (11-20-1913 -   )
CHILDRESS, Eunice S.- (5-15-1931 -   ) {MOM}
CHILDRESS, Carl Trubie- (10-22-1926 - 1-30-1994) {US Army Korea}
CHILDRESS, James W.- (1-1-1920 - 11-18-1976}
CHILDRESS, Woodrow- (3-9-1913 - 11-12-1994)
CHILDRESS, Frank- (1905 - 1979) {US Army WW II}
CHILDRESS, Freddie R.- (1925 - 1975) (US Navy WW II}
CHILDRESS, Joseph S.- (1896 - 1958)
CHILDRESS, Delilah L.- (1885 - 1964)
CHILDRESS, Cecil W.- (3-19-1904 - 1-17-1982)
CHILDRESS, William H.- (4-23-1893 - 4-17-1934)

ROSE HILL CEMETERY
{ Compiled by Jo Ann Tickle Scott }

CHILDRESS, William H.-

CLEMENS, Ruth Meadows- (3-22-1934 - 4-29-1996) {Mother}
CLEMENS, David W.- (3-14-1886 - 3-26-1959) {Father}
CLEMENS, Mary Bowles- (11-21-1896 - 10-27-1964) {Niece}

COLLEY, Cecil Donald- (2-17-1917 - 4-2-1942)
COLLEY, Jean- (7-22-1916 - 7-10-1985)
COLLEY, Cecil, Sr.- (6-10-1918 - 12-11-1989)
COLLEY, Maude- (3-10-1902 - 6-13-1997)
COLLEY, Richard- (11-13-1898 - 8-16-1967)

CONLEY, Carlton M.- (1889 - 2-7-1954)
CONLEY, James W.- (7-3-1928 - 4-26-1996)
CONLEY, Phyllis K.- (5-3-1929 -   ) {Md. 1-6-1950}

COX, Ira- (1-1-1901 - 7-18-1989)
COX, Ethel C.- (11-4-1901 - 1-19-1989)
COX, Duel Dean- (9-28-1921 -   )
COX, Betty Jo- (7-13-1936 - 8-8-1988)

CRESS,   (5-12-1952

CURRY, Maxie Bruce- (7-28-1920 - 9-1-1966) {W/O Wes Curry, d/o John
                    Lee & Bell Thompson Bruce }
DENT, Walter L.- (1935 - 1979)
DENT, Margaret A.- (1944 -   )
DENT, Dewey C.- (10-26-1900 - 7-6-1977)
DENT, Lillie D.- (7-17-1902 - 12-3-1994) {Md. 11-9-1920}
DENT, Dewey C. Jr.- (1928 - 1962) {Father}
DENT, Sheila May- (3-5-1964 - 5-13-1964)
DENT, Barry Wayne- (d. 4-1-1968, age 4months 3 days)

DUNCAN, Virginia Sarver- (12-19-1923 - 7-21-1990)
DUNCAN, Callie- (1879 - 1968)
DUNCAN, Barbara S.- (5-30-1941 - 7-22-1941)

DYKES, Mossie Hyden- (2-20-1900 - 9-14-1975)
DYKES, Wallace E.- (2-21-1923 - 4-11-1969)
DYKES, Pauletta Joyce- (1-26-1943 - 7-28-1943) {Infant d/o Frances &
                                              Wallace Dykes}
ELLIOT, Carl Clay- (11-7-1990 - 4-8-1957)
ELLIOT, Susie Gallaway- (5-5-1895 -   )
ELLIOT, Alfred "Bo" E.- (10-10-1931 - 5-29-1991)
ELLIOT, Juanita E.- (12-1-1929 -   )

ESTEP, Ewel N.- (1899 - 1990)
ESTEP, Della M.- (1905 - 1973)
ESTEP, Donald Junior- (12-18-1939 - 5-21-1984) {Cpl. US Army}
ESTEP, Robert A. "Bob"- (4-24-1915 - 11-24-1968)

ESTEP, Lottie Bailey- (6-2-1917 - 2-18-1996)

FLETCHER, Hazel J. Caudill- (4-7-1911 - 6-23-1966)

GIBSON, Mildred C.- (11-21-1921 - 1-17-1998)

GWYN, James M.- (7-11-1927 - 3-16-1979) {US Army}
GWYN, William C.- (6-7-1897 - 11-3-1945)
GWYN, Hessie- (9-21-1899 - 3-23-1963)

HAGY, Walter C.- (4-17-1907 - 11-8-1980) {Dad}
HAGY, Fannie P.- (2-10-1914 - 6-23-1977) {Mom}
HAGY, Roy C.- (6-4-1934 - 7-2-1982) {Dad}
HAGY, Linda D.- (9-11-1960 -   )
HAGY, Luther D.- (10-22-1946 - 3-19-1991) {Dad}

HALL, Helen G.- (3-10-1928 -   )
HALL, Rebecca Jane- (11-23-1904 - 4-4-1989)
HALL, Harry Frank, Sr.- (1-15-1905 - 9-9-1949)
HALL, Patsy Jean- (8-12-1960 - 8-18-1960)
HALL, Harry Frank, III- (d. 1962) {Lived 13 hours}
HALL, Lula Dorton- (6-9-1882 - 4-25-1958)
HALL, Dave M.- (3-15-1898 - 12-11-1962)
HALL, Franklin C.- (3-17-1925 - 11-17-1971) { USAF Korea & Vietnam }

HARLESS, Christopher Paul- (6-13-1918 - 1-21-1997)

HARMAN, John Douglas- (12-11-1936 - 2-25-1985)
HARMAN, Deborah Kay- (1950 - 1971)
HARMAN, Helen Peery- (1912 - 1968)
HARMAN, J. Hoge- (1-28-1912 - 8-10-1992) {US Navy WW II}
HARMAN, J. Hoge, Sr.- (6-19-1879 - 3-4-1935)
HARMAN, Mary Kitts- (5-12-1883 - 12-8-1960)
HARMAN, C. Woodrow, Jr.- (b. & d. 10-14-1959) {Stillborn}
HARMAN, C. Woodrow, Sr.- (9-5-1913 - 5-7-1972)
HARMAN, Ruby A.- (9-7-1918 -   )
HARMAN, Billy Carter- (12-20-1921 - 8-3-1991) {US Army WW II}
HARMAN, Elfriede- (1-8-1926 -   )

HART, John A.- (5-3-1899 - 2-10-1976)
HART, Ethel- (4-23-1909 -   )

HAVENS, Wiley Brown- (1903 - 1968)
HAVENS, Macie Lucille- (1907 - 1989)
HAVENS, Jewell P.- (5-8-1925 - 9-1-1989) {US Army WW II}

HOOSIER, William Allen, Jr.- (12-1-1953 -   )
HOOSIER, Sandra M. Bivens- (3-24-1957 -   )   {Md. 9-5-1973}
HOOSIER, April Christine- (4-4-1974 -   )
HOOSIER, Arthur W.- (8-18-1900 - 12-5-1983)

HULL, LLoyd C.- (6-23-1905 - 4-2-1979)
HULL, Geneva S.- (1-2-1910 - 5-9-1996)
HULL, Roby- (1902 -   ) {Father}
HULL, Ida F.- (1906 - 1965) {Mother}
HULL, Minnis E.- (9-26-1935 - 2-23-1972) {Brother}
HULL, Ruth Eva- (7-6-1925 - 6-20-1998)
HULL, Danny Ray- (6-7-1951 - 7-15-1995)
HULL, Leora G.- (5-10-1932 - 1-9-1996)
HULL, Emory T.- (8-13-1927 -   )
HULL, Johnny Ray- (1-7-1953 - 5-27-1980)
HULL, Norman F.- (1922 - 1972) {WW II}
HULL, Jessie Rae- (1927 -   )

KIDD, Franklin Chaplin- (1-15-1907 - 4-13-1978) { US Navy WW II}
KIDD, Ollie B.- (1-15-1911 - 3-1-1996) {Md. 5-8-1929}
KIDD, Larry Donald- (2-28-1932 - 7-18-1985) {US Army Korea}
KIDD, Nannie Leedy- (12-1-1875 - 6-3-1973) {W/O Henderson M. Kidd}
KIDD, Henderson M.- (11-18-1867 - 2-11-1947)
KIDD, Carl E.- (9-15-1904 - 6-24-1937) {Air Corps.}

KIRK, Madeline Neal- (8-23-1933 - 11-25-1983)
KIRK, Kathleen Diana- (8-3-1953 - 3-22-1958)

KITTS, J.W. (James Walker)-
KITTS, Ethel Kidd- (
KITTS, Machie Claudine- (
KITTS, Pinkie- (6-18-1915 - 1-14-1978)
KITTS, Straley- (4-24-1907 - 12-18-1977)
KITTS, Linda Joy- (1-13-1955 - 1-15-1955)
KITTS, Estel- (b. & d. 8-17-1939)
KITTS, Buddy Charles- (7-12-1938 - 5-10-1956)
KITTS, Floyd- (1-23-1909 - 7-5-1962)
KITTS, Uva- (8-28-1910 - 3-14-1990)
KITTS, Myrtle Mae Gwyn- (12-2-1914 - 3-12-1990)

LAMBERT, Pete H.- (12-18-1885 - 10-30-1941)
LAMBERT, Minnie V.- (1-1-1885 - 3-20-1953) {W/O Pete H.}

LANE, George J.- (2-14-1907 - 5-30-1981)
LANE, Laura Kate- (8-27-1912 -   )

LEEDY, Eli- (9-15-1807 - 1-19-1899) {There are two stones for Eli
LEEDY. One field stone and one store bought.
LEEDY, Mary- (2-6-1842 - 8-10-1937)

LEFLER, Roby- (6-1-1888 - 1-20-1973)
LEFLER, Gertie- (1-23-1901 - 6-5-197?

LEFTWICH, Roy "Jake"- (5-5-1916 - 3-6-1995)
LEFTWICH, Helen Bruce- (9-2-1922 - 8-7-1989)

LESTER, Taulby M.- (1903 - 1962)
LESTER, Ollie N.- (1899 - 1964)

LESTER, Curtis- (10-1-1933 - 9-7-1998)

LOONEY, Crockett- (1890 - 1969)
LOONEY, Pricy Jane- (1895 - 1966)

LUCAS, Earnest L. "Luke"- (8-5-1914 - 7-24-1992)
LUCAS, Jewell G.- (3-16-1941 -   ) {S/O Luke & Grace Lucas}

MARTIN, Viola E.- (6-27-1909 - 2-10-1090)
MARTIN, Gerald S.- (6-7-1938 - 12-9-1955)

McFADDEN, Myrtle Lee- (4-8-1908 - 5-31-1972)

MCPEAK, Ruth Lane- (4-28-1936 - 3-19-1967)

MEADOWS, Elizabeth- (1855 - 1943) {Grandmother}
MEADOWS, Frank- (1845 - 1912) {Grandfather} {Civil War Veteran}

MILLER, John Edward- (7-20-1939 - 1-12-1991)
MILLER, Beverly Gail Pennington- (3-26-1944 -   ) {Md. 8-26-1960}

MUNCY, Tunis Winston- (7-7-1864 - 10-4-1935)
MUNCY, Hester Ann- (9-19-1863 - 2-4-1953)
MUNCY, Lily Frances- (2-13-1889 - 11-18-1951)

NEAL, Louisa H.- (5-21-1895 - 8-6-1914)
NEAL, Roy Alven- (9-23-1898 - 11-6-1973)
NEAL, Ida Ella Wynn- (7-5-1878 - 2-23-1928)
NEAL, Lafayette- (3-12-1876 - 2-16-1944)

OAKES, C.C.-(1934 - 1964)

PARKS, William M.- (5-29-1910 - 1-31-1998) {Dad}
PARKS, Josephine- (12-7-1915 -   )   {Mom}
PARKS, Monroe F.- (10-13-1873 - 2-23-1954){Spanish American War Vet.}

PARNELL, Ethel N.- (1911 - 1989) {Mother}
PARNELL, Gordon W.- (1898 - 1966) {Father}
PARNELL, Arnold P.- (1955 - 1969)

PATTON, Richard- (4-15-1885 - 3-22-1956)
PATTON, Ella Peery- (12-23-1883 - 4-3-1954)

PEERY, Elizabeth M.- (6-6-1920 -   )
PEERY, Kermit C.- (12-19-1917 - 1-6-1984) {US Air Force Korea, WW II}
PEERY, Jessie C.- (11-18-1899 - 10-26-1949)
PEERY, Gordon H.- (4-16-1880 - 11-4-1947)
PEERY, Lelia E.- (8-4-1882 - 10-11-1965)
PEERY, Thomas Herbert- (2-28-1915 - 12-23-1950} {US Army WW II Korea}

PENNINGTON, Sarah M.- (1896 - 1968) {Mother}
PENNINGTON, J. Garfield- (1889 - 1966) {Father}
PENNINGTON, June- (1-12-1930 -   )
PENNINGTON, Garland S.- (6-20-1920 - 7-17-1996)
PENNINGTON, Nannie Rose- (2-28-1910 - 11-18-1968) {Nee Harman}
PENNINGTON, Shelby Ann- (7-31-1942 - 10-27-1942)
PENNINGTON, Jo Ed- (5-26-1938 - 5-27-1938)

RASNAKE, Johnny David- (8-15-1950 - 8-28-1990)
RASNAKE, Asa-
RASNAKE, Mildred-

RASNICK, James E.- (1894 - 1972)
RASNICK- Mattie B.- (1897 - 1975)

RATLIFF, Elsie V.- (3-25-1912)
RATLIFF, Walter F.- (5-25-1915 - 4-19-1992) {Mother}
RATLIFF, Barbara Dean- (3-5-1993) {Only date}
RATLIFF, Charles Henry- (9-14-1910 - 9-6-1995)
RATLIFF, Mary Pet- (1915 - 1982)
RATLIFF, James Roland- (1938 - 1954)
RATLIFF, Edward- (1-20-1903 - 9-1-1996) {Pvt. US Army WWII}
RATLIFF, Jamie Leigh- (4-24-1962 - 1-4-1978)
RATLIFF, Eden Lawrence, Jr.- (7-1-1923 - 4-21-1981)

ROBINSON, Charles Wes- (9-8-1966 - 3-7-1996) {Son}

ROGERS, Isaia M.- (2-27-1905 - 4-2-1979)
ROGERS, Vicie- (1914 - 1973)
ROGERS, Emitt- (1897 - 1973)

RUDDER, Harry T. Jr.- (9-13-1968) {Only date. A baby.}

SARGENT, William Walter- (1880 - 1964)
SARGENT, Ida Pearl- (11-9-1889 - 2-20-1974) {Mother}

SARVER, Mose- (5-15-1879 - 1-27-1938)
SARVER, Lillie Steele- (1-9-1892 - 6-21-1973)
SARVER, {Picture but no name ordates}

SCOTT, Joe W.- (11-22-1925 - 7-27-1958)

SEXTON, Lafayette- (3-24-1893 - 2-9-1953) {VA Pvt. Engineers WW II)

SHORT, John W.- (10-10-1897 - 8-1-1983)
SHORT, Myrtle (9-15-1900 - 2-19-1989)
SHORT, Paul R.- (1943 - 1943)
SHORT, James R.- (1944 - 1944)
SHORT, James F.- (1910 - 1967)
SHORT, Margaret- (1922 -   )

SHORT, Vicy Childress- (8-11-1865 - 6-30-1951)
SHORT, William Henry- (4-20-1894 - 3-28-1982)

SHUFFLEBARGER, Dave N.(Newton)- 3-21-1893 - 7-25-1969) {US Army WW I}
SHUFFLEBARGER, Elizabeth B.- (2-28-1898 - 4-9-1993) {W/O Dave N.}
SHUFFLEBARGER, Newton S.-(No dates) {CSA marker, hus. of Ann Wygal)
SHUFFLEBARGER, C. Bruce- (11-19-1920 - 6-23-1994) {AKA "Murph"}

SIMPKINS, Ada W.- (1900 - 1972) {Mother}
SIMPKINS, Fred J.- (1901 - 1994) {Father}

SINK, Kevin D.- (9-11-1974 -   )

SLUSS, Ronald- (7-10-1945 - 11-2-1945)
SLUSS, ??? ??   (4-19-1900 - 6-30-1972)
SLUSS, Mary Margaret- (3-29-1908 - 8-18-1980)

SMITH, Marcell- (10-7-1932 - 6-22-1994)
SMITH, Gentry- (2-22-1897 - 5-17-1986) {US Army WW I}
SMITH, Dane D.- 8-5-1897 - 5-22-1978)
SMITH, Nannie J.- (3-12-1891 - 2-25-1970)

STACY, Ronald A.-
STACY, Dorothy L.-
STACY, Malum C.- (5-25-1882 - 10-17-1972)
STACY, Beatrice Q.- (6-6-1894 - 6-5-1957)

STARKS, Larence E.- (12-1-1909 - 6-23-1966)

STEFFEY, Stanley Todd- (3-27-1970 - 5-14-1984)
STEFFEY, Brenda G.- (1955 - 1955)
STEFFEY, Emmett Wilburn- (1921 - 1992)
STEFFEY, Catherine Iola- (12-17-1919 - 11-10-1998) {Age 78}

STOWERS, Earl B.- (3-4-1903 - 1-10-1967)
STOWERS, Kathleen- (5-10-1909 - 3-10-1986)
STOWERS, Ella L. Tolbert- (9-12-1931 - 10-9-1963)

TESTER, Pauleen- (4-8-1908 - 2-16-1979)
TESTER, Bert- (12-8-1902 - 10-22-1978)
TESTER, Karl B.- 11-10-1936 - 10-4-1993)

THOMAS, Denzial A.- (6-9-1920 - 12-31-1993) {Pfc. US Army WW II}
THOMAS, Nellie S.- (12-1-1925 - 11-11-1983)
THOMAS, Arnold- (1-3-1948 - 3-17-1989)
THOMAS, C.E., Jr.- (3-8-1928 - 8-11-1993) {US Navy, Korea}
THOMAS, Clarence E.- (8-11-1893_ - 5-30-1964) {US Air Force}
THOMAS, Bessie Bailey- (9-29-1897 - 7-1-1984)
THOMAS, Ballard- (1869 - 1939)
THOMAS, Jack I.B.- (1895 - 1968)

THOMAS, Sheffie-
THOMAS, Douglas J.- (1932 -   ) {Sgt. US Army Ret. Vietnam}
THOMAS, Jasper E.- 11-1-1901 - 12-28-1954)
THOMAS, Maggie N.- (3-25-1907 - 3-27-1990)
THOMAS, Baby Girl, (born & died 10-1936)
THOMAS, Donald M.- (10-13-1937 - 4-7-1938)

THOMPSON, Tara Jane- (9-19-1971) {Birth or death date?}
THOMPSON, Dewey C.- (8-19-1899 - 6-23-1970)
THOMPSON, Leona C.- (4-28-1906 - 7-24-1971)
THOMPSON, Roy B.- (1894 - 1965)
THOMPSON, Annie B. (1898 - 1984)
THOMPSON, Harry Ray- (1-26-1919 - 12-15-1958)

TOLBERT, Ola P.- (8-18-1905 -   )
TOLBERT, Mason B.- (12-12-1899 - 1-18-1968) {S/O John B. & Mariah T-}

TURNER, Ralph Willis- (9-14-1913 - 1-21-1972) {Husband}
TURNER, Phyllis Bruce- (1-9-1930 - 4-16-1972) {Wife}

VANDELL, Virginia Alice- (9-7-1918 - 3-31-1997)

VANOVER, W. H.- (6-9-1889 - 8-3-1953)
VANOVER, Stella M.- (10-1-1891 - 6-8-1982)
VANOVER, Mary E.- (1916 - 1965)
VANOVER, Johnie L.- (1913 -   )

WALKER, Darren R.- (10-29-1962 - 9-14-1983)

WALTERS, John Bill- (3-20-1909 - 7-26-1992)
WALTERS, Lucille S.- (1-31-1906 - 6-6-1979) {Nee Shufflebarger}

WEDDLE, James F.- (1922 - 1976) {US Army WW II}

WOODY, James F.- (1918 - 1942) {US Army WW II, grave near Gwynn plot}

WYRICK, Rudolph- (9-27-1921 -   )
WYRICK, Betty R.- (1-27-1927 - 1-2-1987) {W/O Rudolph}

24 graves with blank funeral home markers.
1 grave with no marker
1 cinderblock marker, no name or dates.
1 funeral home marker, illegible.
3 field stones
1 field stone and foot stone denoting a child's grave.

HONAKER - TUGGLE CEMETERY
[Located southwest of intersection of I 77 and State Route 61 on
  State Route 52 upon a hill. Near Mining Research and Affordable
  Denture facilities. It is a large cemetery with several field
  stones and is in good condition and is easily accessible by car]
    {Compiled by Jo Ann Tickle Scott January 26,1999}

ANDREWS, Thomas- (1875 - 1953)
ANDREWS, Jessie L.- (5-26-1905 - 2-26-1986)
ANDREWS, Eugene R.- (1935 - 1982) {US Air Force}

BAILEY, Matilda Jarrell- (4-4-1848 - 10-28-1912) {W/O G. G. Bailey,
                                 gave her age as 30 on 1880 Census}
BAILEY, G.G.- (8-9-1842 - 6-5-1893) {Listed as "G.C." on 1880 census)
BAILEY, J. Kenna- (4-7-1875 - 7-19-1877){S/O James & Julia H. Bailey}
BAILEY, Julia Haven- (10-6-1855 - 3-10-1883) {W/O James M. Bailey}
BIRD, Mary J.M.- (1851 - 1936) {W/O J. Harry Bird}
BIRD, J. Harry- (1849 -1941) {Md. 7-29-1869)
BIRD, Carl C.- (4-24-1916 - 11-17-1918) {S/O C.H. & S.H. Bird}

CALDWELL, F. Amy- (1896-   )
CALDWELL, J. Ernest- (1885 -1964)
CALDWELL, Asa Cline- (9-14-1888 - 12-7-1962)
CALDWELL, Myra Grace- (9-9-1894 - 12-7-1932) {W/O Asa C. Caldwell}
CALDWELL, N. N.- (8-26-1836 - 3-14-1917)
CALDWELL, Sarah A.- (7-9-1845 - 3-13-1912) {W/O N.N. Caldwell}
CALDWELL, Oscar W.- (5-13-1877 - 10-14-1935) {Brother}
CALDWELL, Walter C.- (10-8-1880 - 10-14-1935) {Brother}
CALDWELL, Oscar W. Jr., -(5-10-1932 - 12-10-1950)
CONLEY, Anne Brookman- (1890 - 1943) {W/O Joseph Allen Conley}
CONLEY, Joseph Allen- (1889 - 1955)
COX, George D.- (?-28-1903 - ????) {Stone set to deep to read}

DAVIDSON, Mary Tuggle- (1884 - 1964)

GIBSON, Edward- (9-2-1817 - 7-14-1884)

HONAKER, Infant- (10-17-1907 - 10-18-1907) {S/O J.D. & Annie Honaker}
HONAKER, Gaston S.- (12-23-1893 - 8-7-1907){S/O James & Sallie J.}
HONAKER, Juanita J.- (2-26-1901 - 11-6-1902){ S/O James & Sallie J.}
HONAKER, Infant- (b.& d. 4-19-1888) {S/o James D. & Belle B. Honaker}
HONAKER, Infant- (b.& d. 2-28-1889) {D/o James D. & Belle Bailey H--}
HONAKER, James D.- (4-4-1850 - 5-17-1919)
HONAKER, Belle Bailey- (9-22-1850 - 8-3-1903) {W/O James D. Honaker}
HONAKER, James D.- (4-4-1850 - 5-17-1919)
HONAKER, James C.- (1869 - 1934)
HONAKER, Sallie J.- (1869 - 1953) {W/O James C. Honaker}
HONAKER, James Eugene- (12-6-1895 - 8-30-1901)
HONAKER, Sarepta Graham- (10-24-1901 - 6-4-1971)
HONAKER, John Davidson- (3-11-1912 - 9-25-1913)
HONAKER, Eloise- (6-21-1898 - 7-5-1995)
HONAKER, John B.- (5-26-1900 - 10-28-1982)
HONAKER, Joseph H.- (1-28-1841 - 7-6-1844)

HONAKER, Peter C. Jr.- (10-6-1853 - 9-22-1899)
HONAKER, Peter C. Sr.- (10-10-1812 - 12-9-1874)
HONAKER, Mary A.- (8-5-1823 - 4-21-1887)
HURT, Gala Mae- (2-4-1896 - 4-24-1899)

KELLY, Wythe C.- (4-10-1899 - 9-13-1902)

LAMBERT, Elbert T.- (10-26-1875 - 1-17-1957)
LAMBERT, Cora G.- (1-13-1880 - 2-10-1969)
LAMBERT, Clayton- (6-12-1905 - 12-15-1913)
{ Elbert T. KELLY Family written on huge stone}

LINKOUS, Infant- (b. & d. 5-28-1895) {S/O John R. & Lizzie Linkous}
LINKOUS, John Rabourn- (5-6-1851 - 12-20-1899)
LINKOUS, Izzie Virginia- (5-20-1861 - 4-7-1945) {W/O John Rabourn}

NUNN, George- (6-11-1919 - 6-20-1919) {S/O James J. & Martha}
NUNN, James J.- (1880 - 1966)
NUNN, Martha B.- (1893 - 1977) {W/O James J. Nunn}

STEWART, Everet C.- (7-21-1907 - 9-20-1907)
STEWART, Arthur Wade- (4-16-1885 - 12-8-1957)
STEWART, Annie Effie- (3-26-1886 - 7-9-1971)
SMITH, Syble J.- (11-10-1922 - 11-20-1922) {D/O Bentley & Jane Smith}
SMITH, J. D.- (1875 - 1959)
SMITH, Ethel J.- (1870 - 1959) {W/O J. D. Smith} {FHM}

TALBERT, Albert B.- (4-9-1920 - 4-10-1920)
TUGGLE, Steven Allen- (3-28-1953 - 12-16-1994)
TUGGLE, John R.- (7-31-1914 - 7-20-1985) {Sgt. US Army WW II}
TUGGLE, Martha G.- 1927 - 1991) {W/O John R. Tuggle}
TUGGLE, Elizabeth Mustard- (12-12-1918 - 6-5-1988) {D/O James C. &
                              Rose Mustard Tuggle}
TUGGLE, Mary Louise- (12-21-1918 - 6-5-1988){D/O Rose Mustard Tuggle}
TUGGLE, James Conrad- (1881 - 1966) {H/O Rose Mustard}
TUGGLE, Rose Mustard- (1883-1968){D/O W.N. & Eliz C.Newberry Mustard}
TUGGLE, James C. Jr.- (1-10-1917 - 2-9-1917) {S/O James & Rose}
TUGGLE, Raleigh R.- (4-26-1887 - 10-14-1906)
TUGGLE, Matilda J.- (1-22-1860 - 5-4-1944) {W/O J. M. Tuggle}
TUGGLE, J. M. - (10-5-1856 - 5-17-1936)
TUGGLE, Joan- (6-10-1930 - 6-17-1930) {D/O W.D. Tuggle)

WALL, Claud- (7-29-1915 - 9-18-1915) {D/O D.D. & A. M. Wall}
WALL, Samuel- (1862 - 9-28-1920)

WATTS, Rev. Richard W.- (8-11-1880 - 3-22-1946){H/O Darcie}
WATTS, Darcie Maud- (4-29-1887 - 3-4-1987) {Md. 4-17-1921}

WOLPEN, Cora Ellis- (1878 - 1963) {FHM}

WOODYARD, Izzie Estelle- (7-30-1905 - 1-2-1906)

SUNNY POINT CEMETERY
[Located north of State Route 61 about 3 miles west of intersection
with I-77. There is a sign in front and stone steps leading up to the
site which is on the side of a steep hill. There are at least 50-60
field stones. The cemetery is well kept. Once there was a Sunny Point
Church in this vicinity.]
{ Compiled by Jo Ann Tickle Scott, February 26, 1999 }

BELCHER, Mollie S.- (1878 - 1951)

BURTON, Ballard James- (4-17-1898 - 8-23-1968)
{ A stone face down which I could not lift. Probably w/o Ballard J.}
BURTON, Marvin Earl- (10-4-1931 - 8-26-1985) {Brother}

DUNCAN, Bogle H.- (1895 - 1958)
DUNCAN, Ada G.- (1911 - 1941) {W/O Bogle H. Duncan}
DUNCAN, Silas N.- (5-24-1857 - 4-8-1917)
DUNCAN, James A.- (7-29-1828 - 4-22-1907)
DUNCAN, Mary A.- (9-22-1827 - 12-4-1903) {W/O James A. Duncan}
DUNCAN, Lillie Myrtle- (8-17-1884 - 8-24-1903)

FRENCH, James Clayton- (3-15-1915 - 9-5-1965)

GIBSON, Edward J.- (5-11-1908 - 2-14-1957)
GIBSON, Samuel E.- (8-15-1881 - 5-19-1955) {Father}
GIBSON, Rosa Neal- (7-31-1889 - 3-19-1968) {Mother}

HUNT, Lelia Gibson- (8-20-1910 - 12-7-1942)
HUNT, George Glen, Jr.- (4-10-1931 - 3-19-1954)

LINKOUS, Sallie Stowers- (12-8-1883 - 10-8-1974) {Mother}
LINKOUS, James M.- (1883 - 1959) {Father}

PRUETT, Gracie May- (12-28-1845 - 5-11-1917) {W/O W.W. Pruett)
PRUETT, W.W.- (7-29-1885 - 10-18-1918)
PRUETT, David Pierce- (5-16-1919 - 1-25-1990) {AKA Roscoe}
PRUETT, Ruby Burton- (11-26-1922 - 6-15-1991)
PRUETT, Wiley W.- (2-14-1911 - 1-12-1979)
PRUETT, Linda Darlene- (11-20-1954 -   ) {Wife/Mother}
PRUETT, Jerry Lee, (6-16-1951 - 11-20-1984) {Husband/Father}
PRUETT, M.- (11-15-1981) {Birth or death date?}
PRUETT, Louisa- (7-29-1884 - 1-20-1962) {Wife}
PRUETT, Sam- (4-11-1883 - 3-19-1937) {Husband}
PRUETT, Edgar W.- (12-3-1904 - 8-25-1973) {S/O Louisa & Sam}

REED, Phillip Edward, Jr.- (8-30-1952 - 8-20-1995) {S/O M.A. & M.I. }

RICHARDSON, Infant (1913) {S/O W.H. & M. A. Richardson}

SHRADER, T. Lafayette- (3-23-1882 - 5-6-1918)

SMITH, Earl Henderson- (9-14-1919 - 8-21-1927) {S/O John E. & Sarah}
SMITH, Clarence Elmer- (9-5-1925 - 1-27-1928)

SMITH, George Lockard- (5-19-1872 - 4-6-1944) {Father}
SMITH, Susie Catherine- (3-10-1884 - 6-11-1962) {Mother}
SMITH, Sarah Jane Stowers- (3-21-1903 - 9-2-1975)
SMITH, John Ed- (5-29-1899 - 6-2-1977)

STOWERS, Henry W.- 1-8-1872 - 8-15-1906)
STOWERS, Mason L.- (1-17-1886 - 3-1-1947)
STOWERS, James Harvey- (1848 - 1927)
STOWERS, Mary P.- (died 11-19-1902) {Age 72 years}
STOWERS, Jackson- (no dates) { Co F, VA Inf. CSA}
STOWERS, Irene- (3-7-1904 - 7-5-1912)
STOWERS, G. H.- (8-19-1879 - 4-4-1954)
STOWERS, Roy B.- (9-7-1912 - 1-8-1972) {Father}
STOWERS, John M.- (1-24-1883 - 12-11-1968)
STOWERS, Charles B.- (3-17-1921 - 3-29-1963)
STOWERS, Stella B.- (10-8-1921 -   ) {Md. 3-28-1943}
STOWERS, Margaret Sue- (8-21-1941 - 1-28-1942)
STOWERS, Richard Keith- (3-1-1959 - 7-19-1980)
STOWERS, Hazel Gay- (1-16-1908) {Daughter. Birth or death date?}
STOWERS, Gaston B.- (4-19-1889 - 3-12-1959) {Father}
STOWERS, Onnie Mae- (8-25-1882 - 12-20-1971) {Mother}
STOWERS, Daniel W.- (10-16-1883 - 9-21-1952) {Father}
STOWERS, Milda Beatrice- (11-5-1885 - 4-23-1961) {W/O Daniel W.}
STOWERS, Benton- (4-3-1907 - 11-16-1959) {Father}
STOWERS, Nannie B.- (10-13-1908 - 7-14-1996) {Mother}

THOMPSON, Mary Jane- (5-28-1869 - 9-12-1933) {W/O M. A. Thompson}
THOMPSON, M. A.- (11-4-1859 - 12-25-1940)
THOMPSON, Lacy Carrell- (8-15-1911 - 3-9-1913) {S/O R.M & wife}
THOMPSON, Eugene T.- (died 5-5-1902) {Age 2mos & 2 days}
THOMPSON, William E. G.- (9-22-1887 - 6-30-1990)

WALTERS, James W.- (4-20-1873 - 8-22-1956)
WALTERS, Sallie B.- (2-23-1876 - 9-22-1960)

WILEY, Ella Ollie- (10-6-1868 - 9-9-1945)
WILEY, Newton J.- (8-29-1869 - 1-16-1931)
WILEY, Attelia- (5-27-1860 - 6-11-1884)
WILEY, William A.- (10-3-1885 - 7-24-1883)
WILEY, Susan A.- (10-21-1829 - 3-12-1907) {W/O James Edward}
WILEY, James Edward- (10-6-1830 - 3-18-1914)
WILEY, J. L.- (3-8-1855 - 9-29-1921) {S/O James E. & Susan A.}
WILEY, A. J.- (5-10-1900 - 1-28-1955) {AKA "Orb"}
WILEY, Bess J.- (5-10-1905 - 3-3-1965) {W/O A. J. Wiley}
WILEY, Flossie Bowles- (12-10-1928 - 6-9-1969)
WILEY, Connie B.- (4-24-1900 - 3-6-1978) {Mother}
WILEY, R. S.- (7-4-1858 - 3-36-1915)
WILEY, George E.- (12-10-1897 - 10-12-1907) {S/O R.A. & M. E. Wiley}

STIMSON FAMILY CEMETERY

[Cemetery is located about 4 miles west of the intersection of I-77 north of Star Route 61. It is beside of, what appears to be an old church, and just before you cross a cement bridge. There are 3 houses close by. It is in excellent condition and is easily accessible.]
{ Compiled February 26, 1999 by Jo Ann Tickle Scott. }

ASHWORTH, William W.- (8-2-1821 - 6-7-1909)
ASHWORTH, Julina- (10-12-1819 - 1-24-1892) {W/O William W.}
ASHWORTH, Mary Rosalie- (6-16-1878 - 3-23-1914)
ASHWORTH, Infant-(3-20-1914){Child of Mr. & Mrs S.R. Ashworth}

ATKINS, William M.- (3-29-1852 - 11-10-1947){H/O Cynthia N. Atkins}

BAILEY, Lucie B.- (4-29-1886 - 3-15-1905)
BAILEY, William G.- (2-21-1887 - 9-12-1885)
BAILEY, Infant- (4-27-1904 - 5-3-1904) {D/O J. March & Effie V.}

BIRD, John, Jr.- (9-4-1920 - 7-9-1958)
BIRD, Sidney- (3-7-1895 - 3-9-1895) {S/O Johnson B. & Luvicy}
BIRD, Johnson B.- (10-4-1861 - 9-13-1935)
BIRD, Luvicy V.- (11-7-1862 - 2-22-1949) {W/O) Johnson B. Bird}
BIRD, John J.- (6-29-1891 - 9-25-1946) {Masonic emblem}
BIRD, Archie Willard- (8-23-1907 - 12-27-1954) {Husband}
BIRD, Poliny- (1-28-1907 - 1-16-1981) {Wife}
BIRD, Earl Thompson- (12-24-1901 - 9-26-1956)

BISHOP, Naomi John- (7-10-1826 - 9-11-1898) {2nd w/o William M.}
BISHOP, William M.- (5-11-1824 - 7-29-1897)
BISHOP, Lucy A. Wiley- (1827 - 4-8-1860) {1st w/o William M.}
BISHOP, William Ferguson- (4-2-1859 - 6-2-1879) {S/O William & Lucy}
BISHOP, Ella Morgan- (10-26-1871 - 1-17-1900) {W/O Dr. J.J. Bishop}

BROWN, John W.- 8-31-1830 - 8-3-1902) {H/O Lucy A.}
BROWN, J. Milton- (9-7-1848 - 3-26-1874) {H/O L. Annie}

CALDWELL, Mary Jane- (6-10-1917 - 1-18-1969)

CARVER, Charlie- (1880 - 1959)
CARVER, Lucy Kate- (8-22-1902 - 4-8-1982) {W/O Charlie}

DAVIS, John B.- (1890 - 1958)
DAVIS, Rose E.- (1890 - 1972) {Nee Stimson, w/o John B. Davis}
DAVIS, Kathryn A.- (1-30-1951 - 1-18-1952)
DAVIS, Tyler R.- (2-9-1872 - 4-11-1956) {Husband}
DAVIS, Betty M.- (9-9-1889 - 4-13-1951) {Wife}

FAULKNER, Adam Ray- (D. 4-6-1983) {Twin}
FAULKNER, Michael John- (D. 4-6-1983) {Twin}

FOX, Sallie J.- (12-14-1874 - 8-23-1913) {W/O Tom B.}
FOX, Tom B.- (8-8-1912 - 11-25-1925) {S/O T. B. & Sallie Jane Fox}

STIMSON FAMILY CEMETERY

GUY, Walter Wiley- (10-28-1887 - 12-29-1972)
GUY, Rachel Leah- (3-23-1895 - 1-21-1901) {D/O S. William & Genettie}
GUY, Mollie Kate- (11-14-1892 - 4-24-1942)
GUY, S. William- (9-6-1860 - 7-13-1942)
GUY, Genettie Stowers- (1-2-1854 - 1-21-1936) {W/O S. William}

JONES, Luther D.- (1904 - 1940)

KITTS, Ann L.- (no dates) {Infant d/o J.W. & M. L. Kitts}

LEFTWICH, Lola B.- (12-28-1889 - 7-5-1903) {D/O F.W. & E.M. Leftwich}
LEFTWICH, Eliza M.- (3-1-1855 - 10-17-1918) {W/O F. W. Leftwich}

MOREHEAD, William C.-(7-29-1920 - 4-28-1991){US Army WW II, aka Bill}
MOREHEAD, Beulah Lee- (7-19-1921 -   ) {W/O William C, nee Caldwell}

NEAL, Sam J.- (9-18-1902 - 9-11-1956)
NEAL, Annie E.- (8-13-1913 -   ) {W/O Sam J. Neal}

PRUETT, Sallie Ann Bird Caldwell-(9-21-1887 - 11-1-1978)

ROBINETT, Osie- (3-10-1889 - 12-4-190?) {W/O H.G., nee Laurance}

STIMSON, Samuel Evans- (1848 - 1929)
STIMSON, Mary E. Ashworth- (1850 - 1927) {W/O Samuel Evans Stimson}
STIMSON, Ellis B.- (12-1-1877 - 9-24-1882) {S/O N.B.& P.R.}
STIMSON, J. Wesley- (11-10-1880 - 6-21-1884) {S/O N.B. & P.R.}

STOWERS, Lucy Ann Bishop- (2-24-1854 - 4-26-1927) {W/O William N. L.}
STOWERS, William N. Linticum- (12-28-1889 - 7-5-1903)

TAYLOR, Orville R.- (1-24-1920 - 11-9-1976){US Army WW II}
TAYLOR, Sarah Caldwell- (11-8-1923 - 2-19-1976)

SUITER, Margaret Neel- (1-12-1842 - 12-28-1890)
SUITER, B. M. - (1-18-1830 - 8-3-1902)

THOMPSON, Elvira A.- (died 9-3-1882) { Age 54 yrs 8mos 6 days}
THOMPSON, E. G.- (8-31-1822 - 4-12-1882) {H/O Elvira}

TOLBERT, May Guy- (4-8-1890 - 3-25-1980) {W/O Edgar W.}
TOLBERT, Edgar W.- (10-12-1886 - 2-28-1972)
TOLBERT, John- (2-15-1926 - 9-27-1954) {S/O Edgar & May}
TOLBERT, Danny Ray- (9-1-1941 - 11-3-1957)
TOLBERT, Edd Ray- (4-12-1920 - 4-15-1997)

WOODYARD, Rosa Belle- (9-20-1882 - 1-12-1883)
WOODYARD, William S.- (8-24-1855 - 1-18-1885)
WOODYARD, Levi S.- (11-4-1824 - 11-5-1905)

{ About 20 field stones with no names or dates }

STEELE FAMILY CEMETERY
[Located north of State Route 61 about 8 miles from the junction
with I-77. On a hill north of the homestead. Easily accessed by foot]
{ Compiled by Jo Ann Tickle Scott, February 26, 1999 }

FOX, Jasper Lee- (11-19-1899 - 10-28-1908)
FOX, Ella L.- (3-9-1870 - 4-10-1937)
FOX, Lee J.- (5-9-1865 - 2-19-1943)

GREGORY, S. W.- (7-18-1873 - 3-9-1916)
GREGORY, George R.- (1-15-1868 - 8-16-1890) {S/O T.E. & Martha J.}
GREGORY, Marthe J.- (2-12-1841 - 12-21-1890) {W/O T.E. }
GREGORY, Thompson E.- (5-8-1841 - 2-20-1923)
GREGORY, Mary Ann- (4-6-1879 - 9-18-1908) {D/O T. E. & Martha}
GREGORY, Obed E.- (6-26-1890 - 11-11-1906) {S/O T.E. & Martha J.}
GREGORY, Ruth H.- (1-1-1903 - 1-17-1916)

LOONEY, Glenna Stowers- (12-11-1901 - 12-6-1935)

NEEL, Fred Roy Bogle- (8-30-1897 - 2-24-1899) {S/O J.E. & G.A. Neel}

SARVER, Lois S.- (b & d. 3-7-1930)

SHUFFLEBARGER, Gladys B.- (6-3-1896 - 6-10-1899) {D/O T.L. & Belle}

STARLING, G. W.- (7-23-1853 - 4-10-1933)
STARLING, Rebecca- (12-11-1846 - 2-4-1914) {W/O G. W. Starling}

STEELE, Thomas Eugene- (8-9-1926 - 3-27-1988)
STEELE, James Marvin- (4-14-1893 - 9-21-1956)
STEELE, Alberta Mae- (4-27-1894 - 12-13-1938)
STEELE, Geneva S.- (10-23-1874 - 12-14-1918)
STEELE, James Franklin- (12-26-1864 - 6-8-1954)
STEELE, Truby J.- (10-26-1900 - 12-5-1971)
STEELE, John J.- (7-19-1868 - 12-31-1947)
STEELE, Margaret B.- (11-20-1878 - 1-8-1967)
STEELE, Fannie V.- (10-4-1892 - 11-27-1899) {D/O John J.& Margaret}
STEELE, Mary Jane Wiley- (2-27-1917 - 12-23-1948)
STEELE, Carl Boling- (8-1-1907 - 5-25-1990)

STOWERS, Rebecca J.- (7-22-1866 - 4-22-1903)
STOWERS, Arthur Steele- (9-22-1889 - 8-28-1940) {Father}
STOWERS, Eva L.- (5-12-1912 - 2-21-1975) {Mother}
STOWERS, Andrew D.- (5-26-1914 - 5-28-1980) {US Army WW II}
STOWERS, Bessie M.- (11-21-1902 - 12-8-1990)
STOWERS, Walter- (5-??-1902 - 11-14-1966)

About 40 field stones with no names or dates.

COMPTON FAMILY CEMETERY

[Located north of State Route 52 between Bastain and the I-77 intersection at South Gap. It is enclosed by a red plank fence and can be
accessed by walking or truck. According to family history, there are
3 rows of family members, 1 row of slaves, 1 row of Indians and one
indentured servant. The farm has been in the family since the 1700's,
the house being built in 1804. My thanks to Harry Thompson, grand son
of Francis Marion Compton who now owns this beautiful farm.]
{Compiled by Jo Ann Tickle Scott, February 26, 1999 }

COMPTON, Francis Marion- (8-17-1850 - 2-28-1936)
COMPTON, Jesse T.- (5-19-1880 - 12-18-1911)
COMPTON, Rhoda Ann- (3-26-1853 - 1-8-1932)
COMPTON, James B.- (3-23-1856 - 7-13-1896)
COMPTON, William W.- (4-14-1824 - 4-27-1890)
COMPTON, Nancy C.- (12-10-1822 - 7-15-1910) {W/O William W.}

DAVIDSON, William Alexander- (9-15-1875 - 4-21-1966)
DAVIDSON, Nannie Jane- (6-12-1876 - 9-2-1971)
     { The two above graves are marked by a huge "DAVIDSON" stone.}

HAGER, Polly- (died 2-4-1905) {An indentured servant from England}

HARMAN, C.B- (no dates)
HARMAN, G. B. - (12-1-1854 - 4-22-1914)
HARMAN, Walter S.- (1881 - 1934)
HARMAN, Curtis Lee- (1-26-1925) (Twin) Birth or death date?
HARMAN, Kenneth Lee- (1-26-1925) (Twin) Birth or death date?

KIDD CEMETERY # 2

{ Located north of route 615 n Bastain. It is well fenced and in
excellent condition.}
          [Copied in 1998 by Jo Ann Tickle Scott.]

KIDD, Wiley W.- (4-1-1869 - 8-6-1933) S/O Elbert S.& Clara Muncy Kidd
KIDD, Effie G.- (11-21-1883 - 9-10-1942) {D/O James M. & Margaret Ann
        Martin Kidd. Md. 10-17-1906, Wiley W. Kidd, her 1st cousin.)
KIDD, Addison Winston- (no dates) {Corp. Co. F 8th VA Cav. CSA}
{ Addison Winston Kidd-(3-15-1836 - 3-24-1923) S/O George and Evelina
Suiter Kidd. He md. 1st, 10-5-1870 to Rebecca the widow of his
deceased brother John M. Kidd. He md. 2nd 5-29-1894, to Laura Jane
Muncy, step daughter of Elbert and Clara Muncy Kidd.

A stone in a spot by itself with "In memory of Mother" inscribed on
it.
{ Annotations from "Those Forgotten Ancestors" by Daniel S. Kidd, Jr.
  added by Parke C. Bogle}

H. J. LOONEY FAMILY CEMETERY

{Cemetery located at former Looney property, which now is owned by
the Wolfe Creek Golf Club. The site is North of Route 614 beside the
logging road that goes behind an A frame house directly across form
the Golf Club. The road is passable by 4x4 to the old home site, then
one must walk. There are many rock lilies around the old stones which
are still in good condition and none are broken.}
[Copied in 1998 by Jo Ann Tickle Scott.]

KIDD, Louisa V.- (9-29-1892 - 10-14-1920)

LOONEY, Margaret T.M.- (10-3-1919 - 5-11-1921)
LOONEY, Mary Alice- (10-1-1934 - 9-10-1946)
{ Three small stones with only the following- A.W.; VC; J.H.Looney}
LOONEY, Ida- (12-5-1897 - 1-20-1941)
LOONEY, Mary F.- (6-7-1862 - 4-23-1932)
LOONEY, Henry J.- (2-12-1852 - 9-3-1922)
LOONEY, Clyde Greever- (6-17-1911 - 9-27-1972) {USNR WWII}

REPASS CEMETERY # I

{Cemetery located on North side of Star Route 42, about 5 miles from
 the junction of Routes 42 and 52. Land owned by the Sages.}
[Copied in 1998 by Jo Ann Tickle Scott]

REPASS, James A.- (6-22-1831 - 6-26-1919) Age 79 yrs, 84 days.
{I Could see one more indentation. Cemetery was once much larger. The
only stone was face down. Barbed wire around the cemetery}

REPASS CEMETERY # 2

{ Cemetery is in good conditionand is located on North side of Star
 Route 42 about 6 miles from junction of Routes 42 and 52. One needs
 a 4x4 to reach it. The land is now owned by Bargers.
{ Copied by Jo Ann Tickle Scott in 1998.}

KIRBY, Mozelle M.- (5-7-1921 - 3-29-1939)
KIRBY, Lillie Kate- (1878 - 1943)
KIRBY, Sam B.- (1885 - 1950)
KIRBY, Joseph Blanton- (1880 - 1953)
KIRBY, Charles Norman- (1870 - 1955)
KIRBY, Lou Farley- (1875 - 1954)
KIRBY, John W.- (1839 - 1918)
KIRBY, Cynthia R.- (1847 - 1917)
KIRBY, Infant Son of J.W. & C.E. Kirby. (No dates)

LAMBERT, Ellen Kirby- (19-26-1875 - 8-5-1967)
LAMBERT, W. T. "Tade"- (6-1-1884 - 1-28-1973)

MCCORMICK, Mary Kirby- (1873 - 1933)

REPASS, Frederick- (8-18-1774 - 7-6-1861) { Born Fridrich Rippas, son
                of John Jacob & Anna Gerber Repass}
REPASS, Anna Gerber- (died 6-1801) age 73yrs 1 mo. & 24 days.

REPASS, Samuel- (4-13-1776 - about 1840) { Son of John Jacob and Anna
                    Gerber Repass. {H/O Mari Mateline Tarter}
                    { Mateline Tarter Repass born about 1778}
{ These Repass stones were erected by their descendants in 1997}
REPASS, John Winton- (10-5-1853 - 1-7-1854) {S/O J.S & Eliza Repass}
REPASS, Eliza J.- (9-11-1829 - 4-1-1874) {W/O Joseph}
REPASS, Joseph- (10-6-1825 - 11-28-1861)
{ One stone worn smooth and illegible and one plain field stone}
{ One stone with only the initials " S.R." on it.It may be the foot
  stone to Samuel Repass' grave}

REPASS, Lucinda J.- (1-5-1828 - 3-19-1902) {W/O James A. Repass. Nee
                    Suiter}
SHRADER, William L.- (1877 - 1959)
SHRADER, Mollie K.- (1906 -   ) {Nee Kirby}

STEELE, Charley Preston- (11-6-1887 - 6-20-1888) {S/O H.W. & V.J. }
STEELE, Ella Lee- (11-6-1887 - 10-11-1888) { Charley & Ella are twin
                    children of H.W. & V. J, Steele}
STEELE, James Maden- (5-21-1879 - 1-24-1902) {S/O H.V. & V.J. Steele}

WYRICK CEMETERY
{ Copied by Jo Ann Tickle Scott in July of 1998 }

HANCOCK, G.W- (no dates) { Co. A 1st VA Inf. CSA}

THOMPSON, James Kelly "Tom Cat"- (1937 - 1996)
THOMPSON, Pamela M. Gills- (1935 - 1997)

WYRICK, Lorenzo D.- (no dates) {Co. F, 45th VA Inf. CSA}
WYRICK, Robert Shockley- (3-22-1928) { S/o Dunn T. & Elva. Is it a
                    birth or death date?}
WYRICK, R.S.- (2-19-1924) {Is it a birth or death date?}
WYRICK, Dunn T.- (12-6-1929) {VA Pvt. 314 M.G. Batt. 7 N Div. Is it a
                    birth or death date?}
WYRICK, Ralph B.- (no dates) {Co. F. 45th VA Inf. CSA}

{ One field stone with " A.W.B." (12-25-1946)
{ One field stone with only "R.S.W." on it.}
{ 13 plain field stones and at lease 6 imprints}

OLD MADISON ALLEN CEMETERY
{ Located just across the Bland-Giles County line on Bland
Correctional farm. The Allen house, built in 1840, called "Oakley"
and was made from bricks hauled from West Virginia. Cemetery is in
excellent condition. One must walk to it. }
[Copied in October of 1998 by Jo Ann Tickle Scott]

ALLEN, Madison- (11-14-1808 - 6-13-1872)
ALLEN, Emily Susan Carpenter-(12-3-1834 - 4-28-1909) {2nd w/oMadison}
ALLEN, Madison-(4-27-1864 - 1-22-1966) {S/O Madison & Emily}
ALLEN, Fannie B.- (8-23-1854 - 4-7-1890)
ALLEN, M. Bane- (3-30-1883 - 7-7-1890) {S/O J. P. & Fannie B. Allen}

STROCK CEMETERY
{ Located just southeast of the Assistant Warden's house, near the
picnic area of the Bland Correctional Farm. A member of the Wilson
family says there were once at least 25 stones in this cemetery. }
[Copied in October of 1998 by Jo Ann Tickle Scott]

STROCK, Julia A.G.- (4-16-1853 - 6-7-1891) {Nee Price, 2nd w/o John
        F. Strock. He is buried at Mechanicsburg.
STROCK, George D.- (11-21-1876 - 1-14-1882) {S/O John & Julia}

ROBINETT FAMILY CEMETERY
{ On a hill behind the Ed Wimmer home, at the end of Route 604 }
{Copied by Philip Bogle in 1987. Annotated by Parke C. Bogle}

BROWN, Ballard Preston (Dates obscure) { S/O Col. George W. Brown and
        Emma Crump. He married Lucinda Robinett in 1867.
BROWN, Lucinda Robinett- (dates obscure) {W/O Ballard P. Brown. Dau
        of James and Jerusha Newberry Robinett}
        { Ballard and Lucinda were grandparents of Mrs. Pierce Kegley,
        a teacher in Bland County for many years. }
MUSTARD, James Harvey, s/o John & Lovisa Patterson Mustard, born
        according to family records, was born in 1831 , died May 18,
        1905. Married, by bond issued, 9-9-1856, Marcia Robinett,
        d/o James and Jerusha Newberry Robinett.
MUSTARD, Marcia Robinett- (b. abt 1836, died 6-25-1896) Dates taken
        from Family history. No stone visible for her.
MUSTARD, James Henry, s/o James H. & Marcia Robinett Mustard, was
        born July 14, 1861, died in 1883.

ROBINETT, Jezreal- (1-23-1826 - 4-2-1865) { He was the oldest child
        of James and Jerusha Newberry Robinett. He died a prisoner
        of War at Fort Delaware and buried at Finn's Point, NJ. at
        the close of the Civil War. His body was exhumed and
        brought back and buried here.
ROBINETT, Mary Ann- (4-25-1833 - 11-1-1884) {Nee Ward, w/o Jezreal}

{ Several sunken spots but no markers. The cemetery is beyond
restoration. Jo Ann Tickle Scott reports that some of the visible
stones which were there in 1987 are no longer there.

HICKS CEMETERY

{ According to local historians, Charity Ann Spangler Cameron, returned from Floyd County, Kentucky after the death of her husband, James Cameron who died in 1838. She lived with her son Duncan Cameron and is buried here.} The cemetery is located near Bastain on a steep hill north of State Route 52. Not far from Hicksville Church.}

[Compiled by Jo Ann Tickle Scott]

CAMERON, Duncan- (9-5-1791 - 12-18-1886) {S/O James Cameron}
CAMERON, Margaret Fox- (died 12-8-1892) {2nd w/o Duncan Cameron}
CAMERON, Luvenia Virginia- (no dates) {D/O Duncan & Margaret Cameron}
CARVER, Daniel T.- (12-5-1836 - 3-10-1812) {Md. 4-16-1862}
CARVER, Martha C. Edwards- (1-19-1844 - 8-17-1909) {W/O Daniel T.}
CHILDRESS, Nellie W.- (1906 - 1952) {Mother}
          { Cinder block at grave next to Nellie}

DUNN, Wythe G.- (1850 - 1929)
DUNN, Jane E.- (1854 - 1927) {W/O Wythe G.}
          { 1 fieldstone with no name or dates}

EDWARDS, Martha Coley- (4-22-1810 - 10-31-1866) {W/O William C.}
EDWARDS, William- (6-25-1817 - 12-16-1893)
          {1 field stone, no name or dates}

GOFF, Lelia M.- (7-7-1882 - 4-9-1908)

HICKS, Jennie Henderson- (6-18-1848 - 11-29-1908){W/O Henry G. Hicks}
HICKS, Henry G.- (1-26-1849 - 6-15-1906)
HICKS, Elizabeth J.- (6-9-1834 - 7-29-1862) {W/O Peter R.}
HICKS, Peter R.- (1-22-1829 - 9-14-1912)
HICKS, Mariah H.- (4-7-1814 - 7-2-1889)Aged 75yrs 2mos & 25 das.
          {W/O Joseph T.Hicks }
HICKS, Joseph T.- (3-20-1790 - 5-2-1865) Aged 67yrs 1mo & 12 das.
          { Notice that inscribed dates do not agree with age}

MCCOLGAN, William Frank- (1890 - 1946)
MCCOLGAN, Lois Fern W.- (1896 - 1971) {W/O William Frank}

STAFFORD, Betty J.- (1875 - 1954) {W/O John L.}
STAFFORD, John L.- (5-1-1866 - 4-28-1923) {Our Father}
STARKS, Charles M.- (1868 - 1952) {Father}
STARKS, Geneva H.- (1880 - 1933) {Mother}

WALKER, Howard F.- (5-21-1862 - 3-27-1935)
WALKER, Nina H.- (2-14-1870 - 6-9-1906) {W/O Howard F.}
WALKER, Sidna N.- (1874 - 8-25-1970) Aged 96yrs 4mos & 2das.{ W/O
          David J. Walker. She has 2 stones} {Mother}
WALKER, David J.- (1872 - 1942) {Father}
WALL, { Only word "WALL' on stone}
WYNN, James F.- (4-28-1873 - 8-13-1960)
WYNN, Rosa Etta- (7-27-1877 - 4-?-1961) {W/O James F. Wynn}
WYNN, Joseph- (no dates) {Co. F. VA. INF CSA}

CEMETERY NEAR BECKNER'S STORE ON WOLF CREEK
{ Also known as the Burress Cemetery }
[Copied in 1991 by Parke C. Bogle. Checked again in 1998 by Jo Ann
  Tickle Scott.]

BECKNER, Rev. Leroy H.- (11-5-1913 - 1-11-1996)
BECKNER, Thomas D.- (8-15-1966 - 9-30-1992)

BRITTEN, F.E.- (1942 - 1986)

BURRESS, Charles Leon- (5-29-1928 - 5-2-1964)
BURRESS, Ethel- (1-20-1912 - 6-20-1933)
BURRESS, Cora L.- (10-14-1891 - 3-3-1963)
BURRESS, James R.- (11-7-1882 - 11-9-1931)
BURRESS, Julia B. Thompson- (5-12-1858 - 6-20-1941)
BURRESS, Wiley W.- (5-21-1869 - 1-28-1896)
BURRESS, George W.- (4-8-1896 - 10-12-1904)
BURRESS, Harvey G.- (1883 - 1950) Father
BURRESS, Robert Ray- (11-20-1857 - 6-2-1940) Father
BURRESS, Maggie Tabor- (11-22-1876 - 12-12-1921) Mother
BURRESS, Dave- (12-17-1915 - 2-11-1981)
BURRESS, John Wesley- (6-24-1918 - 3-29-1990)
BURRESS, Sam- (4-27-1922 - 5-10-1991)

BURTON, James M.- (1-15-1928 - 6-24-1982) [James Marvin Burton]

CHRISTIAN, Hiram- (1879 - 1965)
CHRISTIAN, Anna F.- (1877 - 1922)
CHRISTIAN, Gabriel- (8-6-1907 -   ) {No death date}
CHRISTIAN, Hester V.- (6-27-1914 - 4-1-1992)
COOK, Bertie S.- (died 6-9-1879, age 1 yr, 5 months)
COOK, James T.- (died 10-1856, age 23 years)
COOK, Z.- (died 2-29-1880, age 57 years)
COOK, Thos.?- (died 3-3-1880, age 67 years

KIDD, Sally Bell- (2-13-1900 - 4-27-1960)
KIDD, Kelly Marvin- (9-16-1897 - 3-29-1976)
KIDD, John- (1929 - 1987)

THOMPSON, George W.- (4-8-1896 - 10-12-1904)
THOMPSON, Julia- (5-12-1858 - 6-20-1941)
THOMPSON, Wiley W.- (5-21-1869 - 1-28-1896)

WOLF, Ada D. Kidd- (4-24-1874 - 2-12-1964) Wife of D.S. Wolf.
WOLF, Dan S.- (6-19-1877 - 11-23-1944)
WOLF, George L.- (4-10-1902 - 7-21-1968)

{ There are about 30 graves unmarked or marked with plain field
stones with no lettering on them. The cemetery is in good condition.}

ROBINETT CEMETERY
{ Located about 4 miles west of Bland off Route 42 on State Route
615. After turning rightonto 615, the cemetery is about 1/2 mile on
the left of the road. }
[Compiled by Jo Ann Tickle Scott]

BANE, Effie- (12-15-1908 - 5-21-1925) {W/O Wallace C. Bane)
BANE, Stephen Olen- (1913 - 1978)
BANE, Wallace C.- (1903 - 1962)

BOWLES, Hattie B.- (10-23-1903 - 12-13-1903) {D/O G.W. & M.A. Bowles}
BOWLES, Perry W.- (10-27-1903
BOWLES, Fannie M.-
BOWLES, Jasper H.- (9-19-1904 - 12-21-1904)

CLEMENS, Barbara Ellen- (9-13-1875 - 4-7-1956)

CRABTREE, Iva Robinett- 6-1-1902 - 4-4-1963)

CRIGGER, Regina V.- (3-19-1841 - 8-7-1890)
CRIGGER, Mary E.- (12-1-1879 - 8-31-1892)

CROUSE, Lemuel- (4-10-1882 - 10-30-1968)
CROUSE, Sallie Ollie Jones- (5-13-1884 - 10-6-1969)

DILLOW, J. Clarence- (5-27-1906 - 11-22-1972)
DILLOW, E. Gray- (4-5-1910 - 9-27-1987)
DILLOW, Larry L.- (7-17-1940 - 7-5-1993) {H/O Doris Dunn}
DILLOW, Infant twin girls of Clarence & Gray} (no dates)

FARMER, Nicholas B.- (9-15-1871 - 9-2-1956)
FARMER, Mary E.- (11-25-1874 - 12-18-1928)
FARMER, Eugene Foster- (1-7-1907 - 5-23-1909) {S/O Elbert}
FARMER, William Harvy- (12-9-1895 - 10-13-1917)
FARMER, Fannie A.- (1-10-1851 - 4-29-1920) {W/O Stephen M.}
FARMER, Stephen M.- (9-17-1848 - 8-11-1909)
FARMER, Elbert Bird- (2-16-1883 - 1-20-1901) {S/O Stephen & Fannie}
FARMER, Infant- (born & died 11-14-1901) {S/O F.H. & R.J. Farmer}

GEARING, Minnie Belle- (2-11-1881 - 11-29-1914) {W/O Arthur}
GEARING, Arthur- Only a fieldstone at his feet. No dates.

HARMAN, Urbana Robinett- (4-30-1827 - 3-18-1899)
HARMAN, James B.- (11-15-1836 - 1-4-1901)

HALL, Roy E.- 1890 - 1980)
HALL, Fannie E.- (1894 - 1971)

HAYTON, K. Grat- (7-10-1905 - 7-8-1986)
HAYTON, Mabel L.- (2-25-1921 -   )

INGRAM- Ettie- (3-4-1871 - 6-8-1934)
INGRAM, Ossie Mary- (3-26-1902 - 1-4-1920) {W/O Jesse Ingram}

ROBINETT CEMETERY
[Compiled by Jo Ann Tickle Scott]

LAMBERT, Elbert M.- (1907 - 1970)
LAMBERT, Stella H.- (1912 - 1990)
LAMBERT, Luke Sheridan- (11-29-1914 -   )
LAMBERT, Ruby Farmer- (1-5-1906 -   ) {Md. 4-16-1938}

LUCAS, Ethel Ingram- (1905 - 1975) {Lived with Paul Penley}

NEWBERRY, Miller W.- (4-11-1889 - 7-14-1960) {S/O Wythe & Elizabeth
                                        Mustard Newberry}
NEWBERRY, Amazetta L. Robinett- (10-24-1873 - 1-30-1951) {W/O Miller
      Wythe Newberry. D/O Francis Marion & Laulett Lambert Robinett}

PARKER, J. Carl- (3-9-1911 - 3-29-1968)

REPASS, Margaret R.- (born & died 2-9-1925)
REPASS, Arlen B.- (1-25-1932 - 1-5-1933) {S/O Davis & Mayme Repass}
REPASS, Edwin Gray- (6-25-1888 - 9-27-1937)
REPASS, Sena Elizabeth Linkous- (11-8-1895 - 12-29-1944)
REPASS, Wayne Eugene- (10-31-1919 - 11-22-1919)
REPASS, Lois Andella- (born & died 11-27-1931)

ROBINETT, Lucy R.- (8-16-1882 - 9-17-1959) {D/O F. M. & Loulett }
ROBINETT, Malvina Loulett- (3-24-1846 - 11-23-1922)
ROBINETT, G. (F) Marion- (10-14-1833 - 8-14-1904)
ROBINETT, Rebecca- (5-6-1806 - 3-7-1868) {W/O Hiram}
ROBINETT, Hiram- (8-31-1797 - 5-9-1875)
ROBINETT, Daniel W.- 4-25-1873 - 10-30-1913)
ROBINETT, Rebecca E.- (12-29-1844 - 10-22-1918) {W/O Martin J.}
ROBINETT, M. J,- (2-8-1839 - 2-8-1914) {AKA Martin J. Robinett}
ROBINETT, Rush F.- (8-30-1877 - 8-20-1962)
ROBINETT, Fannie D.- (4-6-1876 - 4-4-1954)
ROBINETT, Darthula- (4-29-1818 - 5-15-1868)
ROBINETT, Benjamin F.- (7-20-1825 - 10-19-1859)

SADLER, Infant- (born & died 10-4-1958){S/O Olen & Ola Repass Sadler}

SHRADER, Rosetta- (2-27-1892 - 10-22-1918)

STOWERS, Elmer W. Jr.- (born & died 12-26-1935)
STOWERS, Elmer Wise, Sr.- (12-17-1914 - 9-28-1982)
STOWERS, Eula Tickle- (4-2-1914 - 8-7-197?)
STOWERS, Dall W.- (2-15-1882 - 3-1-1952)
STOWERS, Maude G.- (3-25-1889 - 7-26-1972)
STOWERS, James M.- (1884 - 1974)
STOWERS, Perdidia Gray Robinett- (1877 - 1961)
STOWERS, Hayes G.- (1884 - 1956)
STOWERS, Nellie C.- (1883 - 1972)
STOWERS, Ruby O.- (2-5-1916 - 9-23-1976)
STOWERS, Oscar M.- (2-12-1882 - 10-28-1966)
STOWERS, Jake R.- (1-3-1919 - 11-23-1090) {Pvt. US Army}

ROBINETT CEMETERY

STOWERS, H. Perry- (10-27-1878 - 10-13-1952)
STOWERS, America Robinett- (11-24-1878)

TICKLE, Grant- (3-2-1873 - 2-11-1962)
TICKLE, Lottie Virginia- (10-27-1878 - 5-22-1921)
TICKLE, Jackson Lineberry- (1-8-1909 - 3-9-1990)
TICKLE, Helen Huddle- (8-30-1920 - 8-15-1981)
TICKLE, Ewing- (10-8-1906 - 3-18-1967){AKA "Ira Ulysses Nye Tickle}
TICKLE, Eula Mae Crouse- (11-15-1911 - 2-11-1998)

WINEGAR, Earl William, Jr. (4-17-1927 - 6-30-1986)
WINEGAR, Marjorie Crabtree- (2-4-1929 -   )

KITTS FAMILY CEMETERY
{ A good sized cemetery, judging from the amount of land it occupies.
It is in very bad condition, full of briars, brush and trees. Some
stones are down and could not be lifted up. The cemetery is located
on Wayne Tickle's land on top of a hill in a clump of trees. }
    [Compiled by Jo Ann Tickle Scott in October of 1998.]

BROWN, Magnolia- (2-19-???? - 9-27-1887) {W/O John Brown}

DILLOW, { Only the surname is here. No dates.}

KITTS, Peter- (11-12-1827 - 7-8-1879) {He was 42 on 1870 census.)
KITTS, Mary Ann- (3-10-1814 - 8-7-1888) { W/O Peter. She was 29 on
                                    the 1870 census}
KITTS, Rexie- (11-22-1891 - 2-17-1943)
KITTS, Alice Nicewander- (2-15-1866 - 11-18-1911) {W/O Wythe G. Kitts
            and d/o Jacob Nicewander and Susan Rider Nicewander.}
KITTS, Lena Rose- (4-19-1888 - 8-27-1888){S/O Wythe G. & Alice Kitts}

8 field stones
10 indentations
1 stone that could not be lifted.

STEEL CEMETERY ON WENDLE NEWBERRY FARM
[Located on State Route 617, southwest of Bland Courthouse on land
that was once owned by Crockett Steel and Mary "Polly" Bogle Steel.]
{ Copied in 1993 by Alma Newberry Waddell and Parke C. Bogle }

BROWN, Chapman P.,Sr.- (4-7-1900 - 11-4-1961)
BROWN, Wythe Newberry- (4-16-1871 - 10-14-1942) Father.
BROWN, Edith Newberry- (8-8-1873 - 4-17-1942) Mother. Dau of Henley
        Chapman and Mollie Steel Newberry. Wife of Wythe N. Brown.

NEWBERRY, Infant- (1861 - 1861)
NEWBERRY, Mollie- (1833 - 1892) { Wife of Henley Chapman Newberry
        and daughter of Crockett Steel and his wife Mary Bogle
        Steel. { Archives, State Library lists her death date as
        March 11, 1892, age 57. This does not agree with tombstone
        inscription. }
NEWBERRY, H. C.- (1823 - 1879) Grandson of Rev. Samuel Newberry and
        Eunice Powers Newberry. { Henley Chapman Newberry }
NEWBERRY, Mary E.- (7-27-1889 - 12-17-1957) { Nee Mary Ellen
        Shannon, wife of Albert L. Newberry }
NEWBERRY, Albert L.- (1-30-1869 - 3-25-1948) Son of Henley Chapman
        and Mollie Steel Newberry.
NEWBERRY, Edgar A. (Ashby)- (1865 - 1891) Son of Henley C. & Mollie
NEWBERRY, Paul C. (Chapman)- (1871 - 1930) Son of "   " "   "
NEWBERRY, Myrtle F.- (1888 - 1977) Nee Dunbar, wife of Paul C.
NEWBERRY, Elise Wright- (10-20-1022 - 3-24-1979) Wife of Wendell
        Newberry.
NEWBERRY, Capt. Albert Warren- (1918 - 1962) Son of Albert L. &
        Mary E. Shannon Newberry
NEWBERRY, Becky Wright- (1923 - 1977) Wife of Capt. Albert Warren.
NEWBERRY, Stephen M.- (7-24-1948 - 3-14-1995) {Killed in auto wreck}

STEEL, Polly- (1808 - 1833) Daughter of Robert Bogle and his first
                wife, Rachael Dunn Bogle. Wife of Crockett Steel.
STEEL, Crockett- (1802 - 1857) Son of Robert and Rebecca Oury Steel
STEEL, Mary Telie- (8-18-1874 - 6-5-1951)

EVELYN THOMPSON GRAVE SITE
{ On the old Capt Henry Newberry farm, now owned by Fred Tate, across
the road from the house and near the water is a stone placed there by
Evelyn's family in her memory. This was the spot where she loved to
play as a child. I took pictures of the stone but have lost the dates
that were on it. She was the daughter of Nannie Newberry and George
Thompson. Nannie was a daughter of Capt. Henry Newberry and his
second wife, Laura Porter Newberry. She was unmarried. Jo Tickle
informed me that she was cremated and her ashes had been spread here
also.- Parke Bogle.}

OLD CAPT. HENRY NEWBERRY CEMETERY
(On land now owned by the Tate family)
[Copied in 1989 by Parke C. Bogle and Melissa Lester]

CLAY, Emily Ann, (1855-1937) Black servant of the Newberry family.

HUBBLE, Frank Dexter, b. June 11, 1911, d. October 20, 1914.
{ He was the son of Ossie Newberry and Tiberious Dexter
Hubble and the grandson of Capt. Henry Newberry and his 2nd
wife, Laura Porter.
HUBBLE, Pauline May, b. June 17, 1904, d. August 8, 1930.
{ Grand daughter of Capt. Henry Newberry, being a child of his
daughter Ossie who married Deck Hubble.}

NEWBERRY. Capt. Henry, b. 1828, d. 1914. { He was second son born to
Allen Taylor Newberry and his first wife, Elizabeth Bogle Newberry.
He was twice married. 1st to Elizabeth Robinett and 2nd to Laura
Porter. He was a Civil War Veteran }

NEWBERRY, Frank G.- (1-16-1884 - 7-11-1893) { Son of Capt. Henry
Newberry and his 2nd wife, Laura Porter. There is no
visible stone here for him. The dates were taken from his
obituary, which also stated that he was buried in the
family cemetery. His age was given as " 9 years, 5 months &
15 days". }

NEWBERRY, Laura Porter, b. 1852, d. 1934. { 2nd wife of Capt Henry
Newberry. Daughter of Stephen Porter of Wythe County.}

NEWBERRY, John Henry, b. August 8, 1874, d.March 15, 1904.
{ John Henry was the youngest child Capt. Henry Newberry and his
first wife, Elizabeth Robinett. John Henry married Mable Crabtree and
fathered a daughter named Gladys Newberry.

{ The first wife of Capt. Newberry, Elizabeth Robinett, may also be
buried here. If so, there is no stone here at this time for her.}

[The birth and death dates on these tombstones, differ slightly from
the data in "The Newberry History", written by John Allen Newberry.
He gives Capt. Henry's birth date as August 11, 1828 and his death
date as June 5, 1914. He gives John Henry's birth date as August 8,
1875 and his death date as March 4, 1904. Perhaps Mr. Newberry took
his dates from the Archives of the Virginia State Library. I notice
that their dates do not always agree with Bible and tombstone
records.]

ALLEN, Rev. James L.- (4-26-1895 - 4-2-1964)
ALLEN, Maggie Hudson- (1-10-1861 - 3-8-1901) wife of W.B. Allen
ALLEN, William Bascom- (7-8-1857 - 7-28-1924)
ALLEN, Lillie Foglesong- (3-20-1878 - 1-9-1926) wife of W.B. Allen
ALLEN, Barbara Moore- (1886 - 1983)
ALLEN, William Thomas- (1890 - 1960)

ANDERSON, Rachael X.- (9-14-1866 - 3-18-1936)

ATWELL, Charles Bryson- (2-13-1899 - 6-13-1989)
ATWELL, Ruth- (10-13-1915 -   )

BAILEY, Carrie Repass- (8-24-1861 - 3-24-1945)

BALES, J.W.- (no dates)

BAUGH, Mable C.- (1-7-1908 - 3-1-1927) Dau. of D.M. & G.P. Baugh.
BAUGH, Geneva P.- (died 2-14-1932)
BAUGH, D.M.- (8-14-185? - 10-13-1919)
BAUGH, Nickotie L.- (6-9-1851 - 3-15-1902) Wife of D.M. Baugh.

BLAIR, Julian D.- (1-7-1908 - 3-1-1927)
BLAIR, Helen G.- (11-3-1904 - 2-16-1984)

BOGLE, Andrew N.- (3-11-1856 - 1-30-1941) Son of James B. & Susan
        Raulston Bogle. Grandson of Ralph & Margaret Hutzell Bogle.
BOGLE, Louvenia Pruett- (4-14-1882 - 2-17-1957) Wife of Andrew N.
BOGLE, Fred C.- (3-3-1912 -   ) Son of Andrew & Louvenia
BOGLE, Ruth B.- (5-12-1913 - 1-16-1985){W/O Fred C., d/o Ellis Brown}
BOGLE, Josephine- (5-30-1931 - 10-4-1932)
BOGLE, Alma Mozelle- (11-7-1932 - 11-11-1939)
BOGLE, Eugene H.- (10-7-1903 - 4-2-1948) { Son of Andrew Napoleon &
                    Louvenia Pruett Bogle }
BOGLE, Ray- (3-9-1921- 8-29-1990) { Son of Andrew & Louvinia Bogle}
BOGLE, Mary Wayne-(7-25-1918 - 6-6-1990) Dau. of Andrew & Louvenia.
BOGLE, Marie R.- (6-23-1914 - 5-16-1978)Dau. of Andrew & Louvenia
BOGLE, Edgar B.- (11-9-1901 - 7-17-1942) Son of Andrew & Louvenia.
BOGLE, Lorenza D.- (1880 - 1958) Son of L.D. and Charlotte W. Bogle
BOGLE, Martha C.- 1886 - 1957) Wife of Lorenza Dow Bogle

BROWN, Ellis M.- (11-6-1889 - 10-23-1940)
BROWN, Flora A.- (9-20-1893 - 11-27-1979)
BROWN, Miller- (8-29-1916 - 4-21-1976)

BRUCE, Charles K.- (1867 - 1956)
BRUCE, Susan E.- (1875 - 1944)
BRUCE, Infant son of C.K. & S.E. Bruce-(5-19-1911 - 6-6-1911)
BRUCE, Adam Kent- (10-2-1907 - 10-10-1907)
BRUCE, Milton Ray- (5-16-1906 - 5-26-1906)
BRUCE, Lena May- (4-4-1905 - 4-8-1905)

SHARON LUTHERAN CHURCH CEMETERY
[Above Ceres, Virginia on State Route # 42]

BRUCE, Nellie J.- (4-6-1904 - 5-12-1904)
BRUCE, Margaret J.- (6-13-1838 - 1-24-1910)
BRUCE, Rev. J.M. {Jeheil Milton} (8-16-1838 - 8-18-1898) [Son of
    Josiah and Minerva Justice Bruce.
BRUCE, Margaret J. (nee Foglesong) (8-16-1839 - 1-24-1981) Wife
    of Rev. J.M. Bruce.
BRUCE, Hettie Oregon- (12-4-1866 - 5-10-1873) Dau. of Harrold F.
    and Sarah J. Suitor Bruce.
BRUCE, Forest Langdon- (3-5-1869 - 4-10-1941) Son of Harrold F. and
    Sarah Suitor Bruce.
BRUCE, Daisey Crabtree- (12-12-1889 - 10-30-1968) Wife of Forest L.

BUCK, Margaret A.- (1-2-1840 - 6-26-1912) Wife of Felix
BUCK, Felix- (2-14-1827 - 6-24-1889)
BUCK, Lelia- (9-25-1906 - 10-13-1906) Dau of B.E.L. & I.B. Buck

CASSELL, Mary Lola- (12-29-1876 - 12-15-1913)
CASSELL, Ina Belle- (1-22-1899 - 5-21-1899) {D/O James & Christina}
CASSELL, Christina- (5-??-1850 - 12-6-1890){W/O James F. Cassell
CASSELL, James F.- (10-22-1849 - 3-6-1930)
CASSELL, Mary Spangler- (10-7-1872 - 8-5-1949){2nd W/O James F.Cassel
CASSELL, Susan B.- (1873 - 1971)
CASSELL, Thomas M.- (1873 - 193
CASSELL, Andrew B.- (1905 - 1973)
CASSELL, Emma M.- (2-2-1894 - 2-17-1898)
CASSELL, Charles N.- (5-3-1889 - 9-16-1889)
CASSEOL, Earl C.- (2-13-1901 - 4-2-1903)
CASSELL, Nannie D.- (5-7-1865 - 2-26-1954)
CASSELL, Stephen w.- (5-23-1863 - 9-21-1903)

CHAPMAN, Nora Lee- (10-6-1931 - 9-4-1976)

COMPTON, William K.- (1906 - 1970) Former sheriff of Bland County
COMPTON, Margaret S.- (1911 -   ) {Nee Stowers}
COMPTON, Ann Elizabeth- (2-12-1904 - 7-1-1905) Dau of C.W.& L.K C--
COMPTON, Charles Watson- (1877 - 1931)
COMPTON, Lula Kegley- (1891 - 1931)
COMPTON, J. Francis- (3-14-1915 -   )
COMPTON, Neta U.- (6-9-1918 -   )
COMPTON, Andrew W.- (1911 - 1977)
COMPTON, Minnie Foglesong- (1879 - 1964)

COOLEY, T.J.- (and family [only legible words-"4-1-AD---Forbes"

CRABTREE, Ruth T.- (1893 - 1969)
CRABTREE, Alfred- (1895 - 1976)
CRABTREE, J. Howard- (11-2-1913 -   ) md. 10-26-1935
CRABTREE, Reva A.- (9-9-1918 - 7-31-1989) Md.10-26-1935
CRABTREE, R. Paul- (4-16-1909 - 1-26-1990)
CRABTREE, Nancy B.- (3-11-1906 -   )

CRABTREE, Robert Michael- (12-31-1962 - 1-1-1963) Son of Rodney C.
CRABTREE, Susan A.- (8-24-1872 - 7-17-1965)
CRABTREE, Charles A.- (4-25-1866 - 6-24-1948)
CRABTREE, Willis Edgar- (12-18-1901 - 11-14-1903)
CRABTREE, Kathleen- (12-13-1935 - 4-12-1989)
CRABTREE, Basil M.- (10-1-1885 - 7-23-1976)
CRABTREE, Ethel W.- (9-10-1890 - 10-22-1953)
CRABTREE, Arley M.- (1880 - 1939)
CRABTREE, J. Henry- (1847 - 1914)
CRABTREE, Susan- (1849 - 1936)
CRABTREE, Asa Q.- (2-13-1877 - 8-30-1906)
CRABTREE, Polly A.- (5-15-1830 - 8-11-1891) Wife of Rees Crabtree.
CRABTREE, Rees- (10-28-1832 - 3-29-1902)
CRABTREE, Corah J.- (7-31-1873 - 8-3-1881) Dau of Rees & Polly C---
CRABTREE, John H.- (1-17-1859 - 8-20-1871) Son of Rees & Polly C---
CRABTREE, Caroline "Callie"- (11-1895 - 5-19-1988) Wife of Elbert.
        { Callie was dau of Dunn Bogle Newberry & Arbanna Hancock }
CRABTREE, Elbert S.- (10-26-1868 - 5-5-1947)
CRABTREE, Mary L.- (5-10-1876 - 9--8-1896) Dau of Polly & Rees.
CRABTREE, William Earl- (11-26-1916 -   ) Teacher-Farmer
CRABTREE, William Terry- (1871 - 1957)
CRABTREE, Lillie Virginia Ward- (1874 - 1945)
CRABTREE, Virginia Ruth- (7-31-1912 - 10-6-1989) [Scholar-Teacher-
        Supervisor]
CRABTREE, Elbert Kyle- (5-17-1910 - 11-5-1976)
CRABTREE, Kate Reynolds- (11-4-1906 - 12-5-1980)
CRABTREE, Infant (6-1966) FHM
CRABTREE, Estle, Jr.- (7-9-1924 - 11-9-1925) Son of E.P. & H.J. C--
CRABTREE, Hattie Tilson- (2-23-1891 - 8-17-1987) Mother
CRABTREE, Estle Peter, "Doc"- (10-25-1878 - 8-31-1961) Father
CRABTREE, James- (no dates) Co. G.36 VA Inf. CSA
CRABTREE, Agnes C.- (3-26-1843 - 1-10-1894) Wife of James Crabtree
CRABTREE, Margaret- (failed to copy dates) Dau of James & Agnes
CRABTREE, Leonard- (6-4-1839 - 6-6-1855) Age 16 yrs 23 days.
CRABTREE, Mary Umbarger- (3-20-18?8 - 11-28-18??) Wife of James C--
CRABTREE, John- (4-19-1799 - 9-1-1871)

CRAFTON, Naomi Bogle- (1-1-1914 - 11-10-1975) Dau / Andrew N. Bogle

CREGAR, Edward Randolph- (5-22-1923 - 4-4-1985)
CREGAR, Lewis Alex, Jr.- (10-24-1930 - 12-31-1950)
CREGAR, James Calvin- (6-7-1928 - 7-11-1951)
CREGAR, Louis A.- (1894 - 1976)

CREGER, Edward H.- (7-22-1895 - 2-12-1975)
CREGER, Margaret K.- (4-14-1892 - 10-18-1972)

CREGGAR, Roby S., Sr.- (1-17-1902 - 8-9-1981)
CREGGER, Ida B.- (1914 - 1955)

SHARON LUTHERAN CHURCH CEMETERY
[Above Ceres, Virginia on State Route # 42]

DAVIS, Mary- (4-1830 - 7-16-1903)

DILLMAN, Myrtle May- (5-16-1900 - 8-23-1900)
DILLMAN, Walter Clarence- (2-28-1899 - 3-31-1899)
DILLMAN, Callie M.- (2-10-1871 - 3-5-1911) Wife / J.T. Dillman.
DILLMAN, Katherine T.- (1917 - 1983)
DILLMAN, Harvey L.- (1882 - 1968)
DILLMAN, Fannie E.- (1890 - 1967)
DILLMAN, Charles Greever- (9-7-1870 - 10-18-1870)
DILLMAN, Amanda E.- (1-2-1852 - 10-26-1895)
DILLMAN, Barbara Ann- (5-26-1846 - 7-19-1871)
DILLMAN, John D.- (C.S.A. marker (no dates)
DILLMAN, Infant son of John & Amanda E. Dillman- (No dates)
DILLMAN, Infant son of John & Amanda Dillman (No dates)

DOAK, Amanda- (Died 12-1865, age 77 yrs & 7 months.)
DOAK, Mary Ann- (2-4-1813 - 4-13-1844) Wife of Robert Doak
DOAK, Robert- (5-9-1807? - 7-11-1856)

DOTSON, Napoleon B.- (1845 - 1930)
DOTSON, Euphemia E.- (5-14-1837 - 2-20-1900) Wife of Napoleon
DOTSON, Charlie- (1-10-1875 - 2-22-1875) Son of N.B. & E.E. Dotson.
DOTSON, Mary V.- (7-31-1867 - 10-31-1910) Wife of C.C. Dotson.

DOUTHAT, Henry Y.- (7-14-1814 - 6-8-1868)

DOWLING, Clara Virginia Peery- (7-9-1896 - 5-1-1955)
        { Wife of R.M. Dowling }

DUNCAN, Leonard F.- (7-9-1883 - 4-3-1929)
DUNCAN, Lueezia C. Hayton Hanshew- (10-12-1866 - 6-4-1927)

EDWARDS, Jay Scott- (5-21-1905 - 12-20-1937)
EDWARDS, Florence E.- (12-24-1868 - 7-19-1947)
EDWARDS, Walter C.- (7-20-1886 - 12-9- 1948)
EDWARDS, Charles Michael- (10-31-1907 - 4-28-1979)
EDWARDS, Fern S.- (1900 - 1986)
EDWARDS, James- (1-3-1889 - 4-20-1960)
EDWARDS, C. M.- (8-18-1863 - 1-19-1930)
EDWARDS, Rebecca G.- (1860 - 1906)
EDWARDS, Infant son of Charles & Rebecca (died 1895)
EDWARDS, Charles- (1825 - 1906)
EDWARDS, Martha F.- (1838 - 1874)
EDWARDS, Margaret W.- (1837 - 1879)
EDWARDS, Mitchell H.- (1873 - 1887)

FOGLESONG, Joseph- (12-5-1835 - 1-23-1910) Age 73.
FOGLESONG, Bettie- (5-22-1847 - 3-18-1911)
FOGLESONG, William Ray- (1-10-1907 - 4-6-1983) Married 9-9-1832
FOGLESONG, Verna Repass- (5-9-1909 -   ) "   9-9-1932

FOGLESONG, Ida Myrtle- (12-29-1882 - 9-21-1974)
FOGLESONG, Joseph Kelley- (2-13-1881 - 6-3-1963)
FOGLESONG, Henry- (1-10-1805 - 2-16-1889)
FOGLESONG, Julia A.-(6-??- death date illegible) Wife of Henry
FOGLESONG, Wiley P.- (8-2-1904 - 12-12-1974)
FOGLESONG, Margaret H.- (6-10-1862 - 5-3-1935)
FOGLESONG, Christopher- (4-2-1848 - 10-14-1919)
FOGLESONG, Mollie E.- (7-2-1852 - 11-29-1899) Wife of Christopher.
FOGLESONG, Henry H.- (9-19-1843 - 8-1-1929)
FOGLESONG, Matilda- (4-4? -1856 - 6-19-1914) Wife of Henry H. F--.
FOGLESONG, Infant dau of H.H. & N.M. Foglesong (No dates)
FOGLESONG, Claude S.- (8-15-1912 - 7-16-1922) Son of Hugh & Bessie.
FOGLESONG, Fred F.- (6-24-1922 - 2-15-1940) Son of Hugh & Bessie.
FOGLESONG, Emery Hugh- (5-25-1890 - 9-4-1968)
FOGLESONG, Bessie Boling- (7-16-1891 - 5-24-1969)

[Between the graves of Mollie E. Foglesong and Peter Spangler, are
eight graves of infants, bearing no surnames. They are:

---------, Lucy- (Aug. - Dec. 1871)
---------, John- (Oct. - Nov. 1872)
---------, Lillie- (Sept.- Dec. 1873)
---------, Adam- (Sept. - Feb. 1875)
---------, Edward, (Nov. - July 1882)
---------, Cleveland- (Nov. - Dec. 1884)
---------, Fannie- (March - April 1887)
---------, Infant- (Nov. 17, 1890)
{ If any one knows the correct names for these little children,
please noyify me or your Bland County Historical Society, so that the
can be named correctly. }

FOGLESONG, Walter S.- (1-14-1875 - 4-4-1964)
FOGLESONG, Jennie G.-(5-7-1877 - 4-4-1932)
FOGLESONG, Infant dau.of Henry S. & Mollie A. Foglesong
FOGLESONG, Henry S.- (1832 - 1903)
FOGLESONG, Mollie A.- (1846 - 1904)
FOGLESONG, Charles L.- (6-21-1841 - 10-19-1861) Son of H. & J.F. F-
FOGLESONG, Infant son of E.&S. (Elias & Sophia ?) No dates.
FOGLESONG, Stone only (Late 1860's)
FOGLESONG, Infant of E. & S. Foglesong (No dates) {Elias & Sophia?}
FOGLESONG, Infant of E. & S. Foglesong (No dates) {Elias & Sophia?}
FOGLESONG, Elias- (8-28-1831 - 11-2-1891)
FOGLESONG, Sophia- (2-27-1836 - 4-22-1885) Wife of Elias.
FOGLESONG, A.J.- (1-22-1868 - 8-8-1896)
FOGLESONG, Simon- (died 7-28-1875, age 83 years.)
FOGLESONG, Infant dau of J.H. & Paulina (B & D. 9-24-1939)
FOGLESONG, Twin sons of J.H. & Paulina- (B.& D. 9-24-1954)
FOGLESONG, John Henry- (3-12-1917 - 1-14-1977)
FOGLESONG, Charles John- (10-22-1876 - 11-27-1954)
FOGLESONG, Tillie Mable- (10-3-1887 - 1-6-1969)

SHARON LUTHERAN CHURCH CEMETERY
[Above Ceres, Virginia on State Route # 42]

FOGLESONG, T.L.- (1885 - 1958)
FOGLESONG, Ethel C.- (7-31-1902 - 4-8-1986)
FOGLESONG, Donald Lee- (4-4-1929 - 11-8-1978) Korean War Vet.
FOGLESONG, Thelma S.- (4-26-1920 -   )
FOGLESONG, William R.- (11-14-1887 - 12-3-1973)

GROSECLOSE, Adam Dallas- (12-27-1846 - 8-20-1929)
GROSECLOSE, Parthena Ann Wall- (7-17-1849 - 7-14-1912) Wife of A.D.
GROSECLOSE, Milton- (1-28-1873 - 9-13-1944)
GROSECLOSE, Fannie Neal- (8-30-1881 - 11-17-1961)
GROSECLOSE, Conrad Neal- (11-26-1907-6-21-1977) Son/ Milton & Fannie.
GROSECLOSE, Infant dau.\ Milton & Fannie-(3-3-1918 - 3-4-1918)
GROSECLOSE, Mary J.- (1847 - 1920) Wife of Henry (W.H.)
GROSECLOSE, W.H.- (5-2-1840 - 6-14-1892)
GROSECLOSE, Mary M.- (dates illegible) Wife of Francis
GROSECLOSE- Francis- (1805 - 8-20-1882) Stone broken in 3 pieces.
GROSECLOSE, Jacob- (1834 - 1906)
GROSECLOSE, Nancy- (1836 - 1892)
GROSECLOSe, John H., Sr.- (9-16-1898 - 3-26-1967)
GROSECLOSE, Margaret Victoria- (2-2-1870 - 6-3-1933)
GROSECLOSE, Dexter S.- (8-30-1869 - 2-12-1949)
GROSECLOSE, Jean Victoria- (2-11-1815 - 6-26-1815)
GROSECLOSE, Nancy Elizabeth- (2-21-1852 ? - 7-20-1859 ?) Eroded badly
GROSECLOSE, Eli Stephen- (6-16-1846 - 10-12-1847)
GROSECLOSE, George W.- (2-?-1840 - 7-25-1858) Age 18yrs, 5mos 21das
GROSECLOSE, Jacob- (Dates Illegible)
GROSECLOSE, Mary Clara- (8-28-1904 - 1-1-1981)
GROSECLOSE, John H., Jr.- (2-11-1933 - 12-13-1989) W.W. I Vet
GROSECLOSE, W. Henry- (2-17-1895 - 8-28-1936)
GROSECLOSE, Marybelle Moss- (2-15-1900 - 2-26-1988)
GROSECLOSE, Simon Kent- (3-21-1867 - 4-4-1943)
GROSECLOSE, S. Josephine Muncy- (9-7-1862 - 4-2-1932)
GROSECLOSE, Margaret Elizabeth, infant- (died 1937)
GROSECLOSE, Vivian- (11-30-1893 - 7-5-1894)
GROSECLOSE, Carlos M.- (11-16-1886 - 6-17-1888) son\ D.B. & H.C.
GROSECLOSE, { illegible) (8-28-1875 - 10-1-1944)
GROSECLOSE, Levenia V. Peery- (8-11-1848 - 2-7-1929) Wife/ H.C.
GROSECLOSE, H.C.- (8-15-1843 - 3-21-1894)
GROSECLOSE, May Peery- (1-28-1872 - 6-23-1882) Dau of H.C. & L.V.
GROSECLOSE, Cassie Mable- (10-5-1883 - 1-17-1980)
GROSECLOSE, Dorothy Saxton- (3-5-1896 - 1-3-1947)
GROSECLOSE, Henry C.- (5-17-1892 - 6-4-1950) Founter of FFA
GROSECLOSE, Willis Peery- (4-4-1894 - 1-19-1969)
GROSECLOSE, Mae G.- (8-23-1913 -   )
GROSECLOSE, Cloyd C.- (1902 - 1975)
GROSECLOSE, Elsie B.- (1901 - 1977)
GROSECLOSE, Maurice Madden- (2-17-1880 - 1-21-1887)
GROSECLOSE, Infant dau. of J.A.T. & Eliza J. Groseclose (No dates)
GROSECLOSE, Malinda C.- (3-8-1867 - 3-18-1867) Dau/ J.A.T. & Eliza J
GROSECLOSE, William L.- (8-24-1818 - 7-26-1858)

SHARON LUTHERAN CHURCH CEMETERY
[Above Ceres, Virginia on State Route # 42]

GROSECLOSE, Maryetta- (4-9-1841 - 12-27-1856)
GROSECLOSE, Sarah- (4-18-1847 - 3-26-1855)
GROSECLOSE, Houston- (7-20-1836 - 3-28-1855)
GROSECLOSE, Jezreal- (9-1-1807 - 11-20-1856)
GROSECLOSE, Margaret- (12-20-1813 - 7-30-1858) Wife of Jezreal
GROSECLOSE, William- (4-21-1810 - ?-14-1871)
GROSECLOSE, Adeline C.- (9-5-1815 - 6-?-1885)
GROSECLOSE, E.W.- (10-1-1830 - 9-23-1915)
GROSECLOSE, Joseph- (dates buried under ground when stone repaired.
GROSECLOSE, Grover C.- (9-18-1884 - 2-27-1964)

HALL, Emily J.- (5-19-1848 - 9-15-1884)
HALL, Baiseyn L.M.- (3-28-1985 - 3-28-1985)

HANSHEW, Isaac Blaine- (1884 - 1962)
HANSHEW, Kent- (2-20-1887 - 10-4-1914)
HANSHEW, Samuel S.- (6-30-1846 - 1-8- 1929) Father
HANSHEW, Markum V.- (10-5-1856 - 3-17-1935) Mother
HANSHEW, Henry J.- (6-23-1878 - 7-26-1908) Son of S.S. & M.V. H--

HARNER, Michel- (8- ?-? dates illegible.) { A Michael Harner
married a Barbara Spangler in Wythe County on May 2, 1812, by Rev.
John Stanger. It is not known if this is that same Michael Harner. }
HARNER, Guy F.- (1901 - 1957)
HARNER, Byrd W.- (1857 - 1914)
HARNER, Infant son, (Died 1907)
HARNER, Elijah- (10-18-1846 - 8-10-1916)

HAYTON, John L.- (12-29-1868 - 5-1-1928)
HAYTON, Ellas- (6-12-1880 - 1-24-1949) Carved over date of 1899
HAYTON, Lorena- (5-10-1876 - 12-27-1968)
HAYTON, Thomas- (1843 - 1932) CSA Marker
HAYTON, Louisa Ann- (1846 - 1920) Wife of Charles Henry.
HAYTON, Ellen- (8-22-1870 - 9-28-1879)
HAYTON, William W.- (11-28-1879 - 8-9-1891)
HAYTON, Ollie J.- (10-29-1872 - 1-11-1897)
HAYTON, Sgt. Ralph M.- (9-15-1921 - 9-7-1947)
HAYTON, James C.- (2-26-1883 - 1-2-1953)

HICKS, Nancy Kitts- (5-28-1931 - 9-10-1975)

HUBBLE, Gary Michael- (6-6-1961 - 7-9-1981)
HUBBLE, J. Bruce- (1898 - 1974)
HUBBLE, Annie F.- (1902 - 1958)
HUBBLE, Charles Henry- (1-1-1869 - 1-21-1943)
HUBBLE, Minerva A. Bruce- (11-4-1868 - 7-19-1953) W/O Charles Henry
HUBBLE, William J.- (10-25-1837 - 10-19-1925)
HUBBLE, Margaret V.- (4-17-1839 - 5-18-1912) Wife of William J.

HUDSON, Margie "Nita" Juanita- (4-25-1890 - 2-27-1984)

SHARON LUTHERAN CHURCH CEMETERY
[Above Ceres, Virginia on State Route # 42]

HUDSON, Nellie "Nell"- (No dates)
HUDSON, John M.- (3-23-1852 - 2-15-1914)
HUDSON, Florence Repass- (8-31-1859 - 5-10-1938) Wife of John M.
HUDSON, Isaac- (9-16-1813 - 9-1-1903)
HUDSON, Elizabeth Peery- (7-26-1826 - 1-14-1880)
HUDSON, Louisa V.- (9-23-1846 - 1-17-1880) Wife of T.G. Hudson.
HUDSON, Lillie B.- (8-17-1876 - 12-25-1891) Dau\ T.G & L.V. Hudson
HUDSON, two infants of T.G. & L.V. Hudson (no dates)
HUDSON, Frankie Edith- (11-24-1887 - 9-6-1902)
HUDSON, George- (6-9-1790 - 3-11-1863)
HUDSON, Hannah Shannon- (6-19-1793 - 7-15-1861)
HUDSON, Elizabeth M.- (10-1-1829 - 5-18-1863)
HUDSON, Charles J.- (10-18-1836 - 2-23-1888)
HUDSON, Eliza Groseclose- (3-23-1838 - 4-6-1866)

KEGLEY, Henry M.- (3-5-1900 - 5-22-1968)
KEGLEY, Walter S.J.- (7-14-1897 - 5-29-1903)

KINDER, J.M.- (CSA marker, No dates)
KINDER, Sophia- (3-16-1846 - 1-22-1917) Wife of J.M. Kinder
KINDER, Laura Jane- (11-20-1877 - 12-6-1946)

KITTS, Frank Forest- (5-5-1895 - 1-2-1959)
KITTS, Myrtle C.- (3-25-1899 - 7-3-1972)
KITTS, Stephen- (CSA marker, no dates)
KITTS, Harvey J.- (2-11-1856 - 6-24-1918)
KITTS, Sarah E. Williams- (12-12-1862 - 6-10-1936){W/O H.J. Kitts}
KITTS, Walter Lee- (2-9-1869 - 4-24-1948)
KITTS, Sultana Muncy- (6-26-1875 - 12-12-1956)
KITTS, William Stephen- (7-13-1905 - 4-9-1954)
KITTS, Carrie Lee- (11-21-1912 -   )
KITTS, A. M.- (11-30-1879 - 6-15-1955)
KITTS, H. M.- (5-30-1817 - 1-9-1910)
KITTS, Causby D.- (12-8-1849 - 10-18-1907)
KITTS, Harvey John- (2-28-1876 - 10-2-1956)
KITTS, Eliza Williams- (5-9-1861 - 12-28-1954)   {W/O Newton M. Kitts}
KITTS, Newton M.- (6-10-1850 - 12-29-1923)
KITTS, Henry K.- (7-19-1913 - 7-10-1987)
KITTS, Maxie C.- (10-14-1921 - 1-7-1989)
KITTS, G. Kelley- (12-5-1889 - 10-9-1970) Dad
KITTS, Ada Grace- (1-23-1895 - 11-21-1951) Mom

KIMBERLIN, John J.- (3-1-1855 - 9-9-1912)
KIMBERLIN, Henry- (3-17-1825 - 7-31-1887)
KIMBERLIN, Barbara- (2-10-1828 - 6-4-1891) Wife of Henry.
KIMBERLING, Elizabeth- (Dates illegible)

KING, Josie O.- (7-28-1890 - 9-11-1894) D/O E.W. & M.L. King

KINZER, Edward H.- (7-16-1875 - 6-30-1902)

SHARON LUTHERAN CHURCH CEMETERY
[Above Ceres, Virginia on State Route # 42]

LAMBERT, Cammie C. Munsey- (5-13-1869 - 1-30-1902) { W/O C.W Lambert}
LAMBERT, Etta M.- (9-27-1885 - 2-16-1926) {W/O William J. Lambert}
LAMBERT, George W.- (CSA marker, no dates)
LAMBERT, Savey A.- (1-28-1846 - 1-28-1846 - 12-26-1914){W/O G.W.}
LAMBERT, Jackson J.- (1836 - 3-29-1913)
LAMBERT, Elizabeth Greever- (1-22-1841 - 5-13-1926) {W/O Jackson }
LAMBERT, Velma V.- (4-15-1910 - 9-30-1986)
LAMBERT, Nancy E.- (3-16-1875 - 8-21-1954)
LAMBERT, James H.- (7-23-1873 - 2-6-1933)

LESTER, Orbie Dennis- (10-19-1897 - 8-22-1971)
LESTER, Edith Kitts- (1-11-1900 - 4-11-1957)

MAHOOD, Amanda G.- (5-10-1834 - 4-17-1910)
MAHOOD, Rev. James- (1-1-1833 - 1-6-1914)
MAHOOD, Angeline- (5-14-1874 - 9-27-1913)

MCCLELLAN, Josephine Hubble- (1861 - 1932)
MCCLELLAN, William Marion- (1854 - 1931)
MCCLELLAN, Crystal Virginia- (1889 - 1904)
MCCLELLAN, Ocus- (1885 - 1886)
MCCLELLAN, Attie Mildred- (1878 - 1881)

MCFARLAND, Blanch Warner- (1865 - 1939) {Nee Repass}

MCNUTT, Infant of W. & M.M. McNutt- (B. & D. 7-25-1872)
MCNUTT, Lena R.- (9-13-1871 - 1-18-1879) Child \ W. & M.M. McNutt.
MCNUTT, Lillie M.- (10-12-1874 - 12-4-1874)Child \ W. & M.M. McNutt
MCNUTT, William T.- (10-18-1847 - 2-25-1908)
MCNUTT, Mary M.- (3-25-1848 - 11-12-1884) Wife of W.T. McNutt
MCNUTT, John A.- (10-17-1876 - 1-30-1904)
MCNUTT, James Grayson- (4-5-1901 - 12-17-1903)
MCNUTT, Henry Trollinger- (9-28-1918) Only date on US Navy marker.
MCNUTT, Nannie- (8-1865 - 3-4-1931) { Nee Sadler }

NEAL, Samuel F.- (8-30-1879 - 1-31-1910)

PECK, Christina- (3-20-1828 - 11-30-1901)

PEERY, Jennie- (11-11-1868 - 7-12-1898)
PEERY, William J.- (1873 - 1920)
PEERY, Alia McClellan- (1882 - 1966) Wife of William Peery
PEERY, O. Blaine- (1906 - 1930)
PEERY, John G.- (1849 - 1923)
PEERY, Mary J. Groseclose- (1852 - 1918)
PEERY, William- (died 1910, infant son of Mr. & Mrs. W.J. Peery.)
PEERY, Alfred- (died 1912, infant son of Mr. & Mrs. W.J. Peery.)

REPASS, John- (1-12-1821 - 10-29-1904) Father
REPASS, Minerva A.- (7-20-1832 - 4-4-1918) Mother

SHARON LUTHERAN CHURCH CEMETERY
[Above Ceres, Virginia on State Route # 42]

ROBERTSON, Nina Hayton- (3-1-1892 - 2-1-1977)

SCOTT, Robert B.- (12-16-1904 - 10-30-1980) Married 9-24-1927.
SCOTT, Dixie F.- (8-9-1909 -   ) Married 9-24-1927)
SCOTT, Roy Foglesong- (1-11-1935 - 1-12-1935)
SCOTT, Thomas F.- (11-3-1863 - 1-22-1903)
SCOTT, W. Carl- (9-3-1890 - 6-12-1894) Son of T.F. & M.C. Scott.
SCOTT, Barbara A.- (2-23-1827 - 6-2-1897) Age 70yrs 3mos 9 das.
SCOTT, Cecil F.- (9-4?-1889 - 4-4?-1890) Age 7 months
SCOTT, Nellie Gilmore- (4-16-1891 - 7-15-1894) Age 3yrs 2mos 29das

SHANNON, John- (12-26-1796 - 3-2-1850) Age 63yrs 2mos 5das

SPANGLER, Peter- (8-9-1817 - 10-25-1889)
SPANGLER, Amanda- (1-22-1832 - 9-24-1896) Wife of Peter Spangler
SPANGLER, Catherine- (2-19-1790 - 7-27-1886) MOTHER
SPANGLER, (Illegible)- (5-17-1785 - 11-22-1847) FATHER
SPANGLER, Jacob- (dates illegible)
SPANGLER, Stephen- (12-26-1820 - 4-13-1868)
SPANGLER, Margaret- (1760 - 8-11-1838)
SPANGLER, Jacob- (4-?-1856 - death date illegible)
SPANGLER, Joel H.- (2-25-1833 - 12-3-1889)

STACY- John Jay- (1898 - 1955) FATHER

THOMAS, Ruth Groseclose- (12-9-1915 - 6-14-1989) Wife of J.M. Thomas.
THOMAS, Joseph "J.M."- (7-3-1911 -   )
THOMAS, Josie S.- (8-21-1850 - 8-28-1892)

TIBBS, Mary C.- (2-27-1858 - 12-13-1897)
TIBBS, Margaret A.- (1-13-1882 - 10-11-1966)
TIBBS, Mezappa C.- (2-1-1871 - 8-15-1960)
TIBBS, Willie Peery- (6-2-1895 - 10-31-1971) FATHER
TIBBS, Ella Mae- (6-22-1898 - 3-5-1991) MOTHER

TILSON, Anna- (5-2-180? - 10-10-1878) Wife of Ransom Tilson

UMBARGER, Julia A. Crabtree- (12-21-1863 - 10-5-1897) Wife of Jim
          Umbarger. Buried with her infant son
UMBARGER, Emily M.- (no dates) Dau of A. &. A. Umbarger
UMBARGER, Agnes- (8-30-1815 - 1-15-1863) Wife of Alexander Umbarger
UMBARGER, Mary E.- (d-1-1848 - 7-31-1869) Dau of A. & Agnes   "
UMBARGER, Phillip- (5-13-1786 - 5-11-1869)
UMBARGER, Maria- (3-11-1789 - 5-25-1868)
UMBARGER, John D.- (1863 - 1938)
UMBARGER, Minnie Foglesong- (1879 - 1964)

WADDLE, Vivian M.- (5-5-1896 - 8-12-1897)
WADDLE, Laura B.- (4-23-1873 - 1-14-1899) Wife of J.T. Waddle
WADDLE, Wythe G.- (1848 - 1935)

WADDLE, R. Elizabeth- (1870 - 1945)

WALL, Stephen C.U.- (dates illegible) {S/O Stephen & Sarah Wall}
WALL, Sarah- (9-10-1822 - 3-9-1890)

WALTERS, Everette Glenn- (8-3-1896 - 1-28-1940)

WARNER, Dr. Samuel C.- (1870 - 1898)

WHISMAN, Dora Stellena- (6-3-1906 - 11-14-1908) {D/O C.J. & Mable W-}

WILSON, Elizabeth- (12-25-1832 - 5-2-1909)
WILSON, Dewey Kent- (5-15-1898 - 3-17-1963)
WILSON, Owen T.- (2-17-1922 - 4-22-1943)
WILSON, Ben F.- (6-24-1861 - 4-1-1930)
WILSON, Ellen S.- (1-27-1861 - 7-10-1936)
WILSON, W. Neel- (6-26-1896 - 7-23-1968)
WILSON, Mable H.- (2-2-1896 - 7-31-1965)
WILSON, Eugene Neel- (2-22-1929 - 2-25-1929){S/O W.Neel & Mable W}
WILSON, Josie A.- (6-6-1866 - 9-11-1921) {D/O T.O & M.J. Wilson}
WILSON, Elizabeth Rubamah- (4-3-1863 - 5-13-1886){D/O T.O & M.J. W--}
WILSON, Thomas O.- (3-3-1836 - 4-5-1906)
WILSON, Missouri J. Huddle- (7-4-1837 - 1-16-1901){W/O Thomas O.-
WILSON, James Elias- (1-11-1833 - 7-6-1881)
WILSON, Polly Ann- (3-17-1839 - 2-19-1889) Age 49yrs 11mos 2das
WILSON, Texie M.- (5-31-1870 - 6-7-1942) { Nee Wright, w/o Bud}
WILSON, Crockett A. "Bud"- (4-6-1868 - 1-30-1953)
WILSON, Amanda J.- (7-18-1835 - 7-28-1879)
WILSON, James M.C.- (5-27-1?32 - death date obscured)
WILSON, Rebecca- (8-8-1873 - ?-26-1878)
WILSON, Elizabeth, (Died 4-10-1855, in her 84th year.)
WILSON, Elizabeth- (3-1808 - 1-17-18??)
WILSON, James- (2-?-1797 - 8-?-?? age 78yrs 4mos 22 das.
WILSON, Elizabeth- (5-26-1830 - 2-24-1877) Dau\ James & Elizabeth
WILSON, William E.- (5-4-1864 - 4-2-1870)
WILSON, Infant d/o James and A.J. Wilson- (B.& D. 7-29-1872)
WILSON, Infant d/o M.C. & Armanda Wilson (11-21-1881 - 12-7-1881)
WILSON, Edley- (2-20-1788 - 2-15-1859) Age 70yrs 11mos 23das
WILSON, Rebecca- (2-20-1808 - 5-15-1881) { Audley Wilson married
        Rebecca Maxwell, on Oct. 3, 1828, in Wythe County. By Rev.
        L.L. Marshall. Notice spelling of Audley, Edley's name.
WILSON, John- (died 12-10- dates unreadable)
WILSON, James- (12-12-1738 - *1823) Age 85
WILSON, Audley, Jr.- (died 5-11-1828, age 20 yrs 1 month)

WINGATE, S. Luther- (1896 - 1985)
WINGATE, (Josephine Peery- (1903 - 1973)

WOOLWINE, Andrew Groseclose- (7-13-1903 - 12-19-1953)
WOOLWINE, Mamie Groseclose- (12-4-1880 - 12-31-1969)

SHARON LUTHERAN CHURCH CEMETERY
[Above Ceres, Virginia on State Route # 42]

WOOLWINE, Andrew Bane, MD- (5-3-1874 - 11-3-1945)
WOOLWINE, McCarthy- (2-21-1934 - 3-26-1988)

WRIGHT, Matilda R. Wilson- (12-8-1838 - 9-2-1907) {W/O D.O.Wright}

YOUNG, M. Jennie- (died 5-?-1863, age 1 yr 9 mos 19das)
        {D/O S.W. & M.C. Young.

??????, Les a phil- (12-26-1867 - 9-21-1891) age 23yrs 8mos 25das
??????, William- (dates illegible)

SLUSS FAMILY LEGEND
 Data taken from the stone erected in Sharon Cemetery by Col. Samuel
Howe Williams, a direct descendant of Mary Sluss Williams, one of two
survivors of the terrible massacre of 1774.
JARED SLUSS, age unknown in 1774, killed by the Indians.
CHRISTINA SLUSS, wife of Jared, killed by the Indians.
JAMES SLUSS, age 12, in 1774, killed.
HAZEL SLUSS, age 10, went back to help her brother Marion, and lost
her own life.
MARION SLUSS, age 7, survived the massacre.
MARY SLUSS, age 6 months, was later found where her mother had hidden
her. She survived and lived to maturity. Her descendant, Col. Samuel
Howe Williams, placed the monument in the cemetery on August 2, 1974.

{ There are at least 50 graves in the old section of Sharon Cemetery,
near the church, whose stones are so badly eroded that it is
impossible to read them. We appeal to the residents of Ceres and
surounding places to send to the Bland Historical Society any other
information that is in existence, which might enable us to know who
is buried in these graves. }

[Cemetery data was copied on April 13th and 14th of 1991, by Mrs.
Garman Lester and Parke C. Bogle.]
Information can be emailed to Parke C. Bogle at <parkebog@swva.net>
or mailed to 1117 High Street, Pulaski, VA. 24301

JOHN SAMUEL BERNARD'S CASKET LIST

Copied from an old ledger in the possession of Mrs. Ruth Bernard Atwell, daughter of John Samuel Bernard and his wife, Eula Gordon Bernard. Ruth remembered when she was a small child, playing in the old hearse which was stored on her father's property. The hearse was owned by Mr. Aurelius Vest from White Gate.

The years covered in this list were from 1928 through May Of 1933. What a startling difference in the cost of a funeral during those years as compared to today's prices!! Ruth Bernard Atwell is now deceased and is buried at Mechanicsburg. She graciously allowed me to copy it when I visited with her in 1991. Parke C. Bogle

YEAR OF 1928

DATE	STOCK #	NAME OF DECEASED	PRICE
Jan. 12,	# 2	Isaac Dalton	$25.00
Jan. 31,	# 53	Mrs. Gordon Myers	$75.00
Feb. 14,	# 33	Mrs. Mollie Fanning	$65.00
March 21,	# 72	Mr. Gordon Myers	$------
April 16,	# --	Polly Ramsey	$------
April 20,	# 1	Tony Ramsey's boy	$15.00
May 11,	# 36	M.J. Fanning	$65.00
May 22,	# 3	F. T. Gordon's infant	$20.00
July 25,	#--	H. J. Munsey	$75.00
Sept. 13,	# 63	H. W. Steele	$100.00
Oct. 4,	# 16	Rhoda A. Nicewander	$60.00
Oct. 25,	# 17	George Carr	$35.00
Dec. 15,	# 16	John A. Peaks	

YEAR OF 1929

DATE	STOCK #	NAME OF DECEASED	PRICE
March 10,	# 17B	S.C. Bogle	$35.00
May 29,	# 72	W. V. Morris	$50.00
June 9,	# 3	Everett Wolf's child	$-----?
June 14,	# 4	Mason Burton's child	$18.00
Oct. 7,	# 63	Arbanna Caroline Newberry	$125.00
Sept. 22,	# 20	W. R. Sarver's child	bill
Nov. 12,	# 1	Otho Ramsey's child	$15.00

YEAR OF 1930

DATE	STOCK #	NAME OF DECEASED	PRICE
July 4,	# 17	Paris Pauley	$35.00
August 9,	# 63	Mrs. Nannie Stone	$100.00
August 30,	# 63F	Mrs. John W. Burton	$125.00
October 22,	# 17B	Mrs. Wylie	$35.00

YEAR OF 1931

DATE	STOCK #	NAME OF DECEASED	PRICE
March 17,	??	J.H. (Harve) Corner	$60.00
April 19,-	# 16	George Asbury	$60.00
July 13,	chk & discount for W.V. Morris		$50.00

JOHN SAMUEL BERNARD'S CASKET LIST

YEAR OF 1931, contd.

DATE	STOCK #	NAME OF DECEASED	PRICE
August 25,	# 1A	Clyde Dalton's infant.	$15.00
December 2,	# 53	Mrs. Daisey Helvey	$75.00
December 6,	# 36	Mrs. Ellen Stowers	$75.00
December 7,		Hearse service for Ellen Stowers	-----
December 21,		Mrs. Walt Taylor (Ossie)	$60.00

YEAR OF 1932

DATE	STOCK #	NAME OF DECEASED	PRICE
April 28,	# 53	Ruby Price and services	$85.00
May 24,	# 17B	Mrs. Roxie Abshire	$
June 17,	# 36C	Mrs. Willie A. Ramsey	$35.00
July 4,	#	Robert Brookman	$30.00
July		Roxie Abshire	???
September 29		Carl Wetzel's infant	
October 4,		Mrs. Fannie Munsey + $5.00 service	$40.00
October 11,		Mrs. Hoge Wolfe + hearse service	

YEAR OF 1933

DATE	STOCK #	NAME OF DECEASED	PRICE
January 16,		John C. French (paid $7.00)	$35.00
May 26,		A. W. Price	

THOMPSON CEMETERY- PULASKI, VIRGINIA
Off Cox's Hollow Road on land owned by Mrs. Helen Cecil Hall.
{ Copied May 24, 1995 by Parke C. Bogle and Margie Hall Hurst }

BRYSON, James Luther- (12-22-1905 - 9-30-1961)
BRYSON, Mary Thompson- (4-3-1905 - 1998){Date added from her obit}

COX, Curtis F.- (7-26-1929 -   )
COX, Lois M. Bryson- (11-9-1930 - 8-23-1982)

GILLENWATERS, John Harvey- (11-8-1866 - 10-14-1941)
GILLENWATERS, Hubert C.- (3-30-1903 - 4-1-1974)
GILLENWATER, John Clinton- (10-10-1898 - 3-23-1936)

MILLIRONS, Hugh L.- (1-8-1888 - 5-22-1959)   [FATHER]
MILLIRONS, Mary L.- (4-29-1894 - 6-2-1978)
MILLIRONS, Charles H.- (9-15-1864 - 7-21-1935)

THOMPSON, Albert Glenn- (11-28-1929 - 2-19-1971)
THOMPSON, Edward E.- (6-21-1894 - 4-16-1969) [World War I. marker]
THOMPSON, Myrtle Gillenwaters- (5-28-1900 - 5-28-1988)
THOMPSON, David F. - (9-16-1841 - 8-9-1923) Age 81yrs 10 mos, 23das
THOMPSON, Catherine Y.- (10-25-1836 - 1-31-1922) Age 85yrs 3mo 6das
{ Catherine Young Thompson was the daughter of Jacob and Mary Fanning
Munsey. She was first married to Franklin P. Waggoner who was died a
prisoner of War during the Civil War. She later married David Fleming
Thompson son of James Fleming Thompson and Sarah Hearne Thompson.
They moved from Bland County to Pulaski where they both died and are
buried. }
THOMPSON, Franklin Miller- (6-20-1867 - 8-5-1936) On stone with Eliz.
THOMPSON, H. Elizabeth Millirons- (4-25-1869 - 10-7-1960)
THOMPSON, Madge Craig- (8-19-1899 - 7-31-1979) W/o Clarence.
THOMPSON, Clarence Cecil- (10-9-1897 - 2-7-1970)
THOMPSON, Ernest David- (10-1-1920 - 6-15-1921)
THOMPSON, Clarence Cecil, Jr.- (8-16-1919 - 10-1-1971)
THOMPSON, Michael B.- (1988 - 1988) { Funeral Home Marker }

WITHROW, Cecil Earl- (1927 - 1980)
WITHROW, Mrs. Betty T.- (1931 -1982)
[These two Withrow graves are in front of a pretty white brick wall
which serves as a head stone. Their names and dates of birth and
death are on Funeral Home Markers, from Oakeys Funeral Home, Roanoke,
VA.]

  There appear to be no graves in this cemetery that are without
stones. If there were ever sunken places they have been filled in.
The cemetery has a new chain link fence around it and has been mowed
and well cared for. My thanks goes to Mrs. Margie Hall Hurst for
leading the way to this remote graveyard. The cemetery lays just
above her mother's home off Coxes Hollow Road. This cemetery is
included in the Bland County list because of the Thompson- Munsey
connection to Bland County.

WADDLE FAMILY CEMETERY # 1
{ Located on a hill South of Route 617 on the former L. L. Waddle property, now owned by James Waddle. May be accessed by car.}
[Copied March 27, 1999 by Jo Ann Tickle Scott]

WADDLE, Raymond L.- (10-17-1944 - 12-9-1997)
WADDLE, Wanda D.- (3-2-1944 -   ) {W/O Raymond L. }
WADDLE, Leonard Lawrence- (7-27-1904 - 7-11-1956) {Father}
WADDLE, Claudine Farmer- (11-27-1915 - 10-21-1993) {Mother} [Murdered by two men and found in her burned house.]
WADDLE, Everett Nathan- (1897 - 1970)
WADDLE, Mamie Ellen- (1903-1970) {W/O Everett Nathan}
WADDLE, Elmer Eugene- (5-11-1910 - 2-20-1915)

WADDLE FAMILY CEMETERY # 2
{ Located through the pasture land on a hill North of Route 617 on the Vance Waddle property. There could have been as many as 30 graves there at one time. Itis in poor condition. Cattle have grazed over it and time and the elements have taken their toll. It can be accessed by car. My thanks to Teresa Waddle for her help in finding the site }
[Copied March 27, 1999 by Jo Ann Tickle Scott.]

WADDLE, Mark R.- (1-22-188? - 9-7-1888) {S/O Daniel & Mary Waddle}
WADDLE, Daniel- (3-9-1886 - 3-10-1886) {S/O Daniel & Mary Waddle}
WADDLE, Joseph Daniel Miller- (3-8-1886 - 6-15-1902) {S/O G.A. & A.}

ROBINETT, Elizabeth- (3-12-1799 - 8-23-1874)

{ A field stone with markings "G.R.W- (5-29-1877".

WADDLE FAMILY CEMETERY # 3
{ Located on Vance Waddle property, South of Route 617. Site may be accessed by 4x4 or walk. Thanks to Margaret, Peggy and Teresa Waddle for their help in finding this old cemetery. 15 indentations here. }
[Copied March 27, 1999 by Jo Ann Tickle Scott.]

DILLMAN, Teddie Gertrude- (3-13-1882 - 9-19-1911) {D/O Wm. G & Mary C. Waddle. W/O Harman Dillman }
WADDLE, Vance B.- (10-21-1913 - 12-10-1995) {Father}
WADDLE, Margaret G.- (2-25-1917 -   ) {Mother}
WADDLE, Minnie F.- (1881 - 1959) {W/O Dunn B. Waddle}
WADDLE, Dunn B.- (1872 - 1959)
WADDLE, Rufus Floyd- (4-28-1868 - 12-10-1893) {S/O William & Mary}
WADDLE, Napoleon B.- (11-6-1877 - 8-1-1878) {S/O Wm. G. & Mary}
WADDLE, Edward Luther- (5-12-1892 - 4-16-1914) {S/O D.B. & Grace}
WADDLE, Clive Vernon- (7-25-1906 - 1-4-1908) {S/O Dunn & Minnie)
WADDLE, M.C.W.{ a face down footstone thought to be for Mary C. W/O William G. Waddle. (no dates visible. Could not lift stone}
WADDLE, William G.- (12-12-1845 - 4-14-1921)
WADDLE, Greg E.- (5-22-1870 - 11-5-1924)
WADDLE, Isaac Jefferson- (5-11-1859 - 4-21-1889) {S/O Joseph & Rhoda}

WADDLE-HAYTON CEMETERY

{ Located on a hill North of Route 617 on land formerly owned by
Ephriam Waddle, now owned by B.C. and Margaret Hayton Umbarger. It is
in good condidtion and can be accessed by a 4x4 or walk}
[Copied March 27, 1999 by Jo Ann Tickle Scott.]

HANCOCK, Creolia E.- (5-24-1887 - 3-5-1955) {D/O N.B. and Margaret}
HANCOCK, Margaret Waddle- (4-1-1865 - 4-9-1942) {W/O N.B. Hancock}
HANCOCK, N. B.- (died 3-3-1922, age 69 yrs.) {Md. 5-6-1886}

HAYTON, Minta Careen- (7-5-1897 - 11-21-1975) {W/O Samuel Milton}
HAYTON, Samuel Milton- (7-3-1902 - 5-23-1982)

WADDLE, Amanda- (2-26-1829 - 5-27-1888) {W/O Ephriam Waddle}
WADDLE, Ephriam- (died 7-5-1887, age 69 yrs.
WADDLE, Infant- (born & died 5-3-1888) {D/O N.B & A.}
WADDLE, Hiram- (6-16-1868 - 5-1-1888)

DAVIS FAMILY CEMETERY

{ Located on land owned by John and Eleanor Davis Atwell, formerly
the T.M. Davis property. It is in good condition and can be accessed
by a 4x4 or walking. Copied March 27, 1999 by Jo Ann Tickle Scott. }

BROWN, Deborah (Atwell)- (2-24-1964 - 1-9-1990) {D/O John & Eleanor}
BROWN, unborn baby of Deborah's. {Both killed in car wreck}

DAVIS, Thomas McGinnis- (1901 - 1975)
DAVIS, Virginia T.- (1907 - 1984) {Nee Tickle, w/o Thomas M. Davis}
DAVIS, Randolph Mc.- (4-6-1865 - 12-19-1947)
DAVIS, Elizabeth F.- (10-16-1862 - 6-29-1943) {W/O Randolph M. }
DAVIS, Deco Green- (7-12-1892 - 4-7-1961) {Pvt. WW I }
DAVIS, Robert Lee- (7-13-1896 - 3-24-1987)
DAVIS, Ada Shewey- (8-23-1905 - 2-7-1990)

STEELE, {According to Davis family history, there are 2 graves here.
These are relatives of Tealie and Florence Steele. Names forgotten.}

WHITAKER, William Kale- (11-13-1905 - 10-6-1987)

GRAVE SITES

2 graves on a ridge North of Route 617. Davis historians say that
Isabella Waddle, 1st wife of Calvin Waddle, and her infant are
buried there. They both died when the child was born, March 8, 1854.
They were traveling the old road when she went into labor. Theyd were
buried on the spot where they died. What a sad story!

OVERBAUGH, baby of Stanley & Michelle, on hill South of Route 617.

THOMPSON, Estel Hoge- (1916 - 1998) buried South of Route 42 on a
          hill across the branch from his home.

PENLEY CEMETERY # 2

{ Located near a barn on a hill North of State Route 42, about one mile east of Bland School and behind the S. V. Burton home. The cemetery is in bad condition. Cattle and time have taken their toll on the site. It can be accessed by 4x4 or by walking. My thanks to Mildred Richardson for going with me to find this grave site. }
[Copied March 31, 1999 by Jo Ann Tickle Scott]
{ Annotated by Parke C. Bogle}

MARCUS, Ethel A. M.- (1-14-1885 - 12-9-1885) {D/O R.N. & F.A. Marcus}

PENLEY, Melissa A. Suiter- (3-22-1842 - 11-9-1893) {W/O Braxton H.
        Penley and dau. of George W. and Esther Newberry Suiter.}
{ After Melissa's death, Braxton remarried in 1897 to Ardelia Fanning, daughter of Absolem and Sarah Fanning. There is no stone or marker for him here. In the 1900 Bland Census, Braxton was listed as being 70 years old having been born in March 0f 1830 in North Caroline. He was a brother of Rev. George W. Penley who married Adeline Robinett. His home was next door to Jesse A. Muncy. He died after 1900.}

PENLEY, Arthur N.- (10-14-1878 - 11-20-1906) {S/O Braxton and Melissa
        Adeline Suiter Penley.}

CRABTREE CEMETERY

{ Located on a hill North of State Route 42 as you travel toward Ceres. It is behind the Woodrow Scott home and is partially covered with trees and brush. Tommy Scott now owns the property. It can be accessed by 4x4 or walking.}
[Copied and annotated by Jo Ann Tickle Scott on March 31, 1999]

HANSHAW, Anna- (8-7-1828 - 12-23-1898) { This is the only stone
        visible. She was probably the last person buried here. There
        are about 14 field stones and several indentations here. }

BRUCE - PETREE CEMETERY

{Located South of State Route 42 on a hill in a grove of locust trees almost directly across from the George T. Bird home and on his property. It has been almost destroyed by cattle and the elements }
[Copied March 30, 1999 by Jo Ann Tickle Scott]

BRUCE, Sarah- (died 1-19-1857, aged 72 yrs 10 mos & 11 days.) { Nee
        Hearn, w/o Joshua Bruce.}
{ A stone exactly like Sarah's stone but illegible is most likely the
   stone for Joshua BRUCE-(10-23-1778 - 8-23-1865) Dates taken from
   the Bruce Family History.}{ Possibly 16 graves her at one time.}
BRUCE, Josiah- (3-16-1808 - 11-22-1888) {S/O Joshua & Sarah}
BRUCE, Minerva T.- (6-21-1812 - 3-20-1899) { Nee Justice, w/o Joshua}

PETREE, B. F.(Benjamin Franklin)- (1-13-1839 - 5-18-1909)
PETREE, Amanda- (4-3-1843 - 11-16-1916) {D/o Josiah & Minerva Bruce &
        w/o B.F. Petree. }

CLEAR FORK BAPTIST CHURCH CEMETERY
{Located on West State Route 61, about 11 miles from Interstate 77,
behind the Church. It is well kept but many stones have eroded
rendering them illegible. }
[Copied and annotated by Jo Ann Tickle Scott]

BAKER, Betty J.- (1949 - 1980)

CARTER, Billy- (born & died 6-29-1944) {S/O Virgil & Ruby Carter}

CARVER, Sally B.- (1908 - 1979) { W/O David}
CARVER, David D.- (1904 - 1969)
CARVER, Robert Lee- (6-9-1927 - 12-24-1946) {WW II}

CHRISTIAN, Philip K.- (8-4-1892 - 11-14-1911)

CLARK, Thomas Campbell- (3-2-1924 - 8-4-1994) {Pvt. US Army WW II}

CRABTREE, William J.- (11-5-1910 - 7-13-1914)

DAVIDSON, Elizabeth- (12-19-1896 - 8-7-1917)

DAVIS, E. A.- (9-18-1837 - 6-26-192)
DAVIS, Zarilda A.- (10-19-1851 - 8-18-1884) { W/O E. A. Davis}
DAVIS, Stella O.- (9-26-1892 - 1-24-1906) {D/O Zarilda & E.A. Davis }
DAVIS, Mosby C.- (8-23-1876 - 5-20-1877) {D/O Zarilda & E. A. Davis}
DAVIS, G. H.- (died 6-9-1854, age 2 yrs 5mos 6 days.){S/O P.H. & V.J}
        { The above stone very badly eroded. I am unsure of the dates}
DAVIS, Mary Lee- (2-25-1911 - 3-7-1911)

DILLS, Mary- (died 10-24-1856, age 74 yrs 2 mos 26 days)
DILLS, Peter, Sr.- (died 1-27-1853, age 74 yrs 5 mos 23 days)

FORTUNE, Jane Newton- (died 1-12-1999, age 74)

FOX, Peery Gabriel- (3-25-1912 - 12-8-1912)

GUY, Fannie M.- (3-22-1881 - 2-1-1902)
GUY, Ethel M.- (9-28-1900 - 8-22-1906)

HALL, Robert O.- (7-6-1919 - 1-26-1968) {Mil. Police, WW II }
HALL, Matilda- (5-27-1924 - 7-24-1993)

HULL, Albert R.- (8-19-1890 - 9-26-1918) {S/O J. S. & I. B. Hull}
        { He gave his life for his country}

JARRELL, Charles Edward- (1899 - 1990) {S/O Charlie L. & Mary}
JARRELL, Mary V.- (2-9-1874 - 2-28-1958) {W/O Charlie L. Jarrell}
JARRELL, Charlie L.- (10-25-1873 - 4-6-1946)

KELL, Thurman J.- (11-14-1923 - 4-25-1997) {US Army WW II}

KIMBERLIN, Lonnie P.- (3-15-1937 - 3-30-1937) {S/O Luther}

CLEAR FORK BAPTIST CHURCH CEMETERY

LAMBERT, William E.- (2-25-1888 - 3-25-1971)
LAMBERT, Rosa J.- (8-15-1898 - 8-4-1984) {W/O William E. Lambert}

LOCKHART, Mary J.- (1904 - 1982) {Mother}
LOCKHART, James P.- (6-17-1896 - 11-4-1966) {Father} { US Army WW I }
LOCKHART, Jerry W.- (1-2-1944 - 11-16-1956) {Son}

MONTGOMERY, Rebecca- (2-17-1834 - 3-10-1920)

MORRIS, William Clyde- (11-29-1894 - 9-30-1904) {S/O W.A. & M.L. }

NEAL, Alexander- (5-1-1886 - 8-18-1837) {Father}
NEAL, W. B.- (1-5-1891 - 5-6-1944) {Mother}

NEWTON, Ellen Shannon- (7-3-1897 - 9-4-1988) {W/O Rufus T. Newton}
NEWTON, Rufus Tazewell- (6-22-1901 - 2-16-1983)

THOMAS, Minnie Neal- (6-3-1896 - 9-22-1974)

THOMPSON, Louisa Victoria- (5-4-1851 - 5-25-1905){Age 54 yrs 21 days}
THOMPSON, David F.- (no dates) {Co. F. VA Inf. CSA }
THOMPSON, Nelson- (no dates) {Age 61 years}

WOLFE, Rosa Mae- (9-15-1886 - 1-20-1983) {W/O Wiley W. Wolfe}
WOLFE, Wiley A.- (1-27-1883 - 12-2-1956)
WOLFE, Raleigh A.- (1-24-1916 - 4-21-1916){S/O Wiley P. & Rosa Wolfe}

WOOLF, Stella R. B.- (6-12-1904 - 2-2-1907)
WOOLF, Clarence J.- (died 10-26-1900) {S/O C.B. & C. E. Woolf}

WOODYARD, Rosa M.- (1867 - 1904)
WOODYARD, Elizabeth Angeline- (10-2-1860 - 3-22-1900?)
WOODYARD, Roxie May- (4-3-1888 - 5-24-1899)
WOODYARD, Mary Jennie- (7-23-1897 - 9-22-1899)

2 footstones marked "S.D. and M.D." side by side with fieldstones as
head stones.
At least 30 field stones and several which are illegible.

    { The day I copied this cemetery it was snowing} Jo Scott.

DEATH OF DR. J.H. BOGLE
Sebring, Fla., Nov. 14, 1923

Dr. J.H. Bogle, 55, the second of Sebring's older physicians to answer his last "call" within a month, died Saturday November 10, at 10:21 in the morning, after a brief illness. He was stricken with colitis while in attendance on a patient last week and grew rapidly worse. All that was known to medical science was done in a vain attempt to save his life. Drs. Weems and Cook of this city, with Dr. Mitchell of Moore Haven; Dr. Koker of Arcadia and Dr. Wallace of Tampa, assisted by Mrs. Long of this city and Miss Bush of Tampa, both graduate nurses, were with him until the end. James Harvey Bogle was born in Bland County, Virginia, April 6, 1868. He graduated from The School of Physicians and Surgeons of Baltimore, Johns Hopkins, and practiced medicine for several years in the vicinity of his birthplace. Here he was married on Oct. 7, 1896, to Miss Della Claire Bailey, who survives him. To this union, eight children were born, Kathleen who is studying medicine at Richmond, Va.; Mary; Anna; Edna; James; John Lake and Madelyn, all of this city. One daughter, Verena died in Roanoke at age nine.

Before coming to Sebring four years ago, Dr. Bogle practiced in Roanoke, Va., for thirteen years. He was prominent in medical circles in that communuty, having been president of the Shenandoah Hospital at Roanoke for many years. Ill health forced his removal to Sebring where he has been in active practice.

Besides his immediate family, he leaves to mourn his loss, a sister, Mrs. Paris Saunders of White Gate, Va., and two brothers, George Bogle of Winchester, Ohio and John Bogle of Dublin, Va., all of whom were prevented from attending the funeral by illness in the family. L.P. Bailey, a brother of Mrs. Bogle, came Monday evening and will stay for a week.

Wednesday, all of Sebring, paused from ten o'clock until twelve, to pay it's last honor to all that was mortal of Dr. Bogle, and to show it's sympathy to the bereaved family. Every store, office and factory closed it's doors and the entire city bowed it's head with grief at the passing of good physician, loving friend and faithful counselor.

The funeral services which were held in the M.E. Church, were in charge of the Masonic Lodge. At nine thirty the intimate friends of the family gathered at the home and at ten,

DEATH OF DR. J.H. BOGLE
Sebring, Fla., Nov. 14, 1923

the funeral cortege started for the Church, led by the Sebring Band who played the solemn funeral music. The hearse was followed by an escort of Masons in full regalia, and the flower bearers with the beautiful floral tributes, which were sent from every civic, social and church organization in the city, from the staff of the Shenandoah Hospital and from sorrowing friends and relatives in Virginia, and in this vicinity. Active pall bearers were: Louis Catogni; John Graham; J.W. Ingle; R.H. Hancock; A.L. Butler; W.B. Amy; N.C. Cash; and O.E. Douglas.

The honorary pall bearers were: B.O. Bowden; M.G. Norman; H.O. Sebring; George E. Sebring; Dr. Bannister; E. L. Green; A.L. Marchand; George Whitehouse; W. B. Leatherman; David Lane; P.L. Vinson; John A. Taylor; P.G. Carovasios; W. B. Muff; W.W. Right; W.L. Crews; F. T. Haskins; A.E. Lawrence; B.A. Cope; C.W. Rogers; Charles Lewis; Allan Altvator; Ed L. Hainz; A.C. Heacock; M.M. Smythe; C.F. Saunders; W.P. Babcock; B.W. Field; W.F. Johnson; J. W. Geary; E.P. Brown; J.G. McClurg; C.B. Jones; and H.S. Jones.

The flower bearers who were dressed in white were, the Misses Lucille Christy; Alice Cox; Emilie Auslund; Helen Moyer; Ruth Ingle; Jessie Laird; Emma Whitehouse; Faye Christy; Marjorie Michenor; Dorothy Sebring; Leila Sebring; Faith Catogni; Ellen Heacock and Helen Right. The church services were beautiful and impressive. Rev. L.A. Griggs officiated. He was assisted by Dr. John A. Taylor; Dr. H.A. Brown & Dr. J.R. Andrew, all friends of the family in Virginia. Many tributes were paid to the high sacrificing, unselfishness and staunch loyalty of the deceased Physician. The Methodist Choir rendered most beautiful music. Interment was made in the Pine Crest Cemetery in this city and the largest funeral procession ever seen in Sebring, accompanied the body to it's last resting place.

The Masons took charge of the service at the grave and the impressive Masonic burial service was read by the Worshipful Master, Walter Zachary, assisted by the Chaplain, J.W. Gerry. After the grave had been closed with Masonic Rites, four mounted Klansmen rode silently up and planted on the grave of their loyal brother, the red and white cross and the American flag.

-168

DILLOW-BOGLE CEMETERY

{ Located on the former Bogle, Newberry and Allen property and now owned by the Schoenthal family. Thanks to Donna and Bob Distel, Buzz and Mildred Richardson for going with me to find this old cemetery}
[Copied April 1, 1999 by Jo Ann Tickle Scott]

BLANKENSHIP, William Jackson (no stone) {Age 71 Family information}
BLANKENSHIP, Loutheria Dillow- (no stone)

BROWN, J.C.- (died 8-13-1871 - age 15 yrs 11 mos & 3 das.)

DILLOW, Donald Addison- (died at age 3) { No stone, data from family information} { S/O H.H. and Nannie E. Dillow }
DILLOW, William Addison- (no stone) {born 2-21-1851}
DILLOW, Nancy Elizabeth- (died 2-25-1904) W/O William Addison and d/O Isabella & Calvin Waddle}

KITTS, Elizabeth (Dunn)- (2-26-1826 - 8-30-1885) { D/o Thomas Dunn, Jr. and Catherine Steel Dunn. Married William Kitts, June 7, 1843 in Wythe County.}
KITTS, William born 1819 (No stone) {Family information. H/O Elizabeth Dunn Kitts.}

PAULEY, Polly "Pop"- (no stone) { Mother of Nannie }

RICHARDSON, Bettie L.- (3-12-1851 - 12-2-1910) {W/O C.W. Richardson)
RICHARDSON, Nannie E.- (3-29-1892 - 8-28-1892) {D/O C.W & Bettie L.}

TICKLE, Everette Wade- (4-15-1928 - 4-18-1928) (S/O Lemuel & Ida and twin of Wayne Tickle.} (No stone)

{ At one time there were probably 50 graves here. Due to the ravages of time, the elements and cattle this cemetery is practically destroyed. I will appreciate it if any one can tell me of others who may be buried here.}

SLAVE CEMETERIES

Ben Bird told Frazier Lambert that there was a slave cemetery near his home and was destroyed when State Route was built.

There was a slave cemetery on the Sanders Hamilton farm. It was destroyed and plowed over many years ago.

GRAYSON CEMETERY

{ Cemetery is located North of State Route 42/52 on a hill behind the old homestead on the Stowers farm. Some of the stones are so badly eroded that mistakes were probably made in copying the dates. I will appreciate and documentation which will prove the true dates on these old grave stones. Thanks to James and Sarah Stowers Pauley for their help.} [Compiled by Jo Ann Tickle Scott on April 4, 1999]

DUNN, James Randolph- (11-17-1908 - 8-15-1911) {S/O Frank L. and
        Minnie Wayne McColgan Dunn}

GRAYSON, Nancy L.- (4-2-1843 - 4-22-1845) {D/O Randolph & Cynthia}
GRAYSON, Gordon- (1-13-1810 - 12-20-1811) {S/O Ambrose & Elizabeth}
        [Above dates may not be accurate. Stone is badly eroded]
GRAYSON, Randolph- (1-12-1808 - 12-29-1880)
GRAYSON, Cynthia- (11-19-1816 - 2-17-1902) {W/O Randolph & d/o John &
        Agnes Whitlock Grayson.}
GRAYSON, Charles S.- (6-6-1846 - 5-18-1899) {S/O Randolph & Cynthia}
GRAYSON, John A.- (1-15-1857 - 4-23-1926) { S/O Randolph & Cynthia}
GRAYSON, Ambrose- (6-11-1811 - 11-12-1831) {Age 20 yrs 6 mos 1 day.
        This stone is so badly eroded, dates may not be correct}
GRAYSON, George W.- (4-19-1856 - 7-30-1856)
GRAYSON, Adam Crockett- (9-24-1857 - 11-22-1857)
GRAYSON, James F.- (9-26-1861 - 6-2-1905) { S/O James Wayne & Emily
        Steel Grayson.}
GRAYSON, Lucy A.- (6-6-1863 - 7-21-1918){W/O James F. Grayson & d/o
        John S. & Elizabeth Brabson McNutt.}
GRAYSON, Robert Floyd- (9-1-1905 - 7-15-1906) {S/O James & Lucy}
GRAYSON, William R.- (1-23-1813 - 10-25-1817) {S/O John & Agnes}
        [Above dates may not be correst. Stone is badly eroded.
GRAYSON, Edgar Elizabeth- (8-14-1888 - 1-13-1891){2yrs 4 mos 29 days}
GRAYSON, Mary- (4-3-1895 - 7-13-1897}

HAYES, Mayme McColgan- (5-14-1887 - 12-20-1906) { D/O William and
        Mary Grayson McColgan }

HOGE, Bert- { According to family records this lady is buried beneath
        the fence of this cemetery and the fence of the Stowers
        Cemetery, whose fences are almost touching each other. She has
        no stone. Birth and death dates not known.}

MCCOLGAN, William F.- (11-12-1854 - 3-22-1915) {Father}
MCCOLGAN, Mary Grayson- (11-26-1858 - 8-3-1948) {Mother} {W/O Wm. F.
        and d/o James Wayne & Emily Steel Grayson}

MCGINNIS, Elizabeth W.- (1-27-1852 - 12-31-1926)
MCGINNIS, Lee G.- (1-21-1869 - 3-17-1915)
MCGINNIS, John W.- (8-14-1836 - 2-21-1905)
MCGINNIS, Eliza C.- (1876 - 1965) {D/o Randolph & Cynthia Grayson.
        Last person buried here, is listed 1910 Census as age 33}

SHANNON, John C.- (3-22-1827 - 9-27-1864) {H/O Mary Grayson }
SHANNON, Mary Grayson- (2-28-1838 - 11-12-1912){D/O Rand. & Cynthia}

STOWERS CEMETERIE # 2

{ Located right beside the Grayson graveyard. The fences that separate the two cemeteries are only inches apart. These two Stowers Graves are enclosed in a chain link fence. Thanks to Sarah Stowers Pauley for the information on these grave sites.}

STOWERS, Howard Colby- (2-22-1887 - 7-6-1957) { H/O Bessie L. Robinett and son of George Washington & Sarah Jane Shannon Stowers }

STOWERS, Basil Broyles- (9-25-1920 - 6-15-1922) { S/O Howard C. and Bessie Robinett Stowers.}

STOWERS CEMETERY # 3

{ This Stowers graveyard is located on State Route 61, west of Rocky Gap, in the mountain on Clear Fork. The information came from family records. My thanks to Sarah Stowers Pauley for sharing this with me }
[Information furnished by Sarah Stowers Pauley]

BOLING, Serilda Victoria Stowers- (4-26-1873 - 2-9-1949) {D/O George W. & Sarah Shannon Stowers and wife of Hugh Perry Boling}
BOLING, Hugh Perry (12-9-1870 - 4-13-1945)

STOWERS, George Washington- (4-3-1845 - 4-16-1914) { S/O Colby and & Lockie Burton Stowers.}
STOWERS, Sarah Jane Shannon- (8-29-1847 - 11-26-1911) {W/O George W. Stowers and D/O James & Nancy Compton Shannon }
STOWERS, Lettie- (2-2-1900 - 12-2-1996) {D/O Ballard P. & Missouri Caldwell Stowers }

[Mrs. Scott says that there are many more grave sites in the county. She plans to get a listing of each and every one of them for later publication. Many thanks to her for her energy, kindness and willingness to share her findings during the gathering of this information.] - Parke C. Bogle

ADDENDUM

BETHANY CEMETERY

BRUCE, Claude W.- (1-27-1898 - 11-17-1992) h/o Myrtle S.
COOLEY, Joseph Clark- (7-4-1923 - 10-15-1993)
COX, Infant daughter of Mr. & Mrs. S. S. Cox- (7-1-1946)
NUNN, Mary F. Atwell- (3-15-1908 - 10-3-1993) 2nd w/o Henry Nunn. (1st w/o Leland)
UMBARGER, Charles Palmer- (3-4-1916 - 11-25-1964) h/o Ruth Elizabeth Wagner.
UMBARGER, Laura M.- (9-15-1876 - 9-12-1930)
WILLIAMS, Wilbert W.- (11-16-1916 - 2-7-1996)
WILLIAMS, Kermit L.- (2-12-1929 - 5-26-1994)

BLAND, TEMPLE HILL & MORNING STAR CEMETERIES

BAKER, James C.- (9-21-1922 - 5-24-1995) s/o James & Flora.
BLANKENSHIP, Luther H.- (1918 - 1996)
BLANKENSHIP, Helen (Pauley)- (1922 -   ) w/o Luther.
CROUSE, Elizabeth K.- (8-12-1828 - 7-12-1910)
DILLOW, Thomas G.- 10-25-1877 - 12-16-1957)
DILLOW, Margaret Lou- (9-3-1875 - 3-21-1940)
DUNN, Ella Young- (8-23-1865 - 11-26-1949) (corrected birth date)
GOINS, Johnnie Ethel- (5-5-1908 - 3-18-1936)
GREEVER, Mary N. (Newberry) - (6-15-1923 - 4-9-1996)
HALL, Ervin B.- (10-11-1919 - 7-11-1996)
HANCOCK, Elizabeth Stroupe- (4-26-1943 -) w/o Charles Walter Hancock. Md. 12-26-1959.
HANCOCK, Donald- (12-17-1925 -)
HANCOCK, Anabel- (11-16-1925 -)
HANCOCK, Andrew G.- (8-30-1923 - 4-3-1945) Died at sea.
HARDY, Helen Penley- (1-9-1912 -) W/o Sam L. Hardy.
HURLEY, Elizabeth McLemore- (12-11-1914 - 12-15-1983)
INGRAM, Mary D.- (5-5-1917 -)
INGRAM, William P.- (10-9-1911 - 10-20-1996)
JONES, John N.- (2-16-1892 - 1-26-1919)
KING, Henry W.- (1907 - 1959)
MILLER, Vaden H.- (11-5-1931 -   ) S/O Vaden & Ina Lindamood Miller.
MILLER, Ruth F. (Fannon)- (10-14-1927 - 7-2-1994) W/o Vaden H. Miller.
PATTERSON, Floyd Andrew- (1933 -)
SHOCKLEY, Junior V.- (10-2-1925 -)
SHOCKLEY, Dorthea H.- (2-14-1925 - 7-2-1997) W/o Junior. (Md. 6-7-1947)
SLAUGHTER, Margaret J. "Pee Wee"- (6-4-1924 - 2-28-1994)
SPARKS, Ted- (1927 - 1993)
TAYLOR, Willie Wayne- (10-31-1913 - 8-12-1995)
TAYLOR, James Albert- (4-20-1922 - 12-11-1995)
TIBBS, Dennis K.- (9-20-1926 - 7-10-1995)

TIBBS, Margaret (Dillow)- (2-23-1926 -   ) W/O Dennis

TICKLE, Alice Telie- (1877 - 1958) Misplaced under "THOMPSON".

WILLIAMS, William Eugene- (3-7-1929 - 7-26-1994)

WILLIAMS, Beverly Louise- (1934 -   )

WOLFE, Melvin Douglas- (1947 - 1996)

NEWBERRY CHAPEL (RUDDER-DUNCAN)

RUDDER, Infant daughter-1892. { Also two indentations with no stones }

DUNCAN, No name- (1907)

SHILOH METHODIST CHURCH CEMETERY

GUSLER, Evelyn- (8-29-1917 - 10-16-1991) Complete dates for Ollie Evelyn.

NUNN, Roney L.- (1894 - 1973)

HOGES CHAPEL CEMETERY

BOGLE, Mary Jane Pruitt- (4-25-1865 -   ) Listed as M.J. On page 58.

STEPHENS, Samuel- No stone

STEPHENS, Mary Kitts- No stone. {Family says these two are buried here.}

TICKLE, Ella Palmyra (9-20-1873 - 5-13-1957) {Ella not on stone, added by Jo Scott}

MECHANICSBURG CEMETERY

BERNARD, Mamie Sarver- (7-20-1910 - 8-11-1942) Sister

BROOKMAN, Albert C. (Clayton)- (1901 - 1996) S/o Robert & Emma.

HETHERINGTON, Mary G. (Gillespie)- (W/o Joseph B. Hetherington & 2nd w/o Jack Vest.

JOHNSON, John Smith- (1921 - 1992) FHM

KUYKENDALL, Ronald Newberry- (1932 - 1979) S/o Mary Newberry Granberg.

MCNEIL, Victoria Wohlford- (3-2-1877 - 11-25-1945) Dau of Gordon & Matilda Wohlford.

MCNEIL, Thomas Hoge- (12-18-1875 - 7-27-1973) H/O Victoria Wohlford.

MCPEAK, Earl W.- (3-18-1913 - 11-19-1992)

MCPEAK, Maggie Patton- (1-17-1918 - 7-12-1994) W/o Earl.

PARKS, James Wayne- (9-25-1925 - 7-5-1929)

PARKS, William Augustus- (Born & died 6-18-1923)

SIMMONS, Jay (No dates) Hus. of Ruby Lee Gordon.

SIMMONS, Justin Trevor- (1991 - 1993)

TALBERT, Emory Lane- (12-30-1930 - 2-17-1997)

TALBERT, Mary Loraine Chewning- (12-26-1929 -   ) W/O Emory.

THOMPSON, Clarence C.- (8-15-1920 - 5-13-1994)

THOMPSON, Nancy F.- (2-3-1926 -   ) W/O Clarence.

WALKER, Infant son of Floyd and Mary Walker. (No dates)

BURTON CEMETERY (ROUTE 603)

HANCOCK, Emma L.- (3-17-1855 - 5-20-1911)

HIDDEN VALLEY CEMETERY # 2

CROCKETT, John Lewis- (8-28-1915 - 11-17-1993) No given name on pg. 86.

HARMAN BURYING GROUND AT HOLLYBROOK

RAMSEY, Alvah- (Spelled Anvah on page 91)
RAMSEY, Minnie- (Spelled Winnie on page 91)

L. K. MOREHEAD CEMETERY

LAMBERT, Isaac P.- (1827 - 1861) Hus of Susan Rogers.
MILLER, Rachel Herron (Hearn), {On pg. 92- D/O Wm. & Susannah Hearn. { by Jo Scott}

STOWERS CEMETERY (ROUTE # 42)

BURGE, Paul and Elsie. Not buried here.They are buried in Red Oak Cemetery. (Jo Scott)

MOUNTAIN FIELD CEMETERY (OLD WRIGHT)

RAMSEY, Donnie- (4-9-1958 -)
WOLFE, Dennis Roy- (1-9-1949 - 2-27-1995)
WOLFE, Debra B.- (2-19-1952)
WRIGHT, Jerry David- (6-9-1942 - 8-20-1992)
WRIGHT, Charlotte D.- (8-9-1952 -)
WRIGHT, Donald C.- (11-1-1909 - 12-21-1991)

SALEM CHURCH CEMETERY

DALTON, Frances L.- (3-19-1926 - 2-23-1956)
DALTON, M. Viola- (12-10-1906 - 8-11-1994)

ROSE HILL CEMETERY

AKERS, Joseph Thomas- (3-27-1954 - 8-5-1970) No given name listed on page 120.
BAILEY, Charles J.- (3-30-1874 - 3-13-1959)
CRESS, Nancy B. - (5-12-1952) {No other date}
KITTS, Ethel Kidd- (11-17-1896 - 1-29-1981) W/o James W. Kitts
KITTS, Machie Claudine- (7-19-1927 - 3-14-1965) D/o James W. & Ethel
RASNAKE, Asa- (9-30-1907 - 7-19-1982)
SLUSS, Joe- (4-19-1900 - 6-30-1972) Given name missing on page 127.

STIMSON CEMETERY

EVANS, Tyler R. (On page 133, wrongly listed under name of DAVIS.)
EVANS, Betty M.- (On page 133, wrongly listed under name of DAVIS.)

COMPTON CEMETERY

HARMAN, Walter J.- (1-10-1919) (No other date)

WYRICK CEMETERY

EPPERSON, Adeline Hancock, age 78, d/o G.W. Hancock& w/o E.E. Epperson.
The above information taken from an old obituary. (page 138)

OLD MADISON ALLEN CEMETERY

ALLEN, John Poage- (12-13-1839 - 2-25-1917)

STROCK CEMETERY (On Correctional Farm)

STROCK, John E.- (no dates, stone is broken)

CEMETERY NEAR BECKNER'S STORE (BURRESS)

BURTON, Casondra Mae- (8-14-1988 - 11-8-1988)
CHARLES, Charlie W.- (11-26-1913 - 4-16-1998)
CHARLES, Ocie M.- (4-29-1917 -   )
COOK, Jane- (died 10-1884, age 80.)
COOK, Elizabeth M.- (died 12-4-1869, age 11 years)
COOK, Infant d/0 F. & S.E. Cook- (2-18-1875)

KITTS FAMILY CEMETERY

KITTS, W. G.- (stone is face down, cannot read dates)
{ According to family history Dale Kitts' hand, which was severed, is buried here. He is
buried in the Bland Cemetery }

CLEAR FORK BAPTIST CHURCH CEMETERY

BAKER, James Reed- (8-7-1969 - 3-23-1994)
CLARK, Carl Edward- (10-22-1929 -   )
CRALLE, Frank E.- (11-15-1943 -   ) Hus. Of Sandra.
CRALLE, Sandra N. (Neel)- (3-26-1948 - 4-25-1990)
DILLMAN, Wiley K. (1891 - 1944) Wrongly listed as Willie K. On page 107.

EPPERSON, Daniel A.- (5-2-1853 - 2-11-1922)

HARNER, J. J.- (12-26-1821 - 8-8-1871)

HARNER, E. P.- (4-4-1822 - 11-22-1883)

HARNER, Elmo Rudolph- (2-10-1912 - 6-6-1991)

HARNER, Rebecca Lambert- (1-20-1923 -   ) W/O Elmo.

HENLEY, James L. Sr.- (3-9-1943 - 5-31-1992)

HENLEY, Trula L.- (11-21-1945 -   ) W/O James.

HILTON, Jonathan M.- (7-21-1984 - 5-31-1992)

LAMBERT, James Walker- (1876 - 1966)

LAMBERT, Samuel I.- (1883 - 1965)

NEEL, Freda D.- (9-22-1940 -   ) W/O Larry Neel.

NEEL, John C.- (12-17-1892 - 10-9-1964)

NEEL, Silvey Lace- (1922 - 1984)

PECK, Troy B.- (8-26-1926 - 1-5-1989)

UMBARGER, Mary M. (Granny Mollie)- (7-25-1886 - 11-9-1973)

UMBARGER, Bernice L.- (1920 -   ) Md. 11-9-1973.

UMBARGER, Elizabeth- (8-2-1829 - 6-21-1881)

WINESETT, Charles Richard- (8-11-1918 - 4-26-1936)

GREEN VALLEY METHODIST CHURCH CEMETERY

HEDRICK, W.Z.C.- (According to local history, he is the grandfather of LeRoy Beckner and
the first one yo be buried in this cemetery.)

KIDD, C. S.- (1900 - 1971)

KIDD, Lennie, an infant, on home made stone. No dates.

{ These additions and corrections were added by Jo Ann Tickle Scott. They were overlooked in
the first edition. We welcome any corrections or additions. Parke Bogle and Jo Ann Tickle Scott.

MUNCEY
  BEULAH, 86
  EARL, 86
  HARRY THORNTON, 86
MUNCY
  ALMA L., 60
  ANDREW, 25, 29
  ANDREW N., 25
  ANNA JOSEPHINE, 25
  BESS, 25(2)
  BESS REPASS, 25
  C.P., 25
  CHARLES PEERY, 25
  CHARLES PEERY, JR.,
    25
  CYNTHIA D., 25
  D.H., 12
  DAVIS H., 12
  GILBERT CARTER, 25
  GRATTON MUSTARD, 25
  HESTER ANN, 125
  HILARY S., 25
  HOPE LaMOORE, 25
  JACOB, 12(2)
  JAMES B., SR., 25
  JESSE A., 164
  JOHN GORDON, 12
  JOSEPH HOUNSHELL
    "JO-BOY", 25
  JULIA A. STAFFORD,
    12
  LAURA JANE, 136
  LILY FRANCES, 125
  M.E., 25
  MARTHA, 12
  MARY E. McNUTT, 25
  MARY ELIZABETH H.,
    25
  MARY ELLA, 25
  MERLE, 25
  MERLE V., 25
  MERLE VANHOOSE, 29
  MINOR, 25(4)
  MISSOURI HAVENS, 12
  NANNIE ROSE, 25
  PATRICIA R., 25
  SARAH ELIZABETH, 25
  THOMAS J., 25
  TUNIS WINSTON, 125
  WILLIAM M., 25
MUNSEY
  A.M.W., 14
  BOB, 53
  BOWMAN, 14
  C.A.K.M., 14
  CECIL W., 14
  E. MARVIN, 14(2)
  E.G.M., 14
  E.L.M., 14
  EMILY F. [KITTS], 14
  ETTIE G., 14
  FANNIE, 14, 160
  FAYETTE LEE, 14
  FRANK E., 11
  GERTRUDE, 72
  H.J., 159
  H.J.M., 14
  HARVEY J., 14
  INFANT, 14
  J.H., 14(2)

  J.P., 88
  JACOB, 92, 161
  JAMES H., 14
  JANE, 51
  JOSEPH P. (PATTON),
    60
  JOSIE FOLEY, 60
  LOLA F. [FOGLESONG],
    14
  LOUISE M.
    [McSPADDEN], 14
  MARGARET H., 14
  MARGARET HUTZELL,
    14
  MARGARET L.
    [HUTZELL], 14
  MARGARET LOUISE, 14
  MARY FANNING, 92,
    161
  MARY JANE, 11
  N.K.M., 14
  NANNIE H., 110
  NORA KELLY, 14
  OCTAVIA V., 62
  OLD ZAZHARIAH, 51
  OLIN, 14
  OLIN M., 14
  PATTON, 14
  PEARL, 60
  R. EZRA, 72
  R.K.M., 14
  ROBERT O., 14, 53
  RUBY KATE, 14
  SALLY DORN, 93
  SKIDMORE, 53
  VIRGINIA, 90
  WILLIAM B., 110
  WILLIAM HARRY, 14
  WILLIE SUE
    [MOREHEAD], 60
MUSTARD
  ALBERT, 72(2)
  ALLEN, 101(2)
  ANN PATTERSON, 102
  ANNA M., 97
  ANNAH P., 97
  ANNAH [PATTON], 97
  BARBARA INDIA, 97
  BASCOM, 102
  BASCOM N., 102
  BASCOM NEWTON, 102
  BETTY JANE, 72
  BETTY ROSE, 72(2)
  BETTY ROSE
NEWBERRY,
    73
  BILLY B., 75
  BILLY SUE, 66
  BLANCHE, 66
  C. BASCOM, 102
  CALLIE MAY, 102
  CHARLIE, 72
  CHARLIE L., 72(2)
  CLANIE BIRD, 65, 72
  DAISEY PEARL, 102
  E.C., 102(5)
  EDWARD BROWN, 97
  EFFIE, 25
  EFFIE W., 72
  EFFIE W. [WAGNER],

    26
  ELISHA, 10
  ELIZ. C. NEWBERRY,
    130
  ELIZ. CAROLINE
    NEWBERRY, 102(2)
  ELIZABETH, 103
  ELIZABETH DAVIS, 63
  ELLA C., 72
  ELLA CROCKETT, 72,
    77
  ELWOOD, 72
  ESSIE NOWLIN, 72(2)
  ESTEL CAMPBELL, 97
  ESTOL SHELL, 72
  EVA, 72(3)
  EVA MOORE, 72
  FANNIE, 72
  FANNY M. [STUART],
    97
  FORD ROBINETT, 72(2)
  FRANCES, 72
  FRED MASON, 72
  FRONZINIA C., 72
  GARLAND, 59, 77
  GEORGE ELLIS, 72
  GEORGIA BYRNES, 72
  GRAT HARVEY, 72
  GRAT., 72
  H. (HARVEY) R., 97
  HARVEY R., 67,
    72(2), 76, 97(2)
  HENRIETTA, 72
  HENRY, 72
  INA, 72(2)
  INA WOHLFORD, 72
  INEZ SNIDER, 72
  INFANT, 102
  IRENE LYNN, 72
  J. (JAMES) THOMAS,
    97
  J. (JOHN) JASPER, 97
  J.C., 72
  J.H., 11, 25, 70, 72
  J.N., 63
  JACK HUNTER, 72
  JACOB A., 25
  JACOB ANDREW, 25
  JAMES, 101(3)
  JAMES D., 63
  JAMES GARLAND, 72
  JAMES H., 139
  JAMES HARVEY, 11,
    139
  JAMES HENRY, 139
  JASPER, 72
  JERRY D., 72
  JEZREAL, 72(3), 73,
    77
  JEZREAL ROBINETT, 72
  JOHN, 10, 73, 78,
    101(3), 103, 139
  JOHN C., 25(2)
  JOHN G. (GRATTON),
    102
  JOHN JASPER, 97(4)
  JOHN T. (THOMAS),
    101
  JOSHUA, 63
  JULIA, 59

  KING, 72
  KING HANSON, 72(2)
  LARRY OWEN, 72
  LOUISA ROBINETT, 36
  LOUVISA, 78
  LOUVISA PATTERSON,
    103
  LOVISA, 73
  LOVISA PATTERSON,
    101, 139
  LUVICIE [PATTERSON],
    101
  M.E., 63
  MAGGIE CAROLINE, 72
  MARCIA, 11, 70, 72
  MARCIA ROBINETT, 11,
    25, 139(2)
  MARIAH W., 67, 76
  MARIAH WOHLFORD,
    97, 101
  MARIAH [WOHLFORD],
    97
  MARY C., 97
  MARY JANE P., 72
  MATTIE, 102
  MATTIE CRABTREE, 102
  MYRTLE BLANCHE, 97
  NARCIE, 22, 66
  NARCIE MILLER, 72
  NEWTON SHELL, 66,
    72(8), 77
  ORA STAFFORD, 72
  OREN S. (JACK), 72
  PAULINA, 72, 78
  R.G. (ROBERT GRAY),
    72
  ROB, 65
  ROBERT, 72
  ROBERT G., 72(2)
  ROBERT GRAY, 72
  ROBERT HENRY, 72(2)
  ROSE, 130
  ROSEBUD MARTIN, 25
  RUBY AGNES, 11
  RUSH, 48
  SALLY, 76
  SAMUEL PATTERSON,
    97
  SARAH, 101
  SARAH MUNSEY, 101
  SARAH [MUNSEY], 101
  SEGAL, 66
  THOMAS H., 72
  THOMAS HARVEY, 72
  VERA IRENE [WALKER],
    72
  VICKI C., 97
  W.N., 102(6), 130
  W.N. (WESLEY
    NEWTON), 102
  W.T., 22, 66
  WALTER E., 72(2)
  WAYNE, 72(3)
  WAYNE ELWOOD, 72
  WESLEY NEWTON, 102
  WILLIAM, 10, 97(3),
    101, 102
  WILLIAM NEWBERRY,
    102
  WILLIAM P., 36

EVERETT, 159
GEORGE L., 141
TEXAS M., 10
WHITLEY M., 10
WOLFE
  ALBERT, 49
  ALBERT, JR., 49
  BARBARA, 49
  CATHY, 33
  CHARLES O., 82
  CHARLES SAMMY, 33
  DEBRA B., 174
  DENNIS ROY, 174
  E.C., 48
  EMMA ANN, 10
  EVERETTE C., 48
  FAYE ANN, 49
  GAYE ANN, 49
  GEORGE, 48
  HOGE HARVEY, 82
  HOGE, MRS., 160
  JUDY, 49
  JUNE DILLOW, 33
  KATHY, 33
  KELLEY W., 48
  MARIA, 49
  MELVIN DOUGLAS, 173
  NANNIE, 48
  NANNIE SHRADER, 48
  RALEIGH A., 166
  ROSA, 166
  ROSA MAE, 166
  SAMMY, 33
  SONDRA, 49
  VERNIE, 62
  VERNIE E., 62
  VIOLA [MUSTARD], 48
  WALTER WARD, 49
  WARD, 48(2)
  WENDY, 49
  WILEY, 166
  WILEY P., 166
  WILEY W., 166
  WILLIE, 62
  WILLIE K. [KIRBY],
    62
  WM., 49
WOLPEN
  CORA ELLIS, 130
WOODS
  HATTIE, 78
  HATTIE PEARL
HAVENS,
    78
  JOHN, 78
  JOHN WINFIELD, 78
  L.M. (LEATHA
    MUSTARD), 78
  REBECCA, 36
  T.W. "TOMP", 78(2)
WOODY
  JAMES F., 128
WOODYARD
  ELIZABETH ANGELINE,
    166
  H.W., 78
  HETTIE, 78
  IZZIE ESTELLE, 130
  JAMES W., 78
  LELIA, 78

LEVI S., 134
MARY JENNIE, 166
ROSA BELLE, 134
ROSA M., 166
ROXIE MAY, 166
SALLY E. [MUSTARD],
  78
WILLIAM S., 134
WOOLF
  C.B., 166
  C.E., 166
  CLARENCE J., 166
  STELLA R.B., 166
WOOLWINE
  ANDREW BANE, M.D.,
    158
  ANDREW GROSECLOSE,
    157
  MAMIE GROSECLOSE,
    157
  McCARTHY, 158
WRIGHT
  "DOCTOR" WILLIAM
    McCOMAS, 105
  A. ELWOOD, 49
  A.A., 105
  ALLIE, 105
  ALMA LOIS, 49
  ALVIS DEWEY, 105
  ARTHUR C., 49
  C.M., 63, 78(2)
  CARL REID, 33
  CECILIA SUSAN, 78
  CHARLES H., 49
  CHARLOTTE D., 174
  CHESTER EARL, 49
  D.O., 158
  D.W.M., 105(2)
  DAISY E., 105
  DAVID OLIVER, 49(2)
  DELLA RUTH, 105
  DONALD C., 174
  DOROTHY L., 105
  EDNA J. [GUSLER], 49
  EDNA MYRTLE, 105
  ELLIE SHRADER
    [WRIGHT], 65
  ETHEL MEADOWS, 33
  EUGENE WELLINGTON,
    49
  FAIRLY CLIFFORD, 49
  FRANCIS D., 105
  FRANK JAMES, 33
  GEORGE A., 49
  GROVER C., 49
  HALLIE LAWRENCE, 49
  HOMER NEAL, 105
  IRENE MEADOWS, 49
  J.B., 105
  J.R., 65
  JAMES ELBERT, 49
  JAMES W., 49
  JERRY DAVID, 174
  JOHN B., 49
  JONATHAN K., 49
  L.J., 105
  LEE J., 105
  LESSIE R., 105
  LILA J., 49
  LUCILLE GUSLER, 49

LUCY E., 49
MACIE SPANGLER, 49
MARGARET L., 105
MATILDA E., 105
MATILDA R. WILSON,
  158
MICKY D., 49
MINNIE B. [BURTON],
  105
MINNIE EDITH RAMSEY,
  49
NED, 49
NELLIE F., 105
NELLIE R., 49
NINA F., 105
OLLIE MAE, 105
OTIS, 105
OTIS, JR., 105
ROBERT F., 49
ROBERT L., 105
SALLY L., 33
SARAH A. [BRUCE],
  105
TALMADGE LEE, 105
TONY R., 105
VERRENA R., 49
VICKI LYNN, 33
W.G., 49
WESLEY ALLEN, 105
WILLIAM G., 49
WILLIAM LEE, 49
WILLIAM OLNEY, 105
WILMA MAY COX, 49
WYATT
  ALBERT P., 33
  ANNA D., 33
WYGAL
  SALLY [MUSTARD], 63
  T.B., 63
WYLIE
  EDGAR NYE, 33
  MRS., 159
  ROBERT, 33(2)
  ROSE C., 33
WYNN
  A.J., 33(2)
  ANDREW JACKSON, 33
  INFANTS, 33
  JULIA, 33
  JULIA M. HUGHES, 33
  NANNIE S. WALL, 33
WYNNE
  JAMES F., 140(2)
  JOSEPH, 140
  ROSA ETTA, 140
WYRICK
  ANNIE MUNSEY, 14
  BETTY R., 128
  CULES B., 49
  DATURA E., 49
  DAVID EARL, 49
  DUNN T., 138(2)
  ELVA., 138
  HENRY ASA, 49
  LEATHER NATHAN, 49
  LORENZO D., 138
  LOUISE HUNTER, 49
  R.S., 138
  RALPH B., 138
  ROBERT SHOCKLEY,

138
  RUDOLPH, 128(2)
WYROCK
  ASA, 81

-Y-

YATES
  CHARLIE H., 115
  PEARL D., 115
  RUBY [BILLIPS], 78
YOUNG
  JOSEPH E., 8
  LULA V., 8
  M. JENNIE, 158
  M.C., 158
  S.W., 158

-Z-

ZACHARY
  WALTER, 168